D[evotions] for the Christian Public Servant

James D. Slack, Editor

Christopher Sean Meconnahey,
Associate Editor

William (Bill) Dudley
Associate Editor

Foreword by
James A. Davids

EMETH PRESS
www.emethpress.com

Devotions for the Christian Public Servant

Copyright © 2015 James D. Slack

Printed in the United States of America on acid-free paper.

Library of Congress Cataloging-in-Publication Data

Devotions for the Christian public servant / James D. Slack, editor ; Christopher Sean Meconnahey, associate editor ; William (Bill) Dudley, associate editor ; foreword by James A. Davids.
    pages cm
Includes index.
ISBN 978-1-60947-086-9 (alk. paper)
1. Employees—Prayers and devotions. 2. Civil service—Miscellanea. 3. Work—Religious aspects—Christianity—Meditations. I. Slack, James D., 1952- editor.
  BV4593.D485 2014
  242'.68—dc23
                              2014042001

Photos on the front and back cover are some of the *Christian* public servants who contributed devotionals for your inspiration and blessing.

Contents

Foreword / v

Preface / vii

Acknowledgments / ix

Daily Devotions (Week 1, Day 1 through Week 52, Day 5) / 1

About the Contributors / 297

Subject Index / 311

About the Editors / 317

Foreword

This book is honestly labeled *Devotions for the Christian Public Servant*. Each devotional is intended to refresh and encourage public servants spiritually, to start each workday with the proper focus – honoring God and loving others as we love ourselves. Each entry bears the good news that, although man is prone to misdeeds, the sacrifice of Jesus has washed the slate clean with God.

When I served as Deputy Director and Counsel for the U.S. Department of Justice's Faith-Based Initiative during the first two years of the George W. Bush administration, people sometimes asked me why the Initiative was important and, more fundamentally, why it was important for Christians to be involved in publicly funded social service agencies. Often I would point to the Executive Order signed by President Bush that established the following policy:

> Faith-based and other community organizations are indispensable in meeting the needs of poor Americans and distressed neighborhoods. Government cannot be replaced by such organizations, but it can and should welcome them as partners. The paramount goal is compassionate results, and private and charitable community groups, including religious ones, should have the fullest opportunity permitted by law to compete on a level playing field, so long as they achieve valid public purposes, such as curbing crime, conquering addiction, strengthening families and neighborhoods, and overcoming poverty.[1]

Toward the end of my work at the Department, I could turn for this answer to a speech my boss (and now colleague in the Robertson School of Government at Regent University), former U.S. Attorney General John Ashcroft gave to a group of persons interested in learning more about the Initiative. Gen. Ashcroft stated:

> When he traveled through America more than 100 years ago, Alexis de Tocqueville, the great French observer, was struck by the American

---

[1] George W. Bush, *Executive Order 13199 - Establishment of White House Office of Faith-Based and Community Initiatives*, January 29, 2001. Online by Gerhard Peters and John T. Woolley, *The American Presidency Project*. http://www.presidency.ucsb.edu/ws/?pid=61481.

spirit of service to one another. He said, "The Americans'... regard for themselves, constantly prompts them to assist one another and inclines them willingly to sacrifice a portion of their time and property for the welfare of others." This spirit of service and community has existed as long as America has existed, and it remains deeply rooted in our faith traditions.

Towards the end of the 19th century, the streets of American cities were lined with liquor shops, houses of prostitution, and gambling houses. They were littered with addicts, orphaned children, and destitute immigrants struggling to make a life for themselves and their families.

The first Americans to step forward and address these dire conditions weren't government officials but volunteers from private institutions of charity and assistance - the first of what have come to be known as faith-based and community organizations. Disease was treated by church-run hospitals. Children were sheltered by church-sponsored orphanages, and educated by church-sponsored schools. Families were fed and lives were saved by ordinary Americans who reached out to those in need.

Over the years, many of these private charities have been replaced by government-run social services programs. But even today, the majority of social services are not administered by Washington bureaucrats but by many of the same people who fed the hungry a hundred years ago - compassionate citizens in churches and neighborhoods across the nation. . .[2]

People who have vocationally decided to serve others, whether they are in religious organizations or in government, are motivated by compassion, by a desire to improve the conditions of those less fortunate. This compassion, in turn, is motivated by a spiritual dimension for many -- as Christ loved them, they are to love others.

This spiritual dimension, like the physical dimension, needs food. *Public servants, feast on the following devotions!*

James A. Davids, J.D., Ph.D.
Former Deputy Director and Counselor
Task Force for the Faith-Based & Community Initiative
U.S. Department of Justice
Washington, D.C. USA;
currently Associate Professor
and Director of the LLM and MA Programs
Regent University School of Law
Virginia Beach, Virginia USA.

---

[2] John D. Ashcroft, *Speech on Faith-Based Initiative*, Denver, CO (Jan. 13, 2003), electronic copy on file with author.

Preface

The idea of a daily workplace devotional for Christian public servants emerged in September 2012. Obeying the Great Commission (*Matthew* 28:18-20), the Robertson School of Government at Regent University wanted to start a ministry for public servants. The term "public servant" includes people working in all levels of government, the nonprofits, education, healthcare, social work, public safety and defense, as well as in faith-based service agencies and church management. The word "Christian" includes everyone in the Body of Christ – regardless of denomination and faith-practice.

We solicited initial devotionals from alumni, friends and colleagues. We collected e-mail addresses of public servants -- addresses published openingly on websites – and subscribed them. A listserve was built and maintained with the continual guidance and expertise of Keith Alston, Senior Systems Engineer in the Information Technology Department at Regent University. Without the technical knowledge and prayers of Keith Alston, nothing would have gotten off the ground and nothing would be working today.

The daily e-mail devotional, called *The Christian Public Servant*, was first sent on November 5, 2012 to 300 subscribers. Based strictly on devotionals submitted by volunteers, the e-mail version continues to grow. It now has over 10,000 subscribers on six continents.

This printed volume contains selected entries from the e-mail version. Each devotional is workplace- or profession-oriented and written conversationally – as if you and the author are enjoying a coffee break. Entries cover a variety of topics that public servants face. Scriptures come from the New Living Translation. Each devotional is designed for a quick read by busy people.

Some entries may seem a bit out of place, in terms of season and temperature, and that is for two reasons (1) people will read this volume in both the northern and southern hemispheres and (2) the reader may begin the devotionals at any time of the year. Hence, Week 1, Day 1 does not necessarily mean January 1 for each reader, nor does it mean summer or winter. Because entries do not fall on specific calendar dates, none are dedicated to holidays.

Finally, please note that royalties are being donated to a student scholarship fund in the Robertson School of Government at Regent

University. We pray that the royalties will help prepare the next generation of *Christian* public servants!

Pax Christi,
The Editors
    James D. Slack
    Christopher Sean Meconnahey
    William (Bill) Dudley
    Robertson School of Government
    Regent University
    Virginia Beach, Virginia USA

Acknowledgments

We recognize our amazing families whose wisdom, grace, and love inspire us each day: the Slack family — wife Janis, and children Sarah and Samuel; the Meconnahey family — mother Cathy, father Joseph, and grandmother June; and the Dudley family – wife Annette, and children Stephen, David, and Tiffany.

Finally, we wish to acknowledge Dr. Eric Patterson, Dean of the Robertson School of Government at Regent University. We are grateful for his vision, leadership, and support.

Week 1, Day 1

BOTH RATIONAL AND CRAZY

READING

Matthew 10:16(a) Look, I am sending you out as sheep among wolves.

Proverbs 15:2 The tongue of the wise makes knowledge appealing, but the mouth of a fool belches out foolishness.

2 Corinthians 5:13 If it seems we are crazy, it is to bring glory to God. And if we are in our right minds, it is for your benefit.

REFLECTION

As a court administrator, I know some citizens can be angry and aggressive — and they do so just to test us. Last week a defendant went so far as to create a blasphemous e-mail address to use in messages to staff. How sad he must have been when he realized that we didn't even blink!

Antics like this, of course, are nothing new. Many of us deal with different levels of hostility every day, and sometimes that hostility is directed at our faith. In all situations, we strive as *Christian* public servants to remain calm, polite, patient and, above all, *rational*.

After a day of dealing with that "e-mail defendant," my car radio blessed me with the song, *In Christ Alone*. If anything will wash away the trials of a bad day, it's that powerful hymn! In this particular "live" version, the audience burst into spontaneous cheers at the line "up from the grave He rose again..." Hundreds, perhaps thousands at that concert were moved to cheers of joy at the thought of Christ's resurrection.

It's funny how we can be **both rational and crazy**! We're rational in the face of hostility and busy chaos every workday, and yet we're crazy — moved to irrepressible joy at our personal love for someone who walked the earth for only a speck of time 2,000 years ago.

The secular world — citizens like that "e-mail defendant" — will never understand us. But that really doesn't matter. We choose to be **both rational and crazy**, and that just happens to make us tremendous public servants!

Better yet, being **both rational and crazy** truly makes us *Christian* public servants!!

PRAYER

Lord, thank You for Your love for us and Your deeply personal, powerful reality and presence in our lives. Please help us remember each workday, in the midst of cultural and intellectual dismissal and hostility, that You give us the gifts of reason, self-control, patience and stillness so that we can remain steadfast and

confident in Your love and Your eternal, omnipotent and overwhelming reality. Thank You, Lord. In Your name, I pray. Amen.
—Karl Thoennes III

Week 1, Day 2

BEAUTIFUL FEET

READING

Isaiah 52:7 How beautiful on the mountains are the feet of the messenger who brings good news, the good news of peace and salvation, the news that the God of Israel reigns!

REFLECTION

Let's face it. We have **beautiful feet**.

And our **beautiful feet** are so amazing! They are designed to carry us for a lifetime. There is extra padding and thick, keratinized skin to bear our weight. There are a number of small bones with joints to articulate our movements. Our toes help to provide balance and stability.

Ah, but we usually take our **beautiful feet** for granted. Despite donning socks and shoes daily, we truly notice them only when they hurt or are injured. They just don't make the radar most of the time—and yet, if a problem develops with them, it is potentially devastating for our workday.

It's a shame we neglect them so, given how much care and thought went into their design. It's a shame we don't acknowledge them more, given our largest responsibility with these **beautiful feet** is to spread God's good news.

Today at work, when the opportunity comes to move forward the work of the Holy Spirit, let us not forget our **beautiful feet**. Step lively to the call to bring news of forgiveness, jog to bring joy to the downtrodden, sprint to serve the needy, dash to protect the vulnerable, gallop to comfort the suffering, and race to bring peace to all.

PRAYER

Lord, You have called me to spread Your word and Your love. You have equipped me with **beautiful feet**. Help me to use them to heed the call of the Holy Spirit. In Jesus' name, I pray. Amen.

— Erika D. Doster

Week 1, Day 3

TRUE FEAST, NOT JUST LUNCH

READING

Psalm 103:5 He fills my life with good things. My youth is renewed like the eagle's!

Luke 22:19 He took some bread and gave thanks to God for it. Then he broke it in pieces and gave it to the disciples, saying, "This is my body, which is given for you. Do this to remember me."

REFLECTION

I like lunch! I know it's not the most important part of the workday, but it is an essential step in renewing for the afternoon. On real special occasions, my coworkers and I go to the Baton Rouge restaurant. They have the best steaks in town, and their pasta and seafood are second-to-none. Most workdays, however, we just bring our lunches and chat in the break room. Today I brought a Greek salad with feta cheese and olives. Now, that is going to be a feast!

But another kind of feast is even more essential in *renewing for the afternoon.* I'm talking about the kind of feast that really satisfies my mouth by connecting with Who is in my heart. Naturally, I'm talking about a *spiritual feast.*

Regardless of where you eat and what you eat, this lunchtime give thanks, break, and share with others. As you eat, remember His body is broken just for you. Make it a **true feast, not just lunch**. Feel His presence in that restaurant or in that break room. Understand He will satisfy you until the evening *spiritual feast.* You will not hunger or thirst.

Today be sure you take part in more than just a steak or a salad or something from the machine. Be sure to make it a **true feast, not just lunch**.

PRAYER

Thank You, most heavenly Father, for blessing me with a **true feast, not just lunch**. May my body be renewed and my soul transformed into a beacon of Your light for the rest of the workday. In Your Son's name, I pray. Amen.

— Lyse-Ann Lacourse

Week 1, Day 4

ACCOMPLISH INFINITELY MORE

READING

Ephesians 3:20–21 Now all glory to God, who is able, through his mighty power at work within us, to accomplish infinitely more than we might ask or think. Glory to him in the church and in Christ Jesus through all generations forever and ever! Amen.

REFLECTION

There is a Tanzanian man who, with a wife and 6 children, earns only $8.89 per month. In his impoverished village, there are children going blind from a completely preventable disease. The vaccine costs only 44 cents, yet no one can afford it.

So this Tanzanian man prays constantly, that God will send a wealthy person or agency to start a programme. One day he gets off his knees and finally realizes that God has already sent someone — *God has sent him*. So this poor man finds a way to pay 44 cents each month and, one-by-one, children are vaccinated. Eighty-seven months later, 87 children can see.

As we start this day, let us remember that there are no challenges too great for our God. True in our personal lives, but this is also true in our jobs as *Christian* public servants. Prayers are obviously important, but we need to realize that perhaps He has already answered — and not by bringing another source to help the situation. Perhaps, God has sent us.

Could this be the workday when we practice what we believe? Will we hear Him calling us? Will you and I accomplish infinitely more than what we could have ever imagined?

Be big and bold today, remembering that impoverished Tanzanian fellow.

Be big and bold today, for God *is sending you*!

PRAYER

Heavenly Father, thank You for blessing me with this unique path. I pray today that You will help me reach my full potential in glorifying You and Your glorious plan. As Christian public servants across the world strive to be big, bold and to practice what they believe, I pray they will feel Your comfort and support. In Your holy name, I pray. Amen.

— Stephanie van Straten

Week 1, Day 5

PULLING WEEDS

READING

Matthew 13:28(b)–29 "Shall we pull out the weeds?" they asked. He replied, "No, you'll hurt the wheat if you do."

REFLECTION

I've never met anyone who enjoys **pulling weeds** out of the garden. It's hot, back-breaking work, and I know it will have to be done again in about two weeks. I personally consider it a necessary evil — it's just something I have to do. **Pulling weeds** is truly my least favorite chore at home.

But scripture says we should be careful in **pulling weeds**. Certainly, it's an investment of time and sweat that ensures my family gets the strawberries (and memories) they love. Yet, if I do so carelessly, hating the job, I risk damaging the plants. So my approach to this distasteful job is to: remember the good that comes from the time and sweat; prepare to do the job by first pre-soaking the soil; and then set aside a certain block of time — like the cool of the morning — so this necessary evil is less stressful.

You may not be a gardener, but perhaps you have tasks at work that are like **pulling weeds**. Maybe it's filling out the monthly report. Maybe it's reviewing time sheets. How about processing invoices?

Pulling weeds in the workplace is no different than in the garden. The task must be completed carefully, with preparation, and in a time block that permits comfortable concentration. It requires an investment in the good that will come from doing it well.

Today at work, focus on the *wheat*, and **pulling weeds** will become a manageable evil. Who knows, it may even turn into your most favorite chore!

PRAYER

Lord, help me to work through the patches of weeds that I must face today. May the harvest be worth the effort and pleasing to You. In Your name, I pray. Amen.

— Larry Ketcham

Week 2, Day 1

ONE PARTICULAR PERSON

READING

Galatians 6:2 Share each other's burdens, and in this way obey the law of Christ.

REFLECTION

It's Monday and it starts all over again. Perhaps it never ended during the weekend.

As public servants, we are busy people. Just like mine, your job and its demands can be all-consuming at times. Endless meetings, phone calls and emails can keep you on the move all day.

But as *Christian* public servants, we should never become too busy or self-absorbed to remember that colleague in your office or that one coworker down the hall or that one fellow associate you only see at conferences — that **one particular person** in your unit, organization or profession who is going through difficult times on or off the job. Think about it. I'm sure you know someone who fits this bill today: difficulty with a superior, or problems with the city or county commission, or perhaps in-between jobs, or having a personal or health problem.

As this work-week begins, and before we get too consumed with the tasks before us, reach out to that **one particular person** and let him or her know that you care and are in prayer over the situation. Let it be known that you are "here" to help throughout this difficult time. An encouraging note, email, or phone call will begin to fulfill the law of Christ: to assist others.

Christ calls us to bear each other's burdens. Bear the burdens of that **one particular person** at work. It will make a *world of difference* — for both of you!

PRAYER

Lord, help us to remember those in need and those facing challenges in their personal and professional lives. May You uphold and guide them during this time and work out the situation for their good and Your glory. In Your name, I pray. Amen.

— Sam Gaston

Week 2, Day 2

JUST WAIT PATIENTLY

READING

Psalm 27:14 Wait patiently for the LORD. Be brave and courageous. Yes, wait patiently for the LORD.

REFLECTION

My daughter came into my office to inform me a friend of hers was killed in an automobile accident last evening. She was heartbroken, asking why this happened to someone she loved — someone as young as she. I could do nothing more than try to explain that only God knew why.

I held her as she cried and shared my experience of similar happenings when death is thrust upon us. I told her that if she could have *courage at this time*, and **just wait patiently**, the Lord would give her the *strength to face* what lay ahead.

I realized then that she had reminded me of an important lesson: *get out of His way,* and **just wait patiently**. Expect God to show up — count on it — and **just wait patiently**.

You know, God doesn't just show up in times when death takes loved-ones. He's there in all kinds of disasters and challenges — small and large ones, personal and community-wide ones. He shows up at work — even today, this very minute — as you engage in public service.

So remember this: at work and in every other endeavor, He is faithful in all things. So **just wait patiently**.

PRAYER

God, please help me to be courageous each day, but especially this particular day. Give me strength to serve the citizens of my community and wisdom to not get ahead of You. Lord, You are in control, I am not. Help me to wait patiently on You. In Your Son's name, I pray. Amen.

    — James Grogan

Week 2, Day 3

TOP OF YOUR TASK LIST

READING

Philippians 3:12–14 I don't mean to say that I have already achieved these things or that I have already reached perfection! But I keep working toward that day when I will finally be all that Christ Jesus saved me for and wants me to be. No, dear brothers and sisters, I am still not all I should be, but I am focusing all my energies on this one thing: Forgetting the past and looking forward to what lies ahead, I strain to reach the end of the race and receive the prize for which God, through Christ Jesus, is calling us up to heaven.

REFLECTION

I'm a big fan of goal-setting in the work environment. It helps provide staff a better understanding of the mission, and it also overcomes the stagnancy that threatens progression. While goal-setting takes various forms, I tend to favor the good old-fashioned task list. But, as you well know, sometimes it's challenging to decide just what goes at the very **top of your task list**.

In the midst of creating that task list, checking off completed tasks and striving for excellence in the workplace — it's easy to forget the importance of the ultimate goal in every Christian's life: a heavenly existence. Even — or perhaps especially — at the workplace, that goal of heavenly existence has to remain supreme.

So as this workweek continues — as you continue to task and serve well your agency and your community — do not neglect your relationship with God.

As a *Christian* public servant, is glorifying Him in your workplace *today* — right now — at the very **top of your task list**?

PRAYER

Almighty Father, thank You for allowing us the opportunity to serve people. However, help us, Lord, to remember that our ultimate service and calling is to seek You first in all things; to glorify You in everything. Nothing in this world is comparable to the pursuit of You and Your kingdom. Guide us to an even greater knowledge of You. In Jesus' name, I pray. Amen.

— Courtney Christian

Week 2, Day 4

GOOD GOSSIP

READING

Ephesians 4:29 Don't use foul or abusive language. Let everything you say be good and helpful, so that your words will be an encouragement to those who hear them.

1 Timothy 5:13b They will learn to be lazy and will spend their time gossiping from house to house, meddling in other people's business and talking about things they shouldn't.

REFLECTION

Near the end of the night shift, several of us stand around the nurse's station. It's not a lazy time, but usually a relaxing time — when we complete charts and just chat for a few minutes. Then something's said about someone and this sparks a round of bad gossip. I try to stay out of it, but that's not always easy to do. I know I have a choice. I can join in on the bad gossip or try to extinguish it with **good gossip**.

    Good gossip?? Is there such a thing?

    Last night, *bad gossip* centered on a seemingly unpopular nurse. When it was my turn, I said: "I hear she has the most thorough charting. How does she do it?" There was silence, but then someone else chimed, "When B-wing was short-handed yesterday, she single-handedly put half the hallway to bed. That was awesome!"

    Wow! At that point, *bad gossip* was over. **Good gossip** tipped the scales! It showed me that, even though we are quick to talk about the negative, we could be just as quick to acknowledge the good.

    On your way in to work this morning, think of some *really juicy* **good gossip** to share. It will impart grace to the hearers. It can transform your workplace!

PRAYER

Father, let me be quick to differentiate performance from people. Help me to engage in constructive conversations, and to go out of my way to build up my work neighbors. Guard my tongue from the temptation of bad gossip, and lead me ever toward a more holy speech. In Your Son's name, I pray. Amen.

    — Katherine Zasadny

Week 2, Day 5

GODLY PUBLIC SERVANT

READING

Psalm 72:4 Help him to defend the poor, to rescue the children of the needy, and to crush their oppressors.

REFLECTION

Psalm 72 is a prayer for a just king. As such, it is a prayer for a loving, kind and just public servant. The Psalmist has done us a great favor in describing what should be the concern of a **godly public servant**. His primary concern is with those who are most vulnerable — the poor, the downtrodden, the needy, those unable to be heard or to defend themselves — those here and throughout the world who are oppressed and abused physically, emotionally and spiritually.

In the rush of everyday work, it is very easy to overlook our true task of being a godly public servant. Some days we think that currying favor with that large donor or important foundation is our primary goal. Or, maybe it is contacting an important partner agency so that we can advance our own agency's mission. Or, maybe it's conducting a perfect job analysis on the staff, or writing that finance report to the Board.

Naturally all of these things have value in the workplace. But those activities are simply means to an end. They are not the primary goal in the life of the **godly public servant**.

PRAYER

Lord of heaven, in the rush of my everyday work tasks help me never to forget my primary concern to see the world as You see it ... to always have, as my primary concern, Your most vulnerable children. In Your name, I pray. Amen.

— Tom Duley

Week 3, Day 1

A BIT MORE SACRED

READING

Nehemiah 8: 11 And the Levites, too, quieted the people, telling them, "Hush! Don't weep! For this is a sacred day."

REFLECTION

Today I received an email from a friend. She was fired this morning. I am in shock, angry, and a little frightened for her as she has had to endure a lot of loses in the last five years.

Providing comfort to those who have legitimate cause to grieve, such as my friend, is challenging in that too often comfort sounds like platitude. (It is even more challenging when the cause of action is justified.) The older we get, being fired is not really an opportunity. Therefore, it is hard to raise a voice in song that this is the day the Lord has made. *Today does not feel sacred.*

As I think about how to be a *Christian* public servant and leader, I ponder the appropriate responses toward hurt and pain in the workplace. Is it enough to listen and care, or do I need to be my friend's advocate?

What about the people whose lives I have some authority to change: students who cannot do the work, personnel I have to reprimand or terminate? What am I supposed to learn from my friend's harsh treatment that will cause me to take care of the people I supervise?

What do I need to do differently to show the tender mercy of God in my interaction with coworkers? How do I coach, motivate, direct and maintain a Christian spirit about my work and theirs? And if termination is justified and required, how do I perform such a task in the spirit of Christ so that, for everyone involved, the day feels **a bit more sacred**?

PRAYER

Lord of all private and public spheres, show me the way to demonstrate Christian compassion in all of my work. If I must reprimand or fire, show me how to be instructive rather than cruel. Remind me, my conduct is witness of Your importance in my life. Even on the worst days, You are Lord of my life and every day You give me is a blessing, even if I cannot immediately see that gift. Remind me, oh my Lord, that a disciplined life — a life where stillness exists so that You can speak to me - allows my senses to know the sacredness of Your gifts. In Your name, I pray. Amen.
— Stephanie L. Bellar

Week 3, Day 2

STANDING IN THE FREEZING RAIN

READING

Matthew 14:16c You feed them.

REFLECTION

For several years, I volunteered as a supervisor at an inner city storefront church that ministers to the homeless. On one spring morning, an unexpectedly freezing downpour presented a familiar situation — weather that makes the homeless more desperate also prevents an adequate number of volunteers from showing up.

Because of an always limited supply of food and clothing, and because we wanted to build community, compassion for individual need was seasoned with "tough love" rules to ensure equal access. Now, everyone can be incredibly selfish on a bad day, especially you and me. The same is true with the homeless, and a few might even sell or exchange acquired extra items — that should have gone to others in need — for sex, alcohol or illegal drugs.

On this particular day it seemed like everyone wanted more than his share, thus reducing our ability to give others what they really needed just to survive the night on concrete underneath a city bridge. *I grew annoyed and impatient at the selfishness.*

A truck arrived with fresh bread, and I saw several homeless men helping themselves while a single volunteer frantically tried to get the load off the street and into our kitchen. I quickly found myself **standing in the freezing rain**, trying to take a loaf of bread from a homeless man.

I pulled, and he yanked. I shouted "Let go!" He exclaimed, "This is *my* loaf!"

The tug of war lasted only 10 seconds, but the damage was complete. He looked like he had just learned something about Christian hypocrisy that would remain with him for a long time. Chilling expressions on other homeless men came from my behavior, not the weather.

My God, I thought, what am I doing? Would Jesus take a loaf of bread out of the hands of a homeless man **standing in the freezing rain**? Would He take it out of my own hands? I released my grip on that loaf, apologized, and went to the sanctuary to pray about what I just did.

You know, when it comes down to it, we are all **standing in the freezing rain**. We grasp for bread. As public servants, the bread we seek might be better wages or working conditions. The bread our clients and citizens seek might be better health or more empathy about their life.

The next time someone cries out, whether coworker or citizen, listen a bit more intently — not just for their temporal need for "bread," but also for their eternal need for the *Bread of Life*.

As Jesus commands, I must give them something to eat. As a *Christian* public servant, so must you. We all need the *Bread of Life*, in addition to the worldly loaf, because we are all **standing in the freezing rain**.

PRAYER

Father God, I beg Your forgiveness when I am deaf to the cries of others; when I forget there is nothing separating me from those whom I serve; when I neglect that we are all **standing in the freezing rain**. In Jesus' name, I pray. Amen.

— James D. Slack

Week 3, Day 3

DON'T SLIP AND FALL

READING

Proverbs 10:9 People with integrity walk safely, but those who follow crooked paths will slip and fall.

REFLECTIONS

Although He has already planned our lives, our decisions still have a tremendous effect on the outcome. Will I walk safely with integrity, or will I follow a crooked path? Will you give surrender to temptation and use ill-gotten gains to support your fledgling nonprofit agency? Will you play politics with your organization's budgetary process? Will you cut corners by firing employees just to gain that end-of-the-year bonus?

Choices define you and me. So we need to live worthy of the King — we need to live with integrity. Practicing moral values is hard. After all, it seems public servants are on the news each night due to giving in to temptation. Constant lack of sufficient funds, resources, and support could make many take a crooked path.

When tempestuous situations arise, ask *"Will my choice be pleasing to God"*? Today at work, make sure you take the safe path where you **don't slip and fall**.

PRAYER

Lord, I pray that You give me courage to live a life of integrity. I know that it might seem impossible, especially with the many obstacles and temptations I face each day. But I know that all I need do is to ask for Your help and strength. I pray that You protect and prepare me for the many temptations and obstacles that would otherwise pull me away from You. More than anything, today I do not want to slip and fall. In Your name, I pray. Amen.

— Cassandra D. McLendon

Week 3, Day 4

DO WHAT HE WOULD DO

READING

Matthew 5:38–39 You have heard the law that says the punishment must match the injury: "An eye for an eye, and a tooth for a tooth." But I say, do not resist an evil person! If someone slaps you on the right cheek, offer the other cheek also.

REFLECTION

A friend of mine, in another jurisdiction, applied for the open position of police chief. But there was also an applicant who began to slander my friend's character to the mayor and city manager. My secular mind wanted to help my friend strike back. To do so, however, we would've had to submit to the dirty politics of this world. So my friend said, "No!" He wasn't worried about what the other candidate had to say about him.

Right before his opponent's interview, my friend phoned me. He wanted me to help him pray for his opponent. He wanted me to help him carry whatever had been said about his character and just leave it at the altar. We did just that.

God spoke to me through my friend: in our jobs and in our workplaces, we are to be Christ-like and **do what He would do**. After all, we are *Christian* public servants. And despite the fact we work in environments where God's Will is sometimes obscured by the "eye for an eye" mentality, we cannot forget about turning the other cheek.

Whether or not my friend got the position is no longer the point, is it?

Today, let us all remember the reason we are *Christian* public servants: in our jobs and in our workplaces, we are to **do what He would do**.

PRAYER

Good morning, Heavenly Father! This journey You have planned is mapped according to Your will. Along the way, I will encounter those with a secular mind. Give me strength to reflect Your image and not submit to worldly ways. Give me courage to turn the other cheek and be a light in this dark world. I ask and pray in your Son's most beautiful name. Amen!

— Louis A. Carlos

Week 3, Day 5

REVERSE NETWORKING

READING

Matthew 23:12 But those who exalt themselves will be humbled, and those who humble themselves will be exalted.

READING

While the public service is so very different than the business sector, we do have one thing in common: the art of networking. "Here's my business card." "Connect with me on LinkedIn!" "Befriend me on Facebook."

Sound familiar?

We live in a world of networking, a culture of self-promotion. This happens everywhere, and we all do it. Me? As an elected city councillor, some call me the "king of networking". I have over 9,000 "close personal" friends on Facebook, and many more twitter contacts.

If you're like me, you love to volunteer or connect with other public servants to help those we serve — and that makes networking a good thing. But too often we use networking solely to promote ourselves. I know I sometimes do. That is what most MPA programs teach appointed public servants, and the internet is filled with web pages offering workshops on "networking" for elected officials.

As *Christian* public servants, elected and appointed, we need to keep things in perspective. Do we exalt God and help others in our networking, or do we use it selfishly? What kind of image and reputation are you building? Scripture tells me I need to be humble and, if I am, I will be exalted. Am I as humble as I must be to please Him?

Here's an idea. Today let's all engage in a little **reverse networking** — let's network others who humbly do not network themselves. Let's advance others who are unable to advance themselves. *Sooner than what you think*, your business card will be lost. LinkedIn and Facebook will be technological relics. *Sooner than what you think*, people will have only memories of how you conducted yourself. Will they reflect fondly on your reputation of networking and advancing coworkers and the people you served? And *sooner than what you think*, perhaps even today, they will *exalt you for exalting others*.

Networking? On the market? Looking for that promotion? Need that merit raise? Want to move-up in your professional society? That's fine. Like me, you may also be a king or queen of networking. Perhaps that's necessary.

But as this work-week concludes, let's consider starting next week with a little **reverse networking**. Our Lord promises your success. You will be exalted!

PRAYER

Lord, shape me into a humble servant today. Engage me in quietly doing my best work. Calm me in knowing it will be recognized by those *You* choose to recognize it. If others feel the need to exalt me, that is fine; but let me not exalt myself. Challenge me to advance the works and reputations of others. Today at work, let me practice a little **reverse networking**. Let me humble myself for You. In Your name, I pray. Amen.

— Matt Whitman

Week 4, Day 1

WORK WITHIN THE ATTITUDE OF CHRIST

READING

Deuteronomy 30:19–20a Today I have given you the choice between life and death, between blessings and curses. Now I call on heaven and earth to witness the choice you make. Oh, that you would choose life, so that you and your descendants might live! You can make this choice by loving the Lord your God, obeying Him, and committing yourself firmly to Him.

REFLECTION

As public servants, we face diversity and challenge throughout each workday. Sometimes even the impact of policy decisions can make it difficult to do our jobs. But in the midst of it all, we still have the choice to **work within the attitude of Christ**.

Remember, Jesus withstood all that we face and much more. He withstood it while maintaining His character. In the midst of His journey, He never gave up — never turning His back on God or the people He was tasked to serve. He did not allow anything to impact the choice to serve with Godly character.

So regardless of what happens today at work, you and I have the choice to serve with the character that Jesus exemplified. We have the choice to keep our Example in mind. In its most meaningful sense, our choice to be a *Christian* public servant requires us to serve citizens and clients with absolute love, commitment, and obedience for the Lord. People, decisions, behavior — nothing should compromise our choice to **work within the attitude of Christ**.

PRAYER

Lord, I thank You for offering me the choice! I thank You for giving me the Example to shape my response in today's trials at work. I pray that, even at the most challenging times today, I do not forget the sacrifice You made for me. Lord, I pray that You will continue to show me grace as I set out to be the public servant You called me to be. Help me to always keep my motives in check and focus on what You have tasked me to do and be. In Jesus' name, Amen.

— LaShonda Garnes

Week 4, Day 2

ONLY AFTER IT'S TOO LATE

READING

Ephesians 6:10–12 A final word: Be strong in the Lord and in his mighty power. Put on all of God's armor so that you will be able to stand firm against all strategies of the devil. For we are not fighting against flesh-and-blood enemies, but against evil rulers and authorities of the unseen world, against mighty powers in this dark world, and against evil spirits in the heavenly places.

REFLECTION

Have you ever been on your way somewhere and had that gut feeling you forgot something? Did you remember, but **only after it's too late** to do anything about it? I had that feeling driving to work the other morning. I did a mental checklist, but couldn't figure out what I was missing. Later in a meeting, I glanced for my watch and guess what? No watch!

The fact that I forgot my watch is not bizarre. But why do we remember so many things in life **only after it's too late** to do anything about it? Has this ever happened when you were struggling to serve the Lord?

As *Christian* public servants, whether we like it or not, you and I are in a spiritual battle every minute of the day — a war between light & dark worlds; between good & evil. Satan is hoping we forget to wear the *Armor of God*. When we forget, we become vulnerable to Satan's attacks. He's knows that we will eventually remember, but he's hoping this happens **only after it's too late** to do anything about it.

A stupid watch is one thing. But even (or especially) at work, it's something else to forget the *Armor of God*. As you prepare for work today, don't forget the Lord's protection. Don't remember **only after it's too late**.

PRAYER

Father, You have fought endlessly for my heart and mind; I must fight endlessly for You in this spiritual battle. Help me not to neglect properly dressing with Your Armor so that I am prepared for whatever temptations may come my way in this workday. You are all powerful and mighty, and I know I'm capable, but only with You by my side. In Jesus' name, I pray. Amen.

— Angela Arbitter

Week 4, Day 3

DEEPER QUIET

READING

1 Kings 19:11b–13a A mighty windstorm hit the mountain. It was such a terrible blast that the rocks were torn loose, but the LORD was not in the wind. After the wind there was an earthquake, but the LORD was not in the earthquake. And after the earthquake there was a fire, but the LORD was not in the fire. And after the fire there was the sound of a gentle whisper. When Elijah heard it, he wrapped his face in his cloak and went out and stood at the entrance of the cave.

REFLECTION

In my country, and I suspect yours as well, these are not the best economic times. Words like reduction-in-force, sequestration, and down-sizing become part of the workplace vocabulary. Uncertainty results. You start to fear, "Will I keep my job?" Or, "Will family members keep their jobs?" Most importantly, "what will it mean for the people I serve?"

In times of trouble, uncertainty causes the greatest and most powerful winds to tear apart our personal mountains and shatter our individual rocks before the Lord. Perhaps reality might bring substantially less or tremendously more than the expected earthquakes and fires. We just don't know.

What we do know with absolute certainty is this: the true voice of the Lord comes in that *gentle whisper*. But to hear it, we must enter a **deeper quiet** and simply listen — even as earthquakes crash around us. It is in moments of a **deeper quiet** that we pull our cloaks over our faces and stand at the mouth of the cave.

Christian public servants around the world face many of the same storms, earthquakes, and fires in the workplace. It is the **deeper quiet** that allows each of us to hear His *gentle whisper* so that we can become girded with the Word, reason, thanksgiving, and rest.

Today at work, take time to gain a **deeper quiet**. Hear His gentle whisper. With it, you can go forth in mission and discipleship — regardless of crisis — and lay the next brick of public service that He will use to build His kingdom in His world.

PRAYER

Thank You, Holy Spirit, for Your presence, blessings and grace in times of uncertainty. Abide with and within me as I abide in You. Today at work, allow me time to sit simply in Your presence, letting stray words, mental pictures and thoughts simply pass by. Let me no longer fear the storm, earthquake and fire. Let me yearn to hear Your simple whisper. In Jesus' name, Amen.

    — Allen Stout

Week 4, Day 4

WHEN TO SAY "NO"

READING

Ephesians 5:15–16 So be careful how you live. Don't live like fools, but like those who are wise. Make the most of every opportunity in these evil days.

REFLECTION

Time management is a tool I find crucial in my job. But in an attempt to be a testimony of reliability, and enjoying the excitement of new challenges, I am often tempted to volunteer for additional projects or propose new tasks. I seem to do this despite the added burden it places on my time management skills.

Ever find yourself in this situation?

We end up trying to manage too many tasks (even with good intent), and this can generate tension beyond the workplace: in our health habits, in our relationships at home, in our community outreach (church), and even in our walk with our Lord.

When stress escalates, so much can go wrong. But when added stress is attached to unnecessary tasks, so much can go wrong *unnecessarily*. By caving in to every temptation of doing more, we actually do less. We fail to learn **when to say "no."**

In searching for a season of time for all that God places in our path, remember that the first season of each day — and the last season each night — must be a season alone with Him. Seek His advice about which new opportunities really represent important challenges and which ones are just tangential or irrelevant to the success of your agency, job, family, and (above all) your walk with Christ.

Today at work, go to Him to find out **when to say "no"**.

PRAYER

Father, grant me the wisdom to know when to volunteer, when to propose, and **when to say "no"**. Grant me the wisdom to know when to wait and when to move forward. Father, reveal Your direction for my life and provide the skills to maintain seasons of time-with-responsibility that glorifies You. May You be the manager of my desires and duties, and may my testimony reflect Your nature in all I do. In Your Son's name, I pray. Amen.

— Bill Dudley

Week 4, Day 5

PASS THAT CUP OF HOPE

READING

John 4:13–15 Jesus replied, "Anyone who drinks this water will soon become thirsty again. But those who drink the water I give will never be thirsty again. It becomes a fresh, bubbling spring within them, giving them eternal life." "Please, sir," the woman said, "give me this water! Then I'll never be thirsty again, and I won't have to come here to get water."

REFLECTION

I manage a faith-based service organization that ministers to women who are victims of human trafficking. I am blessed, but frightened at the same time.

How do I share His water with women who have no hope? The "Jesus" they know left them. At least that is what they believe. They are helpless, hopeless and without any will to live, and I am given the responsibility of sharing this hope with them. Me? I was "them" at one time! Why me?

We both know why. Like you, I was led to say, "Send me!" and guess what? He did! So now I must show the women I serve *this precious water called Christ.*

Ministry work is not easy. I am always worried about bills and food and repairs. Yet as long as I am quenching my soul with His living water, I can **pass that cup of hope** on to others.

In your workplace today, you too can **pass that cup of hope** on to others.

PRAYER

Lord, help me to continue to drink of Your water, for as I do I am able to share it with those I serve. Help me share the hope found only in Your living water of life. In Your name, I pray. Amen.

   — Tajuan McCarty

Week 5, Day 1

AUTHORITY I WALK IN

READING

Matthew 8:8–9 Then the officer said, "Lord, I am not worthy to have you come into my home. Just say the word from where you are, and my servant will be healed! I know, because I am under the authority of my superior officers and I have authority over my soldiers. I only need to say, 'Go,' and they go, or 'Come,' and they come. And if I say to my slaves, 'Do this or that,' they do it."

REFLECTION

The foundation of leadership is found in an understanding of delegated authority. The officer honored Jesus' authority due to the importance he placed upon being submitted to authority. Jesus marveled at the officer's faith because faith is tied to submission.

I, too, am an officer under authority. I understand the **authority I walk in** isn't mine alone. I must be submitted to authority for the exercise of it. My submission to higher authority better be evident in how others view my character, action and conversation.

As you face challenges of public management and leadership, remember your commitment to those you follow. The commitment isn't blind but requires truth, respect and honor. Remember also your commitment to follow the Lord also requires truth, respect, and honor. As *Christian* public servants, after all, the authority you walk in is no different from the **authority I walk in**.

So at work today, let your confidence be found in *not strictly in man, but centrally in God*. If you manage and lead well by this principle, all will see your servant's heart in the fruit you bear!

PRAYER

Lord, grant me today a greater appreciation of the **authority I walk in**. Grant me greater submission to Your authority over my work and my life. It is my true desire to have my character, thoughts and actions governed by You. Lord, help me to be the leader You call me to be to my supervisors, my subordinates, and those I serve. In Your name, I pray. Amen.
    — C. A. Mitchell, Sr.

Week 5, Day 2

THE SUBSTITUTION OF LISTENING

READING

2 Timothy 1:13a Hold on to the pattern of wholesome teaching you learned from me.

Psalm 95:7b If only you would listen to his voice today!

REFLECTION

In my country, the sport of baseball remains the "national pastime." Before each game, both team managers make a batting order — a rank listing, or pattern, of who bats before whom. Both managers let everyone know their pattern and, while each can change it throughout the game by making substitutions, neither hopes to do so. The batting order is the pre-game pattern for victory.

I love baseball, and so I call my daily task-list, my *batting order*. It typically includes memos and emails that must be written, subpoenas for documents that I must produce, policies to review and edit, phone calls to make, and meetings to attend. Naturally, there are often deadlines!

The day's tasks can seem overwhelming. I don't know about you, but I don't like interruptions. I consider interruptions as changes in my pattern. Just like a baseball team manager, I prefer to stick with my original *batting order* as it is my pre-game pattern for victory.

But, in the fray of deadlines, what if someone thinks they need my immediate attention? As a *Christian* public servant, shouldn't I be willing to set aside my work and substitute some time for *listening*? Doesn't real victory come from hearing His voice in the needs of those who interrupt?

As a *Christian* public servant, where is *listening* in your batting order? Shouldn't you expect (and desire) it to change so you can hear His voice — even within the midst of deadlines?

Today at work, don't be afraid to change up your pattern. Demonstrate your faith and love in Jesus Christ through **the substitution of listening**.

PRAYER

Father God, it's so easy to get caught up in the busy, pre-planned details of the day. I ask for Your help, not only to hear Your voice, but also to stop and truly listen. Do not let my heart be hardened by the interruptions of others. In Jesus' name I pray. Amen.

— Stephen Pincus

Week 5, Day 3

KNOW GOD IS GOD

Psalm 46:10a Be still, and know that I am God!

REFLECTION

In the busyness of another workday, I find it difficult to be still. In our society, being still is frowned upon. It is associated with being unproductive, inactive, and pacific. My being still seems in opposition to the qualities valued in the workplace — such as haste, being occupied, diligent, hectic, active.

Yet it is essential for me to **know God is God**. In order to recognize His voice, to be acquainted and familiar with Him, to have His friendship — *I must spend time with Him*. This requires that I remain quiet, calm, noiseless, and inactive.

When I am calm and still, I become a more productive employee and a much better representative of my Lord then when I am rushed and loud. As I go about my day, I serve my coworkers and citizens in amazing ways when I have had the chance to be still and to **know God is God**.

Granted, it is so tempting to get busy and put aside stillness. However, let this be a different kind of workday for you and me. Let us both find the necessary moments to be still.

Throughout this particular workday, let us take the time to **know God is God**.

PRAYER

Father in the name of Jesus, I pray that You will guide me in demonstrating to my peers and citizens the value of tranquility and calmness. My prayer is that when I am restful, untroubled, "still," the people I meet will be drawn to the stillness and seek out its source, which is my relationship with You. Jesus, help me in being still so that I may know You more today and every day. Amen.

—Suzanne Denis

Week 5, Day 4

SIMPLIFYING QUESTION

READING

Matthew 16:15–17 Then he asked them, "But who do you say I am?" Simon Peter answered, "You are the Messiah, the Son of the living God." Jesus replied, "You are blessed, Simon son of John, because my Father in heaven has revealed this to you. You did not learn this from any human being."

REFLECTION

An academic colleague asked me, "Why can't you just believe in science? You seem to be such an intellectual, otherwise."

My colleague hoped that his question would tempt me — I mean, all academics want to be seen as "intellectual." But the temptation went further. My answer could've made my day a bit more complex than it had to be. I could've excused my faith and compromised my walk with Christ — just to be viewed as an intellectual!

But God was with me in that moment, and I did not take the bait. No, I replied: "I believe in science, it's just that I *believe in God so much more*." I then explained why my faith in God is the fundamental premise in which I based all my beliefs.

The workplace world demands compromise and complexity when it comes to our faith — especially for the acceptance by others. It would be easy to excuse faith were it not for that **simplifying question** asked by Jesus: **"But who do you say I am?"**

If your answer is like Peter's and mine, does it matter what your coworkers think of you? Does that matter more than what the Son of the living God thinks of you?

If we, as *Christian* public servants, live as we truly believe that Jesus is the Son of the living God, then the complex situations we face become very simple.

So as you work today, answer that **simplifying question** Jesus asked His disciples. Your response will determine just how complex and compromised your day will become.

PRAYER

Lord, grant me the wisdom to put my belief in You first and ahead of the opinions of others. Help all my thoughts, words, and actions reflect who I believe You are, the Son of the living God. In Your name, I pray. Amen.

—Kevin Cooney

Week 5, Day 5

PERSON GOD INTENDED

READING

Galatians 6:8 Those who live only to satisfy their own sinful nature will harvest decay and death from that sinful nature. But those who live to please the Spirit will harvest everlasting life from the Spirit.

REFLECTION

It seems we live in selfish times. Even in the public service, some look out only for themselves. You know the kind of coworker I'm talking about.

Well, I once knew a coworker who was completely the opposite. A custodian, this old guy was always in a good mood. He did his job exceptionally well, and he was always looking for ways to do more than necessary — especially if it would help someone.

One day in the hallway, I got the courage to ask him some questions: Whom was he trying to impress? Since no one was getting a raise that year, why bother? What was it all about?

His answer was embarrassingly simple. He was trying to be that **person God intended**. At work and elsewhere, *he just desired to please our Lord.*

Then he turned and asked me the most amazing questions: Do I feel the Holy Spirit in this hallway? Do I want to be that **person God intended**? At work, do I desire to please our Lord?

That old guy retired shortly thereafter, but his questions remained with me. I started to listen and watch for the Holy Spirit. At first, just at my desk; then when I was sitting next to my clients; then in the break room and hallway; and eventually even in the parking lot. Suddenly I realized what that old guy knew all along: *the Holy Spirit* was inside *me!*

So let me ask you those same questions: Do you feel the Holy Spirit where you are right now? Do you want to be that **person God intended**? At work, *do you desire to please God?*

Have a great workday!

PRAYER

Heavenly Father, let me feel You right now. At work, give me strength to be that person You intend for me to be. I desire to please You today. I pray this in Your Son's name. Amen.

—Malcolm Jones

WALKING IN THE MIDST

READING

Daniel 3:24–25 But suddenly, Nebuchadnezzar jumped up in amazement and exclaimed to his advisers, "Didn't we tie up three men and throw them into the furnace?" "Yes, Your Majesty, we certainly did," they replied."Look!" Nebuchadnezzar shouted. "I see four men, unbound, walking around in the fire unharmed! And the fourth looks like a god!"

Psalm 46:10(a) Be still, and know that I am God.

Romans 8:25 But if we look forward to something we don't yet have, we must wait patiently and confidently.

REFLECTION

While the news around our world seems pretty "predictable," I need things to remain unpredictable in my personal world. Otherwise, I won't survive.

You know what I mean?

You see, I'm **walking in the midst** of the fire. I've been unemployed for almost three years. I volunteer here, do an internship there, but there is no monetary compensation. I've submitted countless applications for jobs in which I know I qualify — but no positive response.

I'm **walking in the midst** of the fire and, by any "predictable" standard, I should be living on the streets. Yet, I have never gone without food or shelter, or without clean clothes, or even without transportation. My God has sustained me and — like the three guys in the fiery furnace — I'm protected, unbound and not hurt. My Lord keeps my life, well, *unpredictable*!

As this supposed workday begins, I know I'm not the only one **walking in the midst** of the fire. Just like me, you are protected, unbound and will not be hurt. Really. You have to believe. Contrary to the world's predictions, You will survive!

No matter what the circumstance — job stress, paycheck stress, or stress in having no job or paycheck — you are protected, my friend. Trust in the God that has called you to be still and wait in patience. Know that, in due time, He will lift you.

In the meantime, as a *Christian* public servant, have faith in knowing that He makes you unpredictable! Have faith in that which you cannot see as you are **walking in the midst** of the fire.

PRAYER

Heavenly Father, I ask that, in times of turmoil, You will allow the Holy Spirit to give me the patience I need to be still and let You work. Remind me in trying times that I am unpredictable by the world's standards; that I am protected by you — the Creator of the universe Who created me in Your very image. In Jesus' name, I pray. Amen.

    —Crystal Featherston

Week 6, Day 2

DONKEY ON WHICH HE RIDES

READING

Matthew 21:5b Look, your King is coming to you. He is humble, riding on a donkey.

REFLECTION

We live in an era that celebrates self-importance and self-improvement. Finances, work circumstances, family life — everything must excel. And when things don't go so well, blame is laid on anyone or anything. Some even point toward spiritual warfare because surely our less-than-stellar performance, and even our failures, must be the result of an attack by Satan.

While I'm not denying Satan's existence, I think there are times he is given too much credit. Ours is a world where people want quick explanations & quick fixes — including in the spiritual realm — that somehow restore wealth, work and well-being. Even a few preachers take this route, and some people just love to hear it: it's Satan's fault.

But this is not necessarily always God's truth, is it?

God works in mysterious ways, and the challenges and failures in our lives can't always be blamed on Satan. For me at work and elsewhere, one of the toughest things to admit is that a particular situation is placed before me, not by demons but by God Himself because He is working to improve me — *not self-improvement, but God-improvement* — to re-mold my character, re-calculate my abilities, to show and teach me something that I neglected in the midst of my self-importance to self-improve and my tendency to blame man and Satan.

Fact is, sometimes there is nothing quick about the challenges and failures He places before me. No one to blame. Just a lot of work to re-align my response to His likeness.

In really trying times, yes in times of failure, I must stop explaining & blaming and just become that **donkey on which He rides**. I must say: Lord, here I am! Come ride on me today. Where do You want me to take You? What do You want me to do for You? I am willing to carry You all day long, because You carry me all my life. I am willing to carry you wherever you lead — even into the humiliating darkness of defeat and failure — no matter how difficult the terrain may be. I blame no one and no thing, human or demon, because I know it's important to You that I traverse that terrain. I don't know why, and I don't need to know why. I just need to understand it's important to You.

Where He leads you today, be willing to carry Him. Regardless of terrain, be that **donkey on which He rides.**

<u>PRAYER</u>

Heavenly Father, I thank You for the challenges and failures in my work and in my life, even when I don't see or understand the bigger picture. Help me embrace them and bear patiently under them by the power of Your Holy Spirit and to the glory of Your name. With blessing rather than blame, I want to be Your donkey. Without explanation and regardless of terrain, what a privilege it is to carry Your presence into the world. May all eyes be upon You and not on me. In Your name, I pray. Amen.
— Thea Coetzer

Week 6, Day 3

ALWAYS RIGHT

READING

Psalms 119:144 Your laws are always right; help me to understand them so I may live.

REFLECTION

Always Right. We can say this without hesitation with respect to God's rules, but our citizens and students surely don't always say this about us — their government, their teachers. On one hand, we have to recognize that our rules we impose upon others are flawed. They're likely rational, or at least they once were, but they're flawed. Yet we are duty bound to our organization, barring unethical or illegal or corrupt activity by others, to enforce our rules.

At least in the short-term, the problem comes *when we inflict pain and discomfort on others* by enforcing our rules. For instance, perhaps we deny someone for social service due to eligibility rules, knowing that the individual or family truly needs support but falls through the cracks in the social service network. Or, perhaps we fail a student in a class due to academic dishonesty, even though they appear genuinely apologetic and remorseful, and we know failing them will change their current life course with the addition of new hardships. We construct rules to allocate scarce resources and to ensure everyone abides by the same standards.

Sometimes it may be tempting to break our rules, to take pity on the situation of another person. But this can create tension in our role as a public servant. I mean, can we create exceptions for everyone? And if not for everyone, can we create loopholes for anyone?

And so we abide by and enforce our rules, sometimes violating our true desire to show compassion, to forgive, to give a second chance. Though our rules may not always seem fair, we must have faith that God's rules *are* fair and just, and that those who appear at first to be harmed by man's rules have the opportunity to *live according to rules beyond man*. This may be shallow comfort when we know our decisions are harming others, but it is a comfort we should keep with us as we live according to the blessings we are given.

Regrettably, as you go to work today, know you are not **always right**.

PRAYER

Dear God, give me wisdom to live by Your rules and to see that our rules remain minor in the whole of our existence. Help me to be just in all I do. Forgive me when I am not. Help me to make and enforce rules that are fair and that help rather than hurt my fellow citizens. Look after and give strength to those whom I cannot help through my own efforts. In Jesus' name, I pray. Amen.

—Thomas A. Bryer

Week 6, Day 4

SEE US AS JESUS

READING

John 12:8 You will always have the poor among you, but I will not be here with you much longer.

REFLECTION

As Christian public servants, we are called upon to work with the poor in any number of settings. That means we must be clear about how God sees the poor and how we are to see the poor. Many times today's reading is used to justify less-than-godly views of the poor. Sometimes it's an excuse that goes this way: "there will always be poor people — Jesus said so." Sometimes it's an explanation that goes something like this: "people are poor because Jesus said there would always be poor people." Either way, the ungodly bottom line is "we can't do anything about it."

But *Christian* public servants know another alternative. Jesus is actually *complimenting* His disciples. He is looking to His crucifixion and beyond. He knew that His time was short. In light of that, what will it be like for the disciples after He is gone?

The answer? It will be much the same for them as it was for Him. Disciples continue in the footsteps of Jesus. Because they do, they will get the same response that He did. Just as the poor flocked to Jesus, they will also flock to the disciples. Jesus saw the poor as *God's people* created in *God's image* just as surely as anyone else is created in God's image.

So when the poor approach today, what greater compliment could a *Christian* public servant receive? When we see the poor as Jesus saw the poor, the poor **see us as Jesus**!

PRAYER

God of us all, help me to accept everyone I meet today as Your child. At work today, help me to see the poor as Jesus saw the poor. Remind me to act and do accordingly. In Your Son's name, I pray. Amen.
— Tom Duley

Week 6, Day 5

FLY THAT FLAG UNCEASINGLY

READING

John 13:34–35 So now I am giving you a new commandment: Love each other. Just as I have loved you, you should love each other. Your love for one another will prove to the world that you are my disciples.

REFLECTION

Driving around town, I see many flags posted on people's homes. Some are patriotic flags, while others are seasonal. Some flags represent various colleges, and others are there just for fun. Each banner identifies a little something about the owner.

Now, Christ gives you a banner to unfurl each day, too. It's a *flag of love*, and it identifies a little something about you — that you are His disciple. You don't necessarily post it on your home, but you are to unfurl it in your heart. Because it tells others that you have His demonstrative love to give to them, He expects you to **fly that flag unceasingly**.

You and I both know it's not always easy to display that banner. It's particularly risky business to unfurl it in a crowd of strangers — and that quite often includes coworkers.

Have courage this today at work to unfurl that banner! Let your love for others identify you as one of His. With Christ, don't let circumstance determine anything — fly it on sunny and rainy days. Fly the flag of God! Let each see and feel that you are His disciple. **Fly that flag unceasingly**!

PRAYER

Lord, give me courage to post Your flag of love everywhere, but especially in my workplace. Let me unfurl it to the one who needs Your love the most, as well as to the one who thinks he needs Your love the least. In Your name, I pray. Amen.

—Chris Summers

Week 7, Day 1

PRACTICE THAT ANSWER

Matthew 6:21 Wherever your treasure is, there the desires of your heart will also be.

REFLECTION

Where is your treasure? As Christians, we know the answer. But still, during the workweek, do you **practice that answer**? To be honest, sometimes I don't. I start to find treasure in the job itself, in my profession, or in my own workplace. And sometimes my desire to excel at what I do overshadows the importance of why I do it.

You know, it's too easy to lose track of where our treasure is when we have truly great jobs. And what about bad jobs? Well, it's easy to forget Who can make them great, too.

Where is your treasure? When we dedicate our everyday activities to the Lord, we remember the answer. Then, our work becomes a sacred prayer and hymn of worship. When it does, He listens to us and we can hear Him. That is where the treasure is found.

Where is your treasure? You already know the answer. Today at work, let's you and me **practice that answer**.

PRAYER

Dear Lord, I pray for the strength, will, and passion to know where my treasure really is. Let me work accordingly each minute of this day. In Your name, I pray. Amen.

—Gary Roberts

Week 7, Day 2

BEGIN THE DAY AGAIN

READING

Psalm 46:10a Be still, and know that I am God!

REFLECTION

Maybe your day begins like mine. The alarm sounds and the busy-ness of the new day is upon me. I scarf down my breakfast, grab a cup of coffee and head out the door. I make haste on my way to the office. I pass the slower cars on the highway. I quickly arrive, move to my computer, and soon find myself busy reading and sending emails. It isn't long before I'm swept away by the mounting list of chores before me. I have trouble keeping my head above the water. Before I know it, my morning has passed.

But something is missing.

And then I suddenly realize what's missing: solitude in order for me to be with and know God. I realize that solitude with God is key to my spiritual life and growth. So I stop, close all the doors and windows in my life and seek Him and His presence alone. The busy thoughts and ideas of my day still pound on the outside screaming to get in. They demand my attention, but He demands my stillness. So I simply chase away the outside until all is quiet.

Now, I can feel the presence of God. Now, I **begin the day again**.

As you continue this workweek, put on the breaks just a tad. Chase the outside away for a moment. Seek solitude with Him. Prayerfully **begin the day again**.

PRAYER

Lord, as I begin this day anew, I seek solitude. In the quiet of my workspace, I seek to be in Your presence. I seek to begin this day in prayer. May I honor You in everything I do this day. In Jesus' name, I pray. Amen.

—H. Frank Holley

Week 7, Day 3

DESPERATELY DEPENDENT
AND PREPARED

READING

John 15:1–2, 5 I am the true grapevine, and my Father is the gardener. He cuts off every branch of mine that doesn't produce fruit, and he prunes the branches that do bear fruit so they will produce even more. Yes, I am the vine; you are the branches. Those who remain in me, and I in them, will produce much fruit. For apart from me you can do nothing.

REFLECTION

Regardless of which hemisphere you live in, fall and winter eventually fade into spring and summer — and these are the seasons of growth. When I see the harvested fruit that comes from months of pruning and nurturing, I realize that nothing beautiful and good can remain outside the living vine and the caring gardener.

As Christians, we are *desperately dependent* on both the Vine and the Gardener. While pruning might feel painful at times, it *prepares* us for the good fruit we are to bear.

As *Christian* public servants, remain **desperately dependent and prepared.** His vision may require unexpected changes in your professional growth. His direction may result in a different twist in your career path. His pruning may mean adaptation in what you do today at work.

Painful, perhaps. Threatening, maybe. Scary, sometimes. Uncertain, always. But just remember, you're joined to the strongest Vine. You have the most caring Gardener. He knows what He's doing and, besides, *you can't do anything without Him*. So hang in there, and don't lose faith.

Today at work, stay **desperately dependent and prepared**. The harvest season draws near.

PRAYER

Gardener, Father, Lord. Thank You for loving me enough not to leave me where You found me but to prune me into something beautiful for Your glory. I ask that, in this season, You help me to be desperately dependent on You while being prepared by You to do Your work today and tomorrow. Thank You for the Vine, my Savior. It is in His name, I pray. Amen.
—Kathryn Saunders

Week 7, Day 4

BLESS THE LISTENER AND
PLEASE OUR LORD

READING

James 3:5 In the same way, the tongue is a small thing that makes grand speeches. But a tiny spark can set a great forest on fire.

Psalm 39:1(a) I said to myself, "I will watch what I do and not sin in what I say."

REFLECTION

My friend met a gentleman who is in prison. They started writing, and she visited him quite often. Gradually, they fell in love and married. (Yes, he remained in prison.) Well, despite working really hard on their marriage, separation eventually took its toll. Sadly, they divorced.

A coworker always tossed *careless comments* toward my friend — usually in front of others in the break room. At first, the coworker's observations centered on the obvious consequences of marrying someone behind bars. Then, when the marriage went south, that coworker had a field day. She put in her two cents wherever possible — appearing sympathetic but actually ridiculing my friend's suffering. As much as the divorce hurt, the coworker's words cut into my friend's heart like a knife.

You know, God created the world and man with His words. And many of Jesus's miracles were performed through His spoken words. Yet scripture also warns us that a little spark can turn into a blazing fire. That spark can be our words and, I wonder, how many people are set afire?

At work today, know that you can use your words to build up or tear down. Any conversation can bring encouragement or discouragement. *It's your choice.* Know also that once words flow from your mouth, there's no calling them back.

So today at work, may the words you speak **bless the listener and please our Lord**.

PRAYER

Jesus, use my mouth to bring blessing to those You have created. May my words glorify You and keep me close to You. In Your name, I pray. Amen and amen!

—Ellen C. Stamm

Week 7, Day 5

AT THE HEART

READING

1 Samuel 16:7 But the Lord said to Samuel, "Don't judge by his appearance or height, for I have rejected him. The Lord doesn't see things the way you see them. People judge by outward appearance, but the Lord looks at the heart.

REFLECTION

I am in prison — on death row.

Since arriving here, God has brought many people into my life. A warden and a chaplain who follow Christ each day. Many guards are truly amazing Christians. There are free-world volunteers who visit so often, bringing Christian fellowship and the promise of the Word. You may be surprised, but the Body of Christ is alive and well where I live. You may call it death row, and it truly is, but I am actually a brother-in-Christ on *life* row. I have found eternal life here through my savior, Jesus Christ.

So I just want to tell you how blessed I am by people like you. People you call *Christian* public servants. The *Christian* public servants around me, those who work here and volunteer here, look less at the outward appearance and, like our Lord, look more **at the heart**. Without excusing my past, they look less at what I did or my rebellious ways. They look less at my shame. Like the Lord, they look more at me as to *where I am* and *where I will someday be*.

Through His Word, and His people like you, my Lord has taught me to look **at the heart** of others. (You might think this is a lesson learned too late in my life, but still it is God's lesson to be learned.) So I am thankful for those who come to work and volunteer here. It's not an easy place to work or visit, I realize that. They have to be here because of me, and others like me, I know that. But they bless me each day. And I am blessed when I can bring our Lord to those around me, including a guard who may be having a terrible day or a free-world volunteer facing challenges of his own.

You are not thanked enough, but the world is blessed by people like you, *Christian* public servants. The world is truly blessed.

You may not work in a prison or volunteer on death row, but there are people around you who are *incarcerated* in some way — *incarcerated* by outward appearances. *Incarcerated* by temptation or by Satan. *Incarcerated* by fear or by shame. *Incarcerated* by the consequences of their own bad choices or godless actions.

Maybe it's the person working next to you? I pray you will look at them less in terms of outward appearances and, like our Lord, look more **at the heart**.

PRAYER

Father, in the name of Jesus, continue to mold my heart like Yours so I can meet brothers and sisters right where they are at. Amen.
—Jimmy Davis, Jr.

Week 8, Day 1

RUN THE RACE PUBLICLY

READING

Hebrews 12:1-2(a) Therefore, since we are surrounded by such a huge crowd of witnesses to the life of faith, let us strip off every weight that slows us down, especially the sin that so easily trips us up. And let us run with endurance the race God has set before us. We do this by keeping our eyes on Jesus, the champion who initiates and perfects our faith.

REFLECTION

Many people watch you because you are a public servant. Some cheer you on, while others ridicule you <u>and</u> the public service. The ones directly in front of you are probably a minority – given media and social outlets, everyone on earth may see you do something.

As Christians, you and I must live out our faith in front of people every day. And as Christian public servants, we do so with the knowledge that we must run the race for His glory in serving those whom God places before us. We run the race publicly -- in full daylight and knowing all eyes are upon us.

As this workweek begins, know people eagerly watch you. Some look to see Jesus in you– to see how God works through you. But others hope that Jesus is missing today.

It doesn't matter why they watch. Just follow Christ as you **run the race publicly**. By completing His work faithfully, you will draw the onlookers closer to God.

PRAYER

Dear Jesus, You have placed me in a public world that is looking for purpose. Please help me to point them to You. Help me be worthy of the Gospel I carry. In Your name, I pray. Amen.
    —Jonathan Lantz

Week 8, Day 2

THOSE TWO SIMPLE WORDS

READING

1 Samuel 15:22 But Samuel replied, "What is more pleasing to the LORD: your burnt offerings and sacrifices or your obedience to his voice? Listen! Obedience is better than sacrifice, and submission is better than offering the fat of rams."

Matthew 4:19 Jesus called out to them, "Come, follow me, and I will show you how to fish for people!"

REFLECTION

At the U.S. Army's Infantry School at Fort Benning, Georgia, stands a grand statue affectionately called "Iron Mike" — depicting a battle captain with his arm extended forward, exhorting his men to "Follow Me!"

Those two simple words, *Follow Me*, have great consequence. They require courage and faith in the person commanding you, as veterans of any nation's military can tell you. And, they leave you with nowhere to hide: either you obey those words or you don't.

As a Christian, you know God delights in your obedience. And, as always, Jesus finds a way to cut to the chase with **those two simple words**. It takes courage and faith, but that's what Christianity is all about. Like me, you really have nowhere to hide.

Today at work, **those two simple words** await both of us. They command us, and they have great consequence. As *Christian* public servants, we have nowhere to hide.

PRAYER

Lord, help me obey and follow You throughout my day. Help me be the servant leader You have called me to be. In Your name, I pray. Amen.
   —David Boisselle

Week 8, Day 3

BE THERE WITH YOUR HEART

READING

I Samuel 16:7b People judge by outward appearance, but the LORD looks at the heart.

REFLECTION

There's a slogan for a famous fish market: "be there!" Now I know that sounds so Madison Avenue, but still it's an important consideration. In our work, after all, we should be attentive and focused in everything we do. At our workplace, we should always be there.

It's one thing to be fully engaged with your mind at work, but shouldn't you also **be there with your heart**?

Today when that person asks for help — that citizen, client, patient, or student — when that person seeks your assistance, is it just your mind that comes into play? And how often does your intellect begin to judge that person? He's too lazy; she's just a complainer; he's inarticulate; she's pretty dumb. They will never make it even with my help.

Sure, your mind is working, but you're not using your heart.

My friend, Jesus is *there* — fully engaged and watching you and me today — every day. He is looking at the hearts of the people we serve — not just their outward conditions. He is also looking at our hearts as *Christian* public servants. He really doesn't care how big your brain is, or how much you use it. Just thinking by itself will not cut it by His standards. As your Heavenly Supervisor, He wants you to **be there with your heart**. He cares enough to have His heart in the game. The question is, shouldn't you?

Today at work, know that problems and situations will not be solved strictly by your intellect. And by your thinking alone, poor judgments may well set in.

So, as that fish market slogan goes: *be there* completely. **Be there with your heart**.

PRAYER

Heavenly Father, thank You for loving me too much to leave me the way I am. Provide me with those Divine Appointments today at work. I will be there with my heart as You work miracles on those I serve. I will fully engage in You as You work miracles on me. In the name of Jesus, I pray. Amen.

—Debra Neal

Week 8, Day 4

PREACHERS, PLUMBERS AND PROSTITUTES

READING

Hebrews 13:2 Don't forget to show hospitality to strangers, for some who have done this have entertained angels without realizing it!

Matthew 21:31(b) Then Jesus explained his meaning: "I tell you the truth, corrupt tax collectors and prostitutes will get into the Kingdom of God before you do."

REFLECTION

In public service, we *meet many different kinds of citizens. Some are dressed nicely, while* others might not have changed clothes lately. Some are clean and well-manicured while others are dirty and, quite frankly, smell. Some would never split an infinitive while others may have trouble saying what they need to say. Some hold high-ranking positions and others, well, not so much. Yes, citizens come in all flavors.

Hectic days can result in quick judgments regarding who is standing before us. Yet when Jesus was on earth, he mingled with everyone — didn't matter if the person was rich or poor, well-educated or not. **Preachers, plumbers and prostitutes** — it didn't matter what kind of sinner they were, His service of salvation was offered to everyone. Then and now, *Jesus embraces everyone equally*.

As a *Christian* public servant, shouldn't I do the same? Shouldn't I value everyone as *Imago Dei* and treat each accordingly? Even in my most hectic moments, shouldn't I follow His example?

As the workweek continues, remember that you may be entertaining angels without knowing it. Some will be **preachers, plumbers and prostitutes**.

PRAYER

Father, You created each person in Your likeness — regardless of earthly circumstance. At work today, help me to remember I am serving Your creation and Your image. Help me to imitate Jesus and follow His example. In Your Son's name, I pray. Amen.
—Stephen Pincus

Week 8, Day 5

ANSWER LIES IN HOPE

READING

Psalm 119:71–72 My suffering was good for me, for it taught me to pay attention to your decrees. Your instructions are more valuable to me than millions in gold and silver.

Galatians 6:9: So let's not get tired of doing what is good. At just the right time, we will reap a harvest of blessing if we don't give up.

REFLECTION

Suffering... At one point or another, everyone suffers. But to be honest, it is never easy to say, "My suffering was good for me!"

Someone is suffering this very moment. You know who it is. Look around. It's someone at work. The question is, how can you encourage a constituent waiting in line, or perhaps a coworker sitting in the next office, when you see and feel just how much that person is suffering? The **answer lies in hope**.

Remember the suffering of our Savior. Recognize that we will all have to bear the cross as He has done. Know the hope we have in His resurrection.

Today at work, encourage that sufferer. Remind her of the promises of God. Tell of His resurrection, and that now is the time you *don't give up*. Renew hope alongside that person who really needs hope. Be mindful that both of you will reap a harvest of blessings — if you both *don't give up*.

Suffering... yes, but today don't give up. The **answer lies in hope.**

PRAYER

Father, thank You for being the example I need to follow! In this Most Holy week, thank You for showing me how to suffer with the spirit of not giving up. Lord, as I press through my suffering, I pray that You will equip my mind, heart, and spirit with the tenacity to endure and the joy of knowing that You are in control. In Jesus' name, I pray. Amen.

—LaShonda Garnes

Week 9, Day 1

TAKE THE STRESS

READING

Ecclesiastes 7:9a Control your temper

Psalm 37:7b And wait patiently for him to act.

Matthew 11:28a Come to me, all of you who are weary and carry heavy burdens, and I will give you rest.

REFLECTION

Last summer, I was an intern with the youth ministry at my church. It was a real blessing and honor to be selected, but there were a few unpleasant tasks. Sometimes I was asked to discipline a youth for acting way out of hand, and sometimes I had to call the parents to tell them their child couldn't go on a field trip. Now, don't get me wrong. My work was a true ministry of love and fun, and most of the kids were respectful while acting their age. But one or two occasionally wore my patience a little thin. On those days, patience became the last thing on my mind after work.

Whoever said, "Patience is a virtue," never drove home after a rough day at work. On those days, I tend to hit every stop light — and each seems to last at least 30 minutes. Then I find myself behind the slowest moving car in the world, and I cannot get a break to pass by. Nothing goes my way, my thoughts become angry, and my patience drains completely.

I don't suppose you've had days like this. Do you **take the stress** with you when you leave work? Right into your car and into your home at night? As *Christian* public servants, we're called to control our temper and wait patiently for Him. But on some days, that's difficult to do.

The thing we can do is let *Jesus* **take the stress**. It's the only way to get rest and to wait patiently for God to act. And if you let Jesus **take the stress** before you even get to work, you may not have it in the car as you drive home after work.

And who knows, maybe that 30-minute red light, or that old lady driving in front of me, is a reminder to control my angry thoughts and just wait patiently for Him to act. Maybe it's a sign that I really need to let Jesus **take the stress**.

Each workday may not be fun, but it should be a ministry of love. Going to work, at work, and coming home from work — keep your patience by letting Jesus **take the stress**!

<u>Prayer</u>

Dear Lord, please be with all of Your servants today, including me. Allow each of us to have patience. Jesus, **take the stress** that may sometimes arise in even the most blessed jobs and internships. Shower us all, who work today, with the hearts of *Christian* public servants. In Your name, I pray. Amen.
      —Samuel Douglas Drake Slack

Week 9, Day 2

BEYOND YOUR JOB DESCRIPTION

READING

Acts 20:35 And I have been a constant example of how you can help those in need by working hard. You should remember the words of the Lord Jesus: "It is more blessed to give than to receive."

2 Corinthians 9:7 You must each decide in your heart how much to give. And don't give reluctantly or in response to pressure. "For God loves a person who gives cheerfully."

REFLECTION

A friend and I recently went to a concert. On that day, my friend had to work late — and this meant we would miss the start of the concert. As we hurriedly drove to our destination, my friend suddenly pulled over near a park. He got out the car and walked toward a man lying on a bench. He gave that man his extra shirt along with $5. Then he got back into the car.

My friend told me he believes in giving to others before he treats himself. He would've felt guilty going to the concert knowing he drove past that man. Turned out, that concert offered much more than good music. It taught me the virtue of selflessness. By my friend's action, I remembered what God says about giving and receiving.

As a public servant, your job entails helping others in some way. But as a *Christian* public servant, you are called to serve others in ways **beyond your job description**.

Today at work, give to others in all that you do.

PRAYER

God, I thank You for lessons on selflessness. Use me to serve others as You have taught. Today, use my gifts as a benefit to someone who needs more. In Your Son's name, I pray. Amen.

—Logan Dickens

Week 9, Day 3

WORKPLACE SHOW & TELL

READING

1 Corinthians 10:10 And don't grumble as some of them did, and then were destroyed by the angel of death.

Philippians 2:14 Do everything without complaining and arguing

REFLECTION

Have you ever worked where it seemed everyone had "baggage"? Grumblings about career challenges, family problems, open disputes with coworkers, issues made public about your supervisor. I'm not talking about people, facing the great unknown each day, who choose to carry their crosses with dignity. I'm not talking about major life crises about which a coworker confidentially opens up with a close Christian friend.

No, I'm talking about petty, selfish people who dump out the contents of their baggage on a table each morning and shout, *"Lookie here what I brought today!"* Then others follow suit. Fact is, baggage begets baggage. All at once, you look around and its **workplace show & tell**.

Today, skip the **workplace show & tell** — don't participate and don't view the content of others' baggage as if it were some kind of spectator sport! Leave your baggage in the trunk of your car. (If you must, go check on it at lunchtime.) Otherwise, you will be unproductive and, worse, you will be seen in poor light as a *Christian* public servant.

Today at work, be blind to grumblings. Ignore the **workplace show & tell**. You may be surprised at how God can change the workplace conversation!

PRAYER

Lord, thank You for the opportunity to serve in places that need my talents! Give me the grace and poise as I avoid looking into the baggage sprawled across the workroom. I need to change the conversation, but I can only do so with Your strength. In Your service, not mine, and in Jesus' name, I pray. Amen!
—David Shultz

Week 9, Day 4

MAKE THINGS WORK

READING

Proverbs 31:25 She is clothed with strength and dignity, and she laughs without fear of the future.

Philippians 4:13 For I can do everything through Christ, who gives me strength.

REFLECTION

Turnovers are stressful! I'm not talking about the cherry or apple kind. No, I'm talking about the human kind — when you have to deal with people leaving the workplace.

It happens for a variety of reasons: personal, financial, a better job on the horizon, bad managers mistreating good employees, or good managers disciplining those who deserve it. Regardless of the reason, it seems that turnovers affect everyone in the workplace.

This week alone we lost several workers in my own office. And now it's my responsibility to find new employees to fill in the gaps and work well with our crew. The process is costly, time consuming, and office morale always wants to head south.

You must have similar days in your office. When they happen, you have to find a way to keep your head up. Even though things will be rougher than expected, know that God is working with you. So keep smiling and show dignity. Don't let anyone see you worried or stressed as that will only hurt morale. Our Lord will give you strength to **make things work**.

Yes, on days like this, let everyone see that He will **make things work**.

PRAYER

Lord, I can't begin to thank You enough for blessing me with the position I hold and the life I live. I ask that You give me strength to **make things work** on this tough workday and keep everyone in good spirits. Please help me show my dignity through Your wisdom, love, and comfort. Only with You will each workday be a little easier. In Your Son's name, I pray. Amen.

—Meredith Pulsford

Week 9, Day 5

ROOTED AND BUILT UP IN HIM

READING

Colossians 2:6–7 And now, just as you accepted Christ Jesus as your Lord, you must continue to follow him. Let your roots grow down into him, and let your lives be built on him. Then your faith will grow strong in the truth you were taught, and you will overflow with thankfulness

1 Thessalonians 5:11, 15 So encourage each other and build each other up, just as you are already doing.... See that no one pays back evil for evil, but always try to do good to each other and to all people.

REFLECTION

Does anyone at work ever try to get under your skin? I bet it doesn't matter how nice you are, you remain the brunt of all his smart remarks. Or, in bragging about her accomplishments, she always finds a way to belittle you. Fact is, some coworkers just need someone to pick on.

I know that's the case. One particular coworker will not leave me alone. In subtle ways, of course —so as not to get in trouble — she always finds new ways to make our eight hours together insufferable. I just didn't understand why until I prayed and read the Word.

Turns out, my coworker probably has issues that go well beyond just messing with me. She is searching for recognition and, just maybe, she has no idea that true recognition comes from God. The bottom line is, she seems not to be **rooted and built up in Him**.

Well, we will never get rid of coworkers who try to get under our skin. But scripture can help you and I remember what our response has to be: encouraging and overflowing with goodness. So today at work, let's react in ways that show we are **rooted and built up in Him**!

PRAYER

Heavenly Father, there are so many people tormented by this world. Today at work, may they be touched in ways that lead them to You. Today at work, may the antagonist finally seek Your face for direction. In Jesus' name, I pray. Amen.
  —Crystal Featherston

Week 10, Day 1

IMPORTANT STUFF

READING

Mark 6:8 He told them to take nothing for their journey except a walking stick—no food, no traveler's bag, no money.

REFLECTION

Over the weekend, I engaged in my once-a-decade ritual: I bought a new wallet. Transferring everything from the old to the new was challenging and exciting. It was challenging because they seem to make wallets smaller each decade; hence, less room for my **important stuff**. The excitement came from rediscovering the **important stuff** I had stashed in the cubby holes of the old wallet — forgotten items that brought back memories.

I found post-it notes from my daughter, marking her maturity over the years, but always the same message: "I love U, daddy!" One of my son's notes: "I enjoyed watching football with you yesterday!" In addition to a love-note from my wife, I found something I had written: the words of *Ephesians* 5:25.

I placed this **important stuff** in my wallet because I knew they were memories I never would discard. *They strengthen me.* I will carry them for another decade, and hopefully collect more along my journey. Ultimately, when my journey ends, those same memories will return to my family and *strengthen them* as they collect that **important stuff** and retire my final wallet.

Each day marks a new leg in our journey. The Lord instructs us to take along nothing but a staff or rod, yet He sends us with plenty of **important stuff**. His love travels through many vessels, including the **important stuff** placed and later found in our wallets and pocketbooks, as well as in our hearts.

On good days and bad, that important stuff is a reminder of why we go to work and why we stay at work until it's time to go home.

PRAYER

Father God, as this workday begins, I thank you for the **important stuff** You give to help me on my journey. In Your Son's name, I pray. Amen.
—James D. Slack

Week 10, Day 2

BUT WHAT ABOUT ME

READING

Matthew 6:3–4 But when you give to someone in need, don't let your left hand know what your right hand is doing. Give your gifts in private, and your Father, who sees everything, will reward you.

REFLECTION

Once upon a time, a nurse loved to work. In fact, she loved to work really hard. She knew hard work pays off, so she would point out her hard work to her supervisors. She did this quite often. Their affirmation made her work even harder. The up side was that patients received better and faster care and, each time she pointed it out, her supervisors gave her even more affirmation. She loved the affirmation. The down side was she became addicted to affirmation; the more praise she got, the more praise she needed.

Then one day, in the midst of all the noise of addiction, she heard a quiet yet firm Voice: "**But what about Me?** Isn't My affirmation sufficient reward?"

And there it was. Her shallow desire for earthly acclaim lay bare.

Since then, the praise from supervisors has grown a little lean. Oh, her patients still receive exceptional care, but now they receive it because that nurse loves being a caregiver. As a *Christian* public servant, she loves working hard on His behalf. She now *excels in secret* without expecting praise from others.

But what about Me? Well, what about you!

It may seem risky, but you and I really need no other reward for hard work than the blessing of our Savior. What about performance reviews, raises, and promotions? Our Lord will reward you and me *openly* when He desires.

So today at work, may we both hear the same quiet yet firm Voice that once got the attention of that nurse. May we both answer pleasingly to His glory at the whisper, "**But what about Me?**"

PRAYER

Almighty God, consider the works of Your servant. Bless Your servant's efforts this day to bring You glory and honor and praise. To seek only Your affirmation, and to let Your hand be evident in Your servant's works. In Your holy name, I pray. Amen.

—Katherine Zasadny

Week 10, Day 3

HOPELESSLY HOMELESS, FRIENDLESS, AND FAMILY-LESS

READING

Acts 28: 2 The people of the island *were* very kind to us. It was cold and rainy, so they built a fire on the shore to welcome us.

Matthew 25:40 And the King will say, "I tell you the truth, when you did it to one of the least of these my brothers and sisters, you were doing it to me!"

REFLECTION

Don't know about where you live, but we're having an unusually cold winter in my part of the world. Last night it happened again: ice, snow, and frigid temperatures coupled with strong winds coming off the ocean.

On nights like that, my thoughts run back to Jerry — a homeless man I met a couple of years ago. Claiming he was ill, Jerry called the station and wanted to go to a hospital. Turned out he was not ill; he just needed to get out of the cold and find a hot meal. We let him in our warm station for a while, and we fed him.

As Jerry and I talked, I realized he was **hopelessly homeless, friendless, and family-less**. He had many problems, yes, but his life was not much different from people who have homes, are not cold, and are not hungry. Like so many, what Jerry really needed on that cold wintry night was the *fire of Christ's love*. I realized that was missing in my night, too. I looked around the station and began to wonder which of my coworkers, because they also lacked the warmth of His fire, were unknowingly and **hopelessly, homeless, friendless, and family-less**. Jerry got warmed-up and his physical hunger left, but he gave me much more to think about as he left the station.

Depending on where you live in the world, you may be driving to work this morning with snow tires humming or turning up the car air conditioning because it's already a scorcher. Doesn't matter. You may be a firefighter, like me, a social worker or teacher, or someone who runs the budget from one of those cubicles in central administration. Doesn't matter.

Remember: what is most needed in your workplace today is the *fire of Christ's love*. That fire is needed by those you serve and by coworkers. It is needed by those who "call in" and claim it, as well as by those who deny they're even cold and hungry.

Bring them into the station. Show extraordinary kindness by lighting the fire. Know that, without the *fire of Christ's love*, we all are **hopelessly homeless, friendless, and family-less**.

PRAYER

Father God, as this workday begins, let me not forget why You called me to be a Christian public servant. I am to serve the physical needs of the citizens, but I am called to do much more for You. Let me show extraordinary kindness to my least brothers and sisters. Let me not forget that we all are Your least and, therefore, we all need You as a home, as a friend and as a family. Let my actions toward others today provide the warmth of Your Son's fire. In Jesus' name we pray. Amen

    —Stephen Pincus

Week 10, Day 4

NEITHER YOUR HEAVEN
NOR YOUR HELL

READING

2 Corinthians 4:16–18 That is why we never give up. Though our bodies are dying, our spirits are being renewed every day. For our present troubles are small and won't last very long. Yet they produce for us a glory that vastly outweighs them and will last forever! So we don't look at the troubles we can see now; rather, we fix our gaze on things that cannot be seen. For the things we see now will soon be gone, but the things we cannot see will last forever.

REFLECTION

Where I live, we've been experiencing unusually wintry days. I like watching it snow, witnessing the glory of God in each unique flake, but the storms prevent me from getting to work. Snow shutdowns make the case files on my desk rise higher than the actual snow! Oh, I get a brief repose, but getting caught up is always taxing. Instead of calling to reschedule, my probation clients randomly show up unexpectedly — and this adds stress to serving those whom already have appointments for the day. Plus, due dates that were a little bit down the road before each storm suddenly stand right in my face. An 8-hour day just isn't enough, and that places stress on the family side. On days like this, I find my eyes fixed on what is on my desk, and not the eternal glory that comes in the end.

Sure, I eventually regain perspective, but only after I realize that *God's Will is my schedule* — not the many tasks or the things I label as my priorities. As this workday begins, whether you are drowning in an improvised schedule or just overwhelmed with daily busy-ness, remember: the mountain of paperwork on your desk is not your end-point. It is **neither your heaven nor your hell**.

Try to embody a spirit of joy and peace while you weather that snowstorm on your desk. As a *Christian* public servant, remember to glorify God.

PRAYER

God, help us honor You through our work. Help us to honor Your Will by not complaining or focusing on the physical. Help us to see our path using our faith in You and Your love for us. In Your Son's name, I pray. Amen.

—Malcolm Jones

Week 10, Day 5

NOT PEOPLE, BUT THE LORD

READING

Colossians 3:23 Work willingly *at* whatever you do, as though you were working for the Lord rather than for people.

REFLECTION

It's been a challenging workweek. Actually, this workweek felt more like a work-eternity — and, believe me, I'm not in heaven! I have an impossible supervisor, and I'm stuck working with three lazy goof-offs. It's such a temptation to reduce my productivity to match theirs. But if I do, my supervisor — Mr. Wonderful — will call me on the carpet. It's easier for some managers to pressure the ones who actually work than to do something with those who play work.

I do my work to the best of my abilities. I try my best to excel — not for the sake of Mr. Wonderful or the Three Stooges. No. What keeps me going are **not people, but the Lord**. If I forget this Bible verse for one instant, I am doomed to mediocrity. And I'm not entering the public service to be mediocre.

What about you? We have not made it yet this week, and I bet you have similar kinds of problems. Is Mr. Wonderful hovering over you? Do you have a task assignment involving Larry, Curly, and Moe?

Let's make it through this week as *Christian* public servants. Forget Mr. Wonderful. Forget about those who pretend to work until break time. **Not people, but the Lord**! Now, that is why you woke up this morning. **Not people, but the Lord**! That's why you came to work.

Not people, but the Lord. That is why you are a *Christian* public servant!!

PRAYER

Heavenly Father, we thank You for employment and for careers. We ask for strength and courage so that, even in the most irrational work environment, we work heartily to honor You. In Jesus' name, I pray. Amen.
    —TaQuesha Brandon

Week 11, Day 1

WHERE IS YOUR BROTHER

READING

Genesis 4:9 Afterward the Lord asked Cain, "Where is your brother? Where is Abel?"

Philippians 2:4 Don't look out only for your own interests, but take an interest in others, too.

REFLECTION

Unless you live under a rock, you know the world is a dangerous place. And the danger that comes from within the workplace — the frequency of shootings, especially at public sector facilities — is hard to ignore. Such events are always tragic, and you may feel powerless in their wake, but there's something we all can do to help prevent this madness.

As *Christian* public servants, we shouldn't focus solely on our own well-being. We must look out for our coworkers; know when they're happy, but also sense when they're troubled.

A *Christian* leader should know when someone is distressed. All *Christian* team members should have an equal feel about each other. If you notice a coworker in trouble, whether it is physical or mental, do your best to get them help before it gets worse.

It's so easy to get lost in our own troubles, our own lives, or our own cubicles. Besides, it's risky if we appear to be intruding into the private affairs of others at work. But doesn't God expect us to be our brother's keeper? Even in the workplace, are we not our brother's keeper?

God asks you all the time, "**Where is your brother**?" You can't just answer, "*I don't know — he's not my problem.*" God says he is your problem. Even at work, He expects you to be an active part of the Body of Christ and care for others.

Tragedies sometimes happen without signs. But they certainly do not happen before God asks quietly, "**Where is your brother**?"

PRAYER

Dear Lord, please let me be Your instrument in recognizing my problems, as well as the problems faced by others today. Guide all through these troubling times, and keep everyone safe in our workplaces. In Jesus' name we pray, Amen.
  —Trevor Nystrom

Week 11, Day 2

OLD-SELF WAY

READING

Philippians 2:5 You must have the same attitude that Christ Jesus had.

Romans 12:2 Don't copy the behavior and customs of this world, but let God transform you into a new person by changing the way you think. Then you will learn to know God's will for you, which is good and pleasing and perfect.

James 1:23, 24 For if you listen to the word and don't obey, it is like glancing at your face in a mirror. You see yourself, walk away, and forget what you look like.

REFLECTION

Occasionally at work I find myself easing back into that **old-self way**.

Ever happen to you?

I'm not necessarily talking about working in a selfish way, like when I really would like to ignore all the e-mails in my inbox and just work on what I want rather than what is needed. And, I'm not talking about those times when I just need to get away for a little while.

What I'm talking about is doing things that make me forget *who I am* now — more importantly, to *whom I belong* now. I'm talking about doing things that make me forget *what I look like* now.

For me, it returns — that **old-self way** — when I say something in a meeting that could have been said with a more civilized tongue, or when I go out of my way to correct a student in the harshest terms. For me, it returns when I find myself not helping someone because I just don't believe they are helping themselves.

Because of Who I belong to now, I get signals from above when I return to acting in that **old-self way**. I realize what I am doing, even before I do it, and I am not very happy with myself after it's done. I know I am not reflecting the image of God. I know He is not at all pleased with me.

But I can recover. Scripture promises me that I can be transformed into something further from that **old-self way**. All I need to do is read His Word more deeply and obey it with greater meaning and understanding. If I don't walk away, I will know Him better and will see Him more clearly in the mirror. I will remember the letters *M-I-R-R-O-R* actually stand for **May I Rightly Reflect Our Redeemer**. When I don't walk away, it is harder to return to that **old-self way**.

Yes, sometimes at work I back slide, and I bet you do, too. Today, let's have the strength not to return to that **old-self way**.

PRAYER

Thank You, Father, for Your grace and forgiveness. Thank You for Your Word and Spirit! In them is the power to transform me into all that You want me to be—with the same attitude Your Son had. It is in His name that I pray. Amen.
—Wilisha G. Scaife

Week 11, Day 3

BOTH STRANGER AND FRIEND EQUALLY

READING

Matthew 22:35-40 One of them, an expert in religious law, tried to trap him with this question: "Teacher, which is the most important commandment in the law of Moses?" Jesus replied, "'You must love the Lord your God with all your heart, all your soul, and all your mind.' This is the first and greatest commandment. A second is equally important: 'Love your neighbor as yourself.' The entire law and all the demands of the prophets are based on these two commandments."

REFLECTION

"Love" is the basis of a godly public service.

Whether in government or the nonprofits, we improve and defend our community because we love it and its citizens. Now, this doesn't mean we should ignore wrong and embrace sin. No, but it does mean we must love **both stranger and friend equally**. I wish we would begin to see one another like that today.

At election time in the U.S., and perhaps in your country too, it is important for citizens to wear "I voted" stickers. Perhaps one day soon in all nations, it will be important to wear a little sign that reads *"I want to be loved — I need to love."*

In every nation whether police officer or teacher, legislator or general, custodian or HR specialist, secretary or social worker — I wonder what tomorrow might bring if *Christian* public servants everywhere spent today loving God and loving others, **both stranger and friend equally**? Oh, the miracles that would happen if we truly committed to *love with all that we are!*

Isn't it great that Jesus made this so simple for us? So why do we make it so hard? Today at work, love God and **both stranger and friend equally.**

PRAYER

Dear Lord, at work today I need You. I want to be so in love with You, and to truly show love to others. Help me in this journey, Lord. Show me Your way of love, to see others as You see them. In Your name, Amen.
    —Kathleen Patterson

Week 11, Day 4

JUST DOESN'T MAKE SENSE

READING

Romans 13:3-4(a) For the authorities do not strike fear in people who are doing right, but in those who are doing wrong. Would you like to live without fear of the authorities? Do what is right, and they will honor you. The authorities are God's servants, sent for your good.

REFLECTION

I once worked for an agency where my boss assigned me a project that was already a big mess. I felt overwhelmed, and I thought it **just doesn't make sense**. He seemed like a good manager, but why did he give me a project that was about to fail? As I dug in, I realized the full extent of the damage. It was simply not salvageable. Now I felt anger. I mean, who was he to set me up to fail? Was he going to throw me under the bus and lay all blame on me?

But then God reminded me that my boss had authority, and I had no choice but to submit. Doomed project or not, I had to do my best with what my boss gave me. And, yes, the project inevitably failed. As I feared, some coworkers blamed me. However, my boss did not throw me under the bus. In fact, he even commended the good work I had done.

Now I realize that evil exists in our world. Even when evil is not in play, some people aren't cut out for positions of authority. There are managers who do search for others to blame in order to veil their own incompetence. And, as for me, I sometimes forget that authority comes from God — not from man. When that happens, I get prideful and rebellious. I start thinking that following a particular assignment **just doesn't make sense**.

But God promises you that good authorities — those who are His servants — don't intend to harm you; rather, they work for your good. So as a *Christian* public servant, your job is simple: do good work and have faith in God's servants known as managers and supervisors.

Today at work, don't question a particular assignment. Just do what is good. Honor Him by submitting to the authority of your supervisor — even when doing so **just doesn't make sense**.

PRAYER

Father, remind me every day that authority comes from You. Lead me to submit to my supervisor as an act of honoring You. I pray that all leaders throughout the world will fall to their knees on this workday and become Your servants. As for me, may I humbly represent You well today. In Jesus' name, I pray. Amen.

 —Zach Jones

Week 11, Day 5

WHO SEES YOUR LIGHT

READING

John 1:4b-5 His life gave light to everyone. The light keeps shining in the dark, and darkness has never put it out.

REFLECTION

The morning comes, we begin our daily routines, checking the hours off one by one. At the end of the day, we rest, and wake up the next day only to begin another routine.

Have you ever stopped to think about everyone who crosses your path each day?

Sure, there are coworkers, friends, and colleagues, but what about those we don't really know — the *security guard* in the building, the *parking lot attendant*, the *cashier* at the coffee shop, or an employee from another office sharing the elevator ride.

Scripture says that our light shines and is never put out. It's not a light switch that we simply flip when we're tired of shining....we are ever-shining! We are shining to those we see, and those who see us.

Consider **who sees your light** each day. Is it a bright or dim light? A kind word, friendly gesture, and even a smile can often be the beam that helps carry someone through their darkness.

At work today, be very aware of **who sees your light**.

PRAYER

Father, thank You for placing Your love within me. I don't want to be selfish with what You so selflessly gave. Help me to be aware of my surroundings today at work. Allow my light to shine for everyone who crosses my path. In Your Son's name, I pray. Amen.
  —Christie Brown

Week 12, Day 1

HIT THE BALL AS HARD AS WE CAN

READING

Philippians 4:8b Think about things that are excellent and worthy of praise.

REFLECTION

You may not know this, but my city's slogan is "igniting excellence". While public relations people probably had something to do with it, the phrase still has a Biblical foundation. Scripture reminds all Christians, including public servants, that we must ignite excellence. Yes, we are supposed to be work examples by doing our jobs in an excellent and praiseworthy way.

Yet, do you work with someone who chooses to ignore excellence? Maybe a coworker opts simply to pass the time. Perhaps a supervisor decides not to ignite her own excellence, and then cannot figure out why subordinates are not motivated as well. Maybe you simply elect not to be that much-needed *work example*.

We play a game in South Africa that is similar to your tetherball. The goal is to hit a ball so that your opponent cannot hit it back. The harder you hit, the faster the ball might pass by and return to you. Naturally, you choose how hard you want to hit the ball. If you want to lose, I guess you can hit it softly. But if we're going to play the game, shouldn't we choose to **hit the ball as hard as we can**?

The same is true with the public service. If you are working, why not be a *work example*? Your community deserves your excellence. The citizens deserve your praiseworthy best. Some days you may fail miserably, but scripture clearly calls you to strive for excellence and praiseworthiness.

So as this workday begins, think about how He expects you and me to be *work examples*. Know that He wants you and me to **hit the ball as hard as we can**!

PRAYER

Dear Lord, I want to be a work example today. Help me to fix on Your will and spread Your love and care to my community and the citizens I serve. Not through my own power and strength, but through You, ignite my excellence. I promise I will give You all the glory. I pray this in Your name. Amen.

—Thea G.D. Coetzer

Week 12, Day 2

RESPONSIBILITY TO BE

READING

Isaiah 1:17a Learn to do good. Seek justice. Help the oppressed.

Micah 6:8 No, O people, the LORD has told you what is good, and this is what he requires of you: to do what is right, to love mercy, and to walk humbly with your God.

REFLECTION

As public servants, we are responsible for taking up the case of those who are unable to care adequately for themselves. Most of us understand this as we enter our careers. Others come to that understanding more gradually. Still others lose their grasp in the heat of battle and retreat from the emotional and spiritual drain of the workplace.

It is difficult and demanding work to which you are called. Those in-need are often socially and emotionally challenged, and anger and suspicion are common side-effects of being oppressed, of being helpless to work effectively in society, of being too hungry or too afraid to learn in a classroom, of being robbed or wronged repeatedly.

The prophets agree about what our responsibility is before God. But, Micah takes the argument a step further. We not only have the *responsibility to do*. We have a **responsibility to be**. We are *to be* public servants who love mercy; *to be* public servants who walk humbly before God. We have a **responsibility to be** *Christian* public servants.

To work with the hardest client or citizen, the most challenging student, and the most difficult coworker or supervisor — requires grace, and *grace is delivered only moment by moment*. As one who has experienced God's grace firsthand, you are well aware of the incredible relief and gratitude that pours into your soul when you realize that *your life matters to God*. Everything changes when you realize that you are cherished beyond your own ability to comprehend and that there is a place and a bright future for you, prepared for you from the beginning of time.

The joy that lies within your grasp is *to be God's agent* of grace and acceptance to those who have never experienced it or have forgotten it. As a *Christian* public servant, you have a **responsibility to be**.

PRAYER

My Lord, sometimes I am overwhelmed by how much You trust me and by how generous You have been in preparing me and giving me a place to serve You. I don't always feel worthy and sometimes I am not able to live up to expectations You have for me. Be very present with me, Lord, in the moments of my work that matter. Create in me the compassion for others that You have for me. Amen.

    —Jim Stephens

Week 12, Day 3

NO LIMITS ON ACTS OF LOVE

READING

Ephesians 5: 1-2 Imitate God, therefore, in everything you do, because you are his dear children. Live a life filled with love, following the example of Christ. He loved us and offered himself as a sacrifice for us, a pleasing aroma to God.

REFLECTION

Christians are called to share the Gospel and make disciples. That duty is a part of practicing the faith. Answering that call can be a challenge in public service as lines of acceptability are drawn in order to be tolerant of all faiths, or no faith. Where spoken words may be deemed proselytizing and not politically correct, there are **no limits on acts of love**.

If we imitate God, and show Christ's love to the people we meet and serve, our actions will serve to be a testimony. The refrain of Peter Scholters' hymn comes to mind. "They'll know we are Christians by our love, by our love. Yes they'll know we are Christians by our love."

Let those we serve see us today with **no limits on acts of love**.

PRAYER

Dear Lord, when I am faced with decisions on how to witness to others about Your love, please help my actions to speak louder than my words. In Your name, I pray. Amen.
—R. Keith Jordan

Week 12, Day 4

ON THE COURT HOT

Revelation 3:15-17 I know all the things you do, that you are neither hot nor cold. I wish that you were one or the other! But since you are like lukewarm water, neither hot nor cold, I will spit you out of my mouth! You say, 'I am rich. I have everything I want. I don't need a thing!' And you don't realize that you are wretched and miserable and poor and blind and naked.

REFLECTION

Lukewarm! Just what do you mean: lukewarm? I seek God. I read scripture. I love people. I tithe 10%. I go to services on Sunday and Wednesday. I feed the hungry and clothe the poor during the holidays. I even profess my Christianity with a fish symbol on the trunk of my car. Look, that fish is in plain view in my work parking place right now! Man, in the break room, I even close my eyes and say a silent prayer before I eat lunch!! Lukewarm????

Kyle Idleman writes about two kinds of people who profess Christianity: fans and followers. At basketball games, fans are "there" in the stands and can play an important part, but the coach really needs a team **on the court hot** to win the game. They do not have to make every shot, but they do have to be **on the court hot**.

Is God calling you down from the stands? Does He need you **on the court hot** today?

In my life, I have lived cold and I have lived lukewarm...yet the sweetest part of life is when I am **on the court hot** and part of His team. Just like any other team, we may not win every game. But when we are **on the court hot** as part of His team, we have already won the championship!

At work today, don't be lukewarm for Him. Choose to find ways to be **on the court hot**.

PRAYER

Jesus, life without You is unbearable. Today I do not want to just sit in the stands and cheer You on. I want to join Your team in my workplace, find out what breaks Your heart when I am dealing with others, and try to change the outcome to please You. I am only one person, yet I am willing. I do not want to be cold, and I will not settle to be lukewarm. It is in Your name, that I pray. Amen.

—Tajuan McCarty

Week 12, Day 5

SET ASIDE SHAME

READING

Matthew 28:19 Therefore, go and make disciples of all the nations, baptizing them in the name of the Father and the Son and the Holy Spirit.

Romans 1:16 I am not ashamed of this Good News about Christ. It is the power of God at work saving everyone who believes — the Jew first and also the Gentile.

REFLECTION

As an inmate, shame is a big thing. At one point or another during the day, and especially at night, everyone feels shame — shame at what they did to get here; shame at the damage they did to the lives of many others; shame at what they did to themselves.

Shame makes it much harder to accept His *Great Commission* and spread His *Good News*. It's not the fear of doing so, even in a place like mine, but it's the shame you feel as a sinner. Shame for claiming something you don't deserve. Shame that someone may see right through you. Shame that you are not holy enough.

Shame is a bondage worse than prison. It made me run from Christ for almost 40 years. It steals your confidence.

Shame is what keeps this world's death row from turning into His world's life row.

But Paul tells you and me to **set aside shame**. He became *bold with confidence* and was not ashamed of Christ's *Good News*. And this is the same Paul who had murdered Christians.

If the murderer Paul can **set aside shame**, can you?

Someone where you work needs you to **set aside shame** today and become *bold with confidence* and tell of Christ's *Good News* — not only so they can believe, but also so they can feel the power of God working in them, relieving them of their shame and saving their soul.

Just like Paul, today will you **set aside shame**?

PRAYER

Father, in the name of Jesus, I pray. You promise that "by his stripes we are healed." Heal me from shame and mold me to be as bold as lions so I can share this Good News of Your Son. Help me not just to ask them to believe, but to show Your power to save their souls. Amen.
    —Jimmy Davis, Jr.

Week 13, Day 1

GIVE THANKS TO HIM

READING

Exodus 35:35 The Lord has given them special skills as engravers, designers, embroiderers in blue, purple, and scarlet thread on fine linen cloth, and weavers. They excel as craftsmen and as designers.

REFLECTION

The Lord has blessed me with a job that allows my beautiful son to rest upon my desk at work while I make just enough money to give him a roof, shoes, clothes, toys, food, and a mommy that goes home stress-free each evening. He has blessed me with the skill to make my work environment beautiful. As I study in graduate school to reach my dreams, He allows me to help undergraduate students reach their dreams.

So I **give thanks to Him** for blessing me with talent, skills, and opportunity.

Before your workday begins, I challenge you to **give thanks to Him**, too.

PRAYER

Dear Lord, with honor and praise I come in Your presence. Thank You for the many blessings in my work and in my life. Thank You for being just who You are: the Provider...my Provider. In Your name, I pray. Amen.

—Krystiana Carr

Week 13, Day 2

BRING CHRIST ALIVE

READING

Matthew 25:40 And the King will say, "I tell you the truth, when you did it to one of the least of these my brothers and sisters, you were doing it to me!"

REFLECTION

Public service is not an easy vocation. Citizens and clients can be difficult to deal with, and sometimes they can be downright cruel. Jesus refers to many whom we serve as the least of these. This brings with it special challenges with their own set of difficulties. Just because people are poor doesn't mean that they are any more (or less) cooperative than anyone else. Their needs are often staggering and just can't be met with available resources. Explanations often fall on deaf ears. And on days when difficulties are most pressing, it becomes tempting to give up in despair.

In those moments, we do well to back off a bit, breathe a prayer, and ask God to bring Christ alive in ourselves so that we might see *the least of these* as He does. We didn't choose this career path because we thought we could change the world all by ourselves. As *Christian* public servants, we are in it because we seek to bring Christ alive in ourselves so we can truly serve one person at a time — warts and all!

Yes, the public service is not an easy vocation, and public service undertaken from the Christian perspective is even harder. It only works if, inside yourself, you **bring Christ alive**.

PRAYER

O God of the least of these, help me to bring Your Son to the forefront of me today at work. Where that is easy, let me count it as a blessing. Where it is difficult, give me pause to look closer for You inside me so that I may have more compassionate eyes and a more loving heart toward those whom I serve. For I know, You are counting on me. In Your Son's name, I pray. Amen.
    —Tom Duley

Week 13, Day 3

FIXERS FIND REPOSE

READING

Matthew 11:28b Come to me, all of you who are weary and carry heavy burdens, and I will give you rest.

REFLECTION

Driving to work on this morning, a million thoughts race through your mind.

How can I respond in love to a coworker who lashes out at me? How can I finish my tasks and take time to listen truly to the needs of those I serve? How can I correct a program or project that seems so uncorrectable? Meanwhile, there is the home front: how can I keep my marriage intact with all the work I have to do? Will I find time today to go to that junior high basketball game? And how can I be the parent I am called to be when I resent my rebellious child?

These thoughts lead to days of anxiety and nights of insomnia. *Will today be any different?* Unfortunately we live in a world that constantly needs fixing. Some people are broken and others seem bent on breaking things. Some actions and programs don't work well, and others seem to do more harm than good.

Fortunately you and I are fixers, or at least we try to be. *This is why we are called to public service.* But because we are the fixers-of-the-world, we tend to grow tired and confused in our personal relations and numb and burned-out in our professional roles.

When I was younger, friends would tease me for being so tireless in my hope in hopeless situations. As I get older and see daily "hopeless" situations, I admit I really do get tired!

Yet as a Christian, I must remember there is ALWAYS hope in Jesus. It is only through Him that we are empowered to be fixers, and only by coming to Him can **fixers find repose**.

Today when no further action can be taken to fix things, when we are simply exhausted in the process of public service or how public service becomes a hurdle in our personal lives, remember that prayer is our strongest weapon. It is only after we pray and put matters in our Lord's hands — surrendering the anxiety and consequence of work and life — that we can find rest and repair. Only through Him, can **fixers find repose.**

PRAYER

Lord, the fixers cannot go it alone today. As a Christian public servant, I become broken by my own toil. I come to You to be fixed. Let me be in prayer when I feel helpless or hopeless at work today — when I become exhausted and overwhelmed with my limitations to improve this world in my personal and professional life. Let me always lay my needs at Your feet, be ready to listen for Your calling, and enable me to take deep rest and repair in Your arms. I pray this in Your name. Amen.

    — Erika D. Doster

Week 13, Day 4

DO WHAT IT SAYS

READING

John 13:34 So now I am giving you a new commandment: Love each other. Just as I have loved you, you should love each other.

James 1:22 But don't just listen to God's word. You must do what it says. Otherwise, you are only fooling yourselves.

REFLECTION

The workplace is the hardest place to **do what it says**.

Sure, as Christians we read scripture and devotionals either the evening or morning before we go to work. Yet as public servants, we see too many people struggling every day — strangers in a bad place in their lives. How many times this week have you ignored them or just went through the motions of serving them? We also see coworkers really challenged by fear of job uncertainty, by insufficient paychecks, or by supervisors who really don't care. How many times have I ignored the crisis facing a coworker this week alone?

Citizen-client or coworker, regardless, we sometimes treat people differently because of the color of their skin or the language they speak or their accent or their ethnic heritage or their gender. Sometimes we even treat people differently because of the god they believe in and sometimes because they don't believe in a god at all. Have you done this? I know I have.

You know you should be more caring toward the citizen-client. You know the plight of that coworker could easily be yours. And perhaps it is your plight, and no one seems to care.

As *Christian* public servants, we must simply **do what it says**. We must let our faith be seen through the work we do. You don't have to show your faith through big, grand gestures. God doesn't take score that way. I mean, if God can move your mountains through faith the size of a mustard seed, then surely your effort, no matter how small, can make an impact today at work.

When you read the Word, just simply **do what it says**.

PRAYER

Lord, I pray mightily that You provide me with the wisdom and knowledge I need to be Your dutiful servant at work today. I pray that You not only give me that sacred wisdom, but You also give me the ability to act upon it. I know that faith without works is dead; therefore, I wholeheartedly accept the responsibility of living a life that is worthy of You. I accept the responsibility to **do what it says** when it comes to Your Word. In Your glorious name, I pray. Amen.

—Cassandra D. McLendon

Week 13, Day 5

FORGET THAT BOX

READING

Psalm 61:4a Let me live forever in your sanctuary

Jeremiah 33:3 Ask me and I will tell you remarkable secrets you do not know about things to come.

REFLECTION

Let's talk about the box.

You know what I mean. For the past decade, answers to all workplace problems can be found either in or out of the box. When times get tough, you think outside of it. At other times, you may stay well inside it. Either way, that box is so important. I mean, how did the public service win World War II, or get to the moon, or cure polio, or teach a child, or feed the hungry — in the days before that box?

Yet, I have to wonder just how safe and effective is that box? We both know there is only one good box at any meeting and, ironically, the space outside it is as limited as the space inside it. You will be faulted when you can't find it first, or if you are first to stay inside or climb out. As for those coworkers who cannot even find the box, you will somehow be blamed for hiding it.

Perhaps we should just **forget that box**. Instead, picture yourself in *His Sanctuary*. Room for everyone, and what a wonderfully safe and productive place to be! There, you can think of great ideas — His ideas —- think of fantastic things — His things — that will advance your agency, and the citizens you serve, in ways that are so unimaginable in or out of that old box.

So on this workday, **forget that box**. *His sanctuary is the place to be!*

PRAYER

Lord, You offer Your protection and learning of things so great and unsearchable if I simply dwell in Your sanctuary. Only the brightest thoughts and clearest ideas will come to me when I dwell there. There is nothing the Evil One can do to remove me, so give me courage not to wander from Your sanctuary on this workday and all others. Forever and ever. In Your name, I pray. Amen.

—Larry Ketcham

Week 14, Day 1

WEAR YOUR HEART FIRST

READING

Proverbs 31:30 Charm is deceptive, and beauty does not last; but a woman who fears the LORD will be greatly praised.

1 Samuel 16:7b People judge by outward appearance, but the Lord looks at the heart.

REFLECTION

I am a social work graduate student, hoping eventually to work for a Christian adoption or children's services agency. I've been blessed with interviews for internships, and even one job opportunity, and so I read a lot about "dressing for success." In today's world, an exorbitant amount of money markets fashion to people, like me, in their 20's. You see it on TV, and you get snail-mail and electronic flyers about expensive beauty creams and makeup, trendy clothes and shoes, and fabulous accessories. I admit, I join my generation in being slightly obsessed with the latest fashions and how those trends can affect my appearance socially and professionally.

Yet I am also a Christian. I know what God says about *outward appearance.* Your heart's intent on glorifying Him is more important than what you put on before you go to work. Having worked with homeless children, autistic children, and a local food pantry for poor families — I realize that the *outward appearance* of the public servant will never give hope or remedy to the lives of those in need. Neither will fashion lead people to Christ.

Everyone spends money on improving appearances, and I'm not suggesting you go to work dressed inappropriately. Some earthly things are nice to have, and they do matter to a degree. But as you prepare for work, internship, or an interview today — do not let *outward appearance* trump your focus on serving others to glorify our Lord. As a *Christian* public servant, **wear your heart first** because God first looks at your heart.

PRAYER

Dear Lord, give me courage to care less about how I look and more about how Your people feel. Give me strength to serve them today. Grant me heart to glorify You. In Your name, I pray. Amen.
—Sarah Ashley Slack

Week 14, Day 2

RUN UP THE DEBT

READING

Romans 13:7-8 Give to everyone what you owe them: Pay your taxes and government fees to those who collect them, and give respect and honor to those who are in authority. Owe nothing to anyone—except for your obligation to love one another. If you love your neighbor, you will stay strong and focus on doing excellent in your job.

REFLECTION

Stay strong and focus on doing excellent in your job.

Now, if this statement were made to a public servant who is uncertain about furloughs today or about even having a permanent job next week, like many public servants in my country, there may well be a dirty look or two coming back your way.

Fact is, citizens in any country, regardless of politics and ideology, depend upon public servants to perform the necessary tasks of society — however "necessary" may be defined & constructed. Fact is, the number of services offered, how they are defined & constructed, and the price for public policy — all are decided by the real bosses in any democracy — the *citizens*.

Regardless of on-going political debates over public debt, government works — wherever you are located today in this world — the real bosses are counting on you to serve them and serve them well. Hence, as a *Christian* public servant, you have a special obligation to **run up the debt** — that *huge debt of love* that all citizens owe each other and often offer collectively to one another via a variety of necessary programs and services.

So, try to forget about the *politics du jour*. Let the real bosses sort that out. Just do your best in completing *what the law has been after all along*. For the citizens, **run up the debt** — that *huge debt of love* — through your excellent work!

PRAYER

Dear God, give all public servants the strength to be their best each and every day. Give each of us strength to **run up the debt** — that huge debt of love — regardless of ideological crisis. Lord, let no one worry about politics and help each remember that the citizen needs us to perform effectively, efficiently and compassionately. In all troubled times, keep intact our sense of duty to the citizen and to You. In Jesus' name, I pray. Amen.

    —Adam Schenkel

Week 14, Day 3

HOW ARE YOU KNOWN

READING

Proverbs 20:11 Even children are known by the way they act, whether their conduct is pure, and whether it is right.

Proverbs 20:7a The godly walk with integrity.

Matthew 25:23c Well done, my good and faithful servant.

REFLECTION

Wow! My recent performance appraisal was fabulous!! Of course, it was I who wrote it.

While we all may say it's hard to brag about ourselves, we do a pretty good job when we submit our accomplishments to our supervisors. The question is, do others really see us as the marvelous creatures we claim to be?

How are you known by your supervisor and coworkers? Are you the dedicated public servant that can be trusted? Do you really have that great work ethic you claim to have? Is your work *pure and right*? As a supervisor, I chuckle sometimes when I read the submissions of some of my subordinates. I think, "Do they really believe what they just wrote?" So I wonder if my supervisor chuckles at my write-up. Or, am I known as a man of *integrity*?

Then I ponder my Christian walk. Do I really live the principles of Christ? As a *Christian* public servant, do I live those principles in the workplace? Or, do people chuckle when they see my life because it does not match what I claim to be?

What is the performance appraisal that God will deliver to you? Will it conclude, "Well done, my good and faithful servant"? Or, will He chuckle at your pretentiousness? Or still, will He condemn you for your fraudulence?

Driving to work today, consider: **how are you known?**

PRAYER

Father, mold me through Your word and through the power of Your Spirit. At work today, and throughout all hours, may I truly be known as Your faithful ambassador. Use my life, Father, as a testimony of the grace obtained through the sacrifice of Your Son, Jesus Christ. Empower me to do mighty works today in Your glory. I pray this in Jesus' name. Amen.
—Bill Dudley

Week 14, Day 4

ALWAYS PREPARING YOU

READING

Leviticus 19:33 Do not take advantage of foreigners who live among you in your land.

Matthew 20:16 So those who are last now will be first then, and those who are first will be last.

REFLECTION

You are still in the probationary period, and it appears that the more senior coworkers only associate with one another. They are not rude, but they are distant. It's like you (as a human being) are really not "there". In return, you are polite and maintain a sense of professionalism, trying to impress them by making every effort to excel in all assigned tasks. But the tasks are not the ones advertised; they seem to be makeshift ones that no senior coworker really wants to do. You feel alone, mistreated, and, well, like a foreigner in a very strange land. You wonder if you should have taken this job in the first place.

Remember, Your Father sees everything that you are going through. In due time, you will no longer be the stranger; it will be your land. He is **always preparing you**, as a *Christian* public servant, to not mistreat the next foreigner — the next new employee.

And in due time, He will do much more. You will be "first." You will become the senior person. When that happens, remember that He was **always preparing you** to lead and manage His workplace!

Know that He is always preparing you.

PRAYER

Eternal Father — Author and Finisher of everything — I ask that You give me strength to excel in uncomfortable situations, like being the new employee. I ask that You give me understanding and memory as to how it feels to be a foreigner in the workplace. I know that, when You place me in uncomfortable situations, it is only temporary. You are always preparing me! I ask that You guide me in developing the skills and wisdom needed to become the Christian public servant you call me to be. In Jesus' name, I pray. Amen.

—Deyonta T. Johnson

Week 14, Day 5

WORK AT LIVING IN PEACE

READING

Hebrews 12:14 Work at living in peace with everyone, and work at living a holy life, for those who are not holy will not see the Lord.

REFLECTION

There are many Muslim brothers in prison, and this can sometimes create tension with the Christian brothers. Some Muslims come to our church services for the wrong reasons, and the same is sometimes true when outside ministries come here on weekends. Some Christian brothers respond with talk that does not reflect Jesus. Not all Muslim brothers act wrong and not all Christian brothers act wrong. But some do on each side, and this doesn't help.

One Muslim brother has been asking a lot of questions about how to handle situations in prison and with his family — but also about Jesus. The Christian leaders have agreed to take him seriously, and to give him the best advice we can. We do not just recite the bible all the time, but we make it a point to **work at living in peace** with him. We try to live a *holy life*.

I don't know what will happen, that's up to God. But I do know he is beginning to view Christians differently. To **work at living in peace** with him — showing a humble heart — is the best way we can tell him about our Father God and His Son, our Savior, Jesus Christ.

At work today, don't get annoyed with others, especially those who are nonbelievers. Keep this verse in your heart and use it throughout the day. When you **work at living in peace**, you are working to live a *holy life*. Your testimony and actions will make a difference in someone's life and in someone's heart.

That person may start to **work at living in peace** with you. Someday he may want to live a *holy life*. Then someday, he will *see the Lord*.

PRAYER

Father, in the name of Jesus, I pray. Give me Your grace of peace and Your wisdom and strength to live a holy life, so I can help others who don't know You; so that they will see You through me and my actions. Amen.

—Jimmy Davis, Jr.

Week 15, Day 1

DO WHAT WE SAY

READING

Hebrews 7:21a The Lord has taken an oath and will not break his vow.

REFLECTION

This week, my 4-year-old daughter blurted out one of those truths that affect us personally, spiritually, and professionally. Her four words stopped me in my tracks: "God keeps his promises!"

Wow, what a reminder. What if we kept our promises? What if your spouse knew you'd call the insurance guy, just like you said you would? What if my kids knew I would fix the tire on their bikes when I said? What if our coworkers knew we would give them the report just like we said we would? What if the citizens we serve knew we would truly look into the issue they brought to our attention?

Honesty and integrity are integral to every part of our lives. It is especially important in public service, and it is quintessentially important when you promise to be a *Christian* public servant. We are expected to *say what we will do*, and **do what we say**.

None of us is perfect, but look at the list of people you admire. Do they keep their word? This world still does respect people who keep their promises.

Yes, God keeps His promises! Let's strive to do the same. At work today, let's try to **do what we say**.

PRAYER

Heavenly Father, You have made countless promises in Your Holy Word. You have either already fulfilled them, or You will. You are my role model; help me to be more like You. There is a place where everyone keeps their word; it's called heaven. Today, help me to bring a little bit of heaven to my home and my workplace. In Your Son's name, I pray. Amen.

—Larry Ketcham

Week 15, Day 2

RUN TO WIN

READING

1 Corinthians 9:24-27 Don't you realize that in a race everyone runs, but only one person gets the prize? So run to win! All athletes are disciplined in their training. They do it to win a prize that will fade away, but we do it for an eternal prize. So I run with purpose in every step. I am not just shadowboxing. I discipline my body like an athlete, training it to do what it should. Otherwise, I fear that after preaching to others I myself might be disqualified.

REFLECTION

Ah, competition. It's true. Everyone at work today is in a race. Like it or not, you are in a competitive environment. It's also true; there are not enough prizes to go around! Only one will get the job, only one will be promoted, the project will either be completed on time or not; only one university will get that prospective student; there will be only one top grade; only one nonprofit will get that grant. Ah, competition!

All the talk about how the workplace can be, well, friendly and sweet, think again! Even in a loving Christian environment — even among brothers- and sisters-in-Christ — there is a race to be the best. While the short-term aim is for a perishable workplace crown — keeping a job, getting a raise, receiving a positive performance appraisal, whatever the prize — that crown becomes much more if and when we strive to **run to win** by glorifying God.

As *Christian* public servants, we must discipline ourselves to run not with uncertainty and fight not as though we are shadowboxing. But rather, we must discipline ourselves to **run to win** in a way that reflects our eternal victory.

For this workday, the starter's pistol is firing. How fast will you come out of the starting blocks? *God wants winners, not wimps!* Are you ready? Don't get disqualified. You can **run to win** in a way that takes the workplace prize and that imperishable crown!

PRAYER

Lord, You have placed me where You want me to be. I accept this race cheerfully and gratefully. I accept this race as a fighter and a winner. I seek Your divine grace to help me **run in such a way** that results in a workplace victory and reflects my eternal victory in You. Thank You, Father. In Your Son's name, I pray. Amen.

　　—David Boisselle

Week 15, Day 3

JUST WHO IS THIS JESUS

READING

Mathew 12:33 A tree is identified by its fruit. If a tree is good, its fruit will be good. If a tree is bad, its fruit will be bad.

REFLECTION

I am a Christian public servant. It feels so good to say that!

As you well know, it's difficult to be a *Christian* public servant. After all, we are especially defined and judged by our actions, reactions and deeds.

In my own job, I mentor at-risk youth. I encounter all types of teens from some of the roughest walks of life. I am yelled at, lied to and tricked — yet I am a *Christian* public servant.

I am disrespected in the most awful ways — yet I remain a *Christian* public servant.

There are plenty of times when I want to lash out in response, but I am called to be *Christ-like*. Even in punishment, I have to provide grace and forgiveness — especially among the least of His. I have to be an example so unbelievers can yearn for the peace, hope and joy I have in my own tribulations. It is my prayer that my *Christ-like* reactions will cause them to ask, **just who is this Jesus** and how can I get to know Him?

How about you? What type of fruit are you producing at work? Is your fruit *Christ-like*? Or, are you responding in some other fashion? Do your words and actions prompt nonbelievers to ask, **just who is this Jesus**?

And, by the way, isn't it wonderful today to proclaim we **are** *Christian* public servants!!

PRAYER

Heavenly Father, in all I do at work today, let me shine Your light. I ask that You give me the strength, the wisdom and the desire to be a practicing Christian public servant. Help me to be a Christ-like example in the workplace, to bear good fruit in trying times. I ask that my work may prompt others to ask, **just who is this Jesus**? I ask for courage to answer that question in ways that glorify You. In Jesus' name, I pray. Amen.

—Crystal Featherston

Week 15, Day 4

TRUST IN THAT POWER

READING

Psalm 107:29   He calmed the storm to a whisper and stilled the waves.

Mark 4:39 When Jesus woke up, he rebuked the wind and said to the waves, "Silence! Be still!" Suddenly the wind stopped, and there was a great calm.

REFLECTION

What workplace ever seems calm? I know mine is not. Somehow academia has become very competitive to the point of being cut-throat. Forget about the "publish or perish" axiom that every professor has to endure. It's beyond that. Recruiting students and protecting program turf, well, it's become "Old Testament" with bodies flying and storms and floods abounding.

My seas are never calm, and I don't even work in an environment like yours. The people you serve might be victims of child abuse or victims of human trafficking. You might work with drug addicts or people so long impoverished that they have forgotten the how and the why of finding their way out. You might work in a finance division and lay awake at night worrying about how your agency will ever be able to continue to serve the public. Your nonprofit may be praying for that one external funder to just say "yes".

If my seas are never calm, your seas are filled with vicious storms.

Yet remember: how powerful is our Lord that He can command the forces of nature to be still. This is the God that loves and equips you and me. This is why we can make it through the storm — have an impact despite the storm — as *Christian* public servants.

In the rush and demands of every workday, and the exhaustion that follows in the evening, I tend to forget that *the power of God is complete*. I need to **trust in that power** and, when I do, I realize that I will not be overwhelmed by the surrounding storm. He truly will hush the waves and calm the wind!

At work today, I need to **trust in that power**. So do you.

PRAYER

Almighty God, help me to always know and honor Your power. Equip me with the courage to defend what You have given to my work unit so that I may help my agency glorify You. Equip me and all Christian public servants with the courage to stand up for justice, to speak for those who are voiceless. Empower each of us to be Your servant in the public and nonprofit square. In Your Son's name, I pray. Amen.

    —Stephanie L. Bellar

Week 15, Day 5

PROFESS A PROTECTOR'S HEART

READING

Romans 13:1 Everyone must submit to governing authorities. For all authority comes from God, and those in positions of authority have been placed there by God.

REFLECTION

Sometimes it's very hard for people to follow rules in a society where kids are taught that the "rules are made to be broken." Because of that, those empowered by God to make sure rules are followed are usually seen by public eyes as their enemies.

Sadly, this is too frequently the case in my country. The "rules are made to be broken" culture can adversely affect the self-perception and self-esteem of many of the 173,000 members of the Colombian National Police. It can also affect how they view their coworkers and their profession. Some see their work increasingly as meaningless. Some get so disillusioned they forget they once had a profession and not just a job. In this kind of setting, it's easy to forget what it was that they professed to God when they entered the profession of public service.

Now, I know my country is not alone. In anyone's career, there may be periods of time when it's quite easy to get disillusioned and view what he or she does merely as a job and not a profession. Routine can lead to mechanical reaction. Self-esteem fades, and so does respect for coworkers. Seeing rules constantly broken can dull professional ethics and scriptural morality. It's easy to forget that we are called to **profess a Protector's heart**. That is, we must work on behalf of others unselfishly and even lay down our lives for others. It means we are obligated to administer justice with discernment and wisdom.

God reminds us that all authority comes from Him. As a *Christian* public servant, He has placed you in your workplace. Your boss is placed there by Him. The coworker, who doesn't always meet your standards, is placed there by God. All are placed there by Him to **profess a Protector's heart**, and that changes the way you look at others and the way you look at yourself. You are placed there to serve God with all your heart.

Are "rules made to be broken"? Regardless of culture and where you work in public service, you are called to rule over those you serve. Do you **profess a Protector's heart**?

Prayer

Lord, place a Protector´s heart in me to deliver justice with wisdom and righteousness. Give me the strength to change how my eyes see coworkers and myself. Let me look at everyone the same way You look at me. In Your name, I pray. Amen.

    —Carlos Villamarin

Week 16, Day 1

WORK WITH ENTHUSIASM

READING

Ephesians 6:7 Work with enthusiasm, as though you were working for the Lord rather than for people.

Colossians 3:23 Work willingly at whatever you do, as though you were working for the Lord rather than for people.

REFLECTION

It's Monday, the start of a new work week. Unfortunately for most people, today marks a day of dread. Kids often suddenly have illnesses on Monday mornings. My sister had a job that she actually hated so much that she became physically ill on Monday mornings. Sound familiar? Most of us do not cope well with Mondays and, to exacerbate things, we work in public and nonprofit organizations. We deal with individuals who may test our patience and leave us frustrated and ready to give up. And it's only Monday!

We might be tempted to fight fire with fire; to treat others as they treat us. But God wants us to take a different approach — **work with enthusiasm!** Our actions should say to others that we are a follower of Jesus Christ and, because of Him, we care about the work that we do, our coworkers, and the people we serve. Regardless of task or the person standing in front of us, we work to impress God, not men. We take the high road because that is the path Jesus has chosen for us.

Work with enthusiasm, *Christian* public servant! Give this Monday to our Lord!

PRAYER

Father, I pray that You bless this Monday. I pray for a productive day at work and, regardless of circumstances, I pray that Your presence is felt in a mighty way. I pray that I will do work that is pleasing to You. In Your Son's name, I pray. Amen.

—Tammy Esteves

Week 16, Day 2

LESSON TO BE LEARNED

READING

1 Peter 5:7 Give all your worries and cares to God, for he cares about what happens to you.

REFLECTION

It was one of those moments. Maybe you've had them as well. You know, where you gaze up at heaven and say "alright God, time to have a little come-to-Jesus meeting." Well, maybe you don't talk to God like that, but yesterday I did. (Now, I fear God enough not to talk too sternly to Him, but I did lay out all my frustrations and fears).

A dear childhood friend is in the battle of her life with a serious illness. I've been praying for her to draw closer to God and for the treatment side-effects to be as limited as possible. Until yesterday, things had been going well. She's been seeking to know more about God, His call on her life, and living her life by faith. But when I got the phone call from her, I was in a state of shock. On top of everything, there may be still another health crisis.

As I got off the phone and sat down to begin my talk with God, I have to admit I was angry at Him. Angry that He could not have done something to stop this from happening. Angry that someone so new in her faith walk would have to endure yet another trial of faith so quickly. As I cried and just simply talked to God, I kept asking *why*. Why, God, *why?*

And then, just as any parent would do, God wrapped His arms around me and reminded me that my understanding of the situation is limited. Only He knows why she has to go through all this. He knows what the new tests will show. He knows what her life will be like tomorrow. The greatest news, He reminded me, was the fact He cares for us and what happens to us!

You may not think this has anything to do with the public service or your particular workplace, but it does. Trials come to strengthen our character and faith. It may be a health issue, but it may be a work issue. It may be both. Instead of asking *why*, we need to ask God to show us the **lesson to be learned**. From every trial and tribulation, there is *something* God wants to teach us.

So whatever crisis you face today, at work or elsewhere, remember that *we are not in control*. Turning to God and taking our hands off the situation can bring peace.

This, my friend, is one **lesson to be learned**.

PRAYER

God, You know the struggles each of us face today. You know who sits next to us at work, or anywhere else, who lives in fear right now. You know when fear takes over our mind, we can't function. The only way to get through is to give our worries and cares over to You. Help strengthen our faith in You so we can let go and let You work. In Your Son's name, I pray. Amen.

— Jenny Sue Flannagan

Week 16, Day 3

Y SHOULD I CARE

READING

Luke 10:34 Going over to him, the Samaritan soothed his wounds... and bandaged them ...and took him to an inn, where he took care of him.

REFLECTION

"I wish sometimes that I never help people in need. Y should I care. I beat some people up for try to make me out of a fool. God never help me enough and make me look like fools. **Y should I care**."

My church invites the homeless to stay overnight, and church members volunteer in a variety of ways. We have a prayer table where men and woman can talk, pray, or where they can leave anonymous prayer-requests in a basket. I found the words above scratched on a piece of paper in that basket.

Y should I care... at first, I was angry. I mean, my church provides dinner, breakfast, showers, fellowship, and a warm, friendly, and secure place to sleep for an entire week — with a team that takes care of their needs around the clock — and this person doesn't understand why he should care? We care and, therefore, he should, too!

Then my anger turned into frustration. I realized that this person has open wounds that need bandaging. More importantly, he has open wounds that require healing. Yet something is wrong. Healing has not occurred. Perhaps we were applying not nearly enough bandages to permit healing. Perhaps we were using the wrong kinds of bandages. Or, in our enthusiasm, were we wrapping the bandages so tight that the breath of God could not enter? Still possibly, does this person keep ripping off the bandages before healing can even begin?

As *Christian* public servants — volunteers and professionals in the public and nonprofit sectors — *we bandage those in need*. In one form or another, that's what we do. Yet we become discouraged when the intended effects of our mortal bandages don't seem to take as quickly as we want. We suffocate healing with our own pride and ambition, and we apply only what we learn in college or through training. We sometimes forget what we learn through our Lord: have *faith* that He will heal the wound in His way through our means.

Y should I care... It's so easy to forget that the man in Jesus' parable was not healed in just one day. But unlike other passers-by, the Samaritan did not lose faith. He gave faith. *Faith is the bandage* that man needed on the road to Jericho. *Faith is the bandage* that homeless man needed on that evening in my church. *Faith is the bandage* we all need right now.

As this workweek continues, do not forget His answer to **Y should I care**... *Faith.*

PRAYER

Father God, you call me to do Your work in my workplace and even where I volunteer. Do not let me forget why I am here and why I should care. I serve and I pray in Your Son's name. Amen.
  —James D. Slack

Week 16, Day 4

HOPE IN THE LORD

READING

Psalm 37:25; 31:24 Once I was young, and now I am old. Yet I have never seen the godly abandoned or their children begging for bread ... So be strong and courageous, all you who put your **hope in the LORD**!

Matthew 10:8(b) Give as freely as you have received!

REFLECTION

When I heard the sound of my coworker's voice, I shed my own tears. She was back to work after burying her husband – a truck driver whose semi went over the side of a bridge. And now, she is alone. New to the region, her family is not near. So young, she and her husband had no life insurance or pension. Soon she began to struggle living on only a teacher assistant's salary.

Yet she comes to work with strength in her heart. Worried, her face also shows confidence. "This is just temporary," she'll say when asked, "I have **hope in the Lord**!" God will not forsake her.

But isn't <u>her</u> hope in the Lord tied to <u>my</u> hope in the Lord?

You may know someone at work in a similar (or worse) situation. It's easy to overlook that coworker-in-need and move on with your day. After all, he <u>has</u> to have a church family helping him, right? Or, she can <u>always</u> get welfare from the government.

But as Christians, are we not the church? In our workplace, aren't we still the Church? Isn't the Body of Christ, even at work, supposed to be a safety net of prayers <u>and</u> hands and feet?

As a *Christian* public servant, freely give <u>your</u> **hope in the Lord**. It was freely given to you.

PRAYER

Heavenly Father, I come to You the only way I know how. I ask You to bless those people who are having a rough time within their jobs. Use me to help them in ways You want. Help me give freely the hope I have in You – the hope You have given me so freely. Let none of Your children have to beg for bread. All these blessings and this prayer, I ask in Your Son's name. Amen.

—Dwayne Plummer

Week 16, Day 5

ALWAYS A MATTER OF HEART

READING

Deuteronomy 13:1-3 Suppose there are prophets among you or those who dream dreams about the future, and they promise you signs or miracles, and the predicted signs or miracles occur. If they then say, 'Come, let us worship other gods'—gods you have not known before— do not listen to them. The Lord your God is testing you to see if you truly love him with all your heart and soul.

REFLECTION

I've never been to Vegas or Hollywood, and I know there are many good Christians living there, but it seems like both settings contribute to a world full of glamorous dreams. TV and movie stars. Rich gamblers. Prophets who find their way into the magazines at checkout lines in grocery stores. All tempt us with dreams of another life style. Even without Vegas and Hollywood, there is so much temptation out there — and that is perhaps why so many choose to live where I work.

Our Father allows us to exercise freewill to draw us closer to Him or for us to push Him further away. You may follow lady-luck, you may seek a fast-track prophet, or you may choose to love and worship your Lord. It may seem complicated at times, but it really is not. The choice is **always a matter of heart**.

Today at work, don't assume things happen by chance. Don't rely on good fortune to get the task done. Don't daydream about false prophets and their enticements.

Even at work, know our God is testing you. He truly wants to see if you choose to love other gods or if you choose to love Him. Know the choice is **always a matter of heart**.

PRAYER

Lord, give me a heart today that chooses to see and know only You. In Your Son's name, I pray. Amen.
—Chris Summers

Week 17, Day 1

PRETTY IMPORTANT

READING

Galatians 6:3 If you think you are too important to help someone, you are only fooling yourself. You are not that important.

Philippians 4:13 For I can do everything through Christ, who gives me strength.

REFLECTION

You know, I really amaze myself. I happen to be the coworker everyone runs to for answers. I get hundreds of emails every day asking for my insights. I've been doing my job so long that my corporate knowledge is what keeps this whole place going. I have all the connections. I am the one that represents the program at all the high-level meetings. Yes, ma'am, I am **pretty important**! How would this place ever function without me?

But then I go on vacation and guess what? The program survives. The missions are met, the deliverables are on time, and all questions somehow get answered. And to think, all that is done without me — without me — the center of the universe!

As a public servant, you may be given experience and expertise, and these can give you the illusion of being **pretty important**. But as a *Christian* public servant, you might just realize that you are special not because of the work you do but because of the work Christ does in you.

The fact that He would even consider you and me worthy of His love, and then trust us with the privilege of steward leadership at work, well now ... it's only through His eyes that we become **pretty important**!

PRAYER

Father, I praise You for the special blessing of being Your child, and I ask for Your strength and wisdom this workday as I serve others through serving You. May my work be a blessing to many and seen as an example of the important love You so graciously provide. May I honor You in all I do. In your Son's name, I pray. Amen.

—Bill Dudley

Week 17, Day 2

WORKPLACE HOPE OF JESUS CHRIST

READING

Ephesians 3:20 Now all glory to God, who is able, through his mighty power at work within us, to accomplish infinitely more than we might ask or think.

REFLECTION

If your workplace is anything like mine, new financial quarters usher in feelings of uncertainty, anxiety, and, at times, discontentment. It is unnerving to place your livelihood in the hands of management and budget analysts who seem indifferent to your true worth to the agency. Instead, they focus merely on balancing numbers in an Excel sheet amid another year of deficit. The whole idea is quite frightening.

You reflect upon the outcomes of previous budget years. You remember all the times you felt misused: overlooked for advancement despite your education and experience, no recognition for personally filling in the shortcomings of coworkers, and job description creep resulting from role changes that are constantly thrust upon you. You're a public servant — you are called to do what you do and you recognize the special challenges of doing what you do — yet this is ridiculous. Your morale deteriorates, your productivity declines, and your fears emerge.

Today I must remember there is hope. Today we all must remember there is hope. There is the **workplace hope of Jesus Christ**. Forget not that He — and He alone — is able to do far more in our workplaces than we imagine. In fact, it is the **workplace hope of Jesus Christ** that permits each of us to do far more than what we ask or think.

So, recognized or overlooked? Shifted or sustained? Deficit or surplus? Doesn't matter. Merely numbers in an excel sheet? Doesn't matter!

What matters today is the workplace hope of Jesus Christ.

PRAYER

Heavenly Father, You are capable of more than I can ask or think. Thank You for Your dominion over my workplace and for the hope it brings. In You, I find stability, peace, and contentment. Forgive me for grumbling. Remind me there is hope before my morale deteriorates, my productivity declines, and my fears emerge. I love you. In Your Son's name, I pray. Amen.

—Melinda Luchun

Week 17, Day 3

MIGHTY WORKPLACE WARRIOR

READING

Judges 6:12, 15 The angel of the LORD appeared to him and said, "Mighty hero, the LORD is with you!" ... "But Lord," Gideon replied, "how can I rescue Israel? My clan is the weakest in the whole tribe of Manasseh, and I am the least in my entire family!"

REFLECTION

There are occasions at work when you just have to ask: "Why ME, Lord?" You have a new task or assignment, and you're not sure you can do it. Someone has judged you to be the appropriate person for the task, but you just don't feel like a **mighty workplace warrior.**

Sometimes we are *too close to ourselves* to see our own gifts. Sometimes we are *too close to ourselves* to see what God sees.

If God has called you to your workplace, then He will equip you. Even if, at the time, you cannot see how you can do it, He will direct you to the spiritual strength and organizational resources to become a **mighty workplace warrior**.

So if called to lead, pray. If called to do, pray even harder!! Just like Gideon, you may want to hide, but God has greater things in mind for you, your agency, and those whom you serve!

Follow His path, and you will be amazed at what He accomplishes *through* you. Today at work, He will be with you, **mighty workplace warrior**!

PRAYER

Lord, I cannot see what You can see. Help me to believe in what You see in me so that I may do what You have called me to do. Also, allow me to encourage my coworkers to do the same. In Your name, I pray. Amen.

—Stan Best

Week 17, Day 4

PASS BY ON THE OTHER SIDE

READING

Luke 10:30-37 Jesus replied with a story: "A Jewish man was traveling from Jerusalem down to Jericho, and he was attacked by bandits. They stripped him of his clothes, beat him up, and left him half dead beside the road. By chance a priest came along. But when he saw the man lying there, he crossed to the other side of the road and passed him by. A Temple assistant walked over and looked at him lying there, but he also passed by on the other side. Then a despised Samaritan came along, and when he saw the man, he felt compassion for him. Going over to him, the Samaritan soothed his wounds... and bandaged them....took him to an inn... 'Take care of this man...' Now which of these three would you say was a neighbor to the man who was attacked by bandits?" Jesus asked. The man replied, "The one who showed him mercy." Then Jesus said, "Yes, now go and do the same."

REFLECTION

The Good Samaritan parable sums up what our walk with Christ is supposed to be — even (or especially) in our workplace and in our careers. All public servants walk the road to Jericho each day and, yes, what we experience en route is often disturbing and overwhelming. We face needs everywhere — needs that most other citizens fail to notice.

Yet how many times do we choose to **pass by on the other side**?

We are supposed to be more than public servants; more than just bureaucrats or staff. We are *Christian* public servants. Jesus instructs us to "love your neighbor as yourself". This is difficult to do if we travel on our own, using only secular maps, strategies and thinking.

If we let Him, the Holy Spirit will help us do the right thing. He will help us help the people in need around us — the people who depend on us — the people whom others too conveniently **pass by on the other side**.

Today at work, as He walks with you toward Jericho, do not **pass by on the other side**.

PRAYER

Our Heavenly Father, thank You for giving Your Son's parable to guide me through today. Help me to be more like You by helping citizens and clients and loving them where they are at. Help me never to **pass by on the other side**. In Your Son's Holy name, I pray. Amen.

—Lyse-Ann Lacourse

Week 17, Day 5

SOMEONE NEEDS TO SEE ME

READING

Psalm 118:24 This is the day the Lord has made. We will rejoice and be glad in it.

REFLECTION

Each morning, my breakfast is cold and half-cooked. It's so noisy around me, with shouting going on from one cell to another, I can't even hear myself breathe. There's a freezing rain, so I won't be allowed the 45 minutes outside. The inmate that hands out the mail just walked past my cell without stopping. I won't see or talk to my family today. And tonight, because of an unexpected cold front, my blanket won't be enough. I will sleep wearing my jacket and toboggan hat.

You might think that prison, especially death row, is a miserable place to live and die. But please don't feel sorry for me. I'm not asking for your sympathy or pity.

You see, life is about choices. Yesterday, I chose something else. Today, I choose to rejoice and *be glad in it*. I do so because each day the Lord renews for me His love, His mercy and His favor.

But I also choose to rejoice for another reason. I know, regardless of how bad my day seems to others, **someone needs to see me** *be glad in it*. Someone needs to see the Lord through my love, my mercy, and my favor. Someone needs to see my joy and my faith. Each morning, I know **someone needs to see me** *be glad in it* so that they can make it through their own day.

When you're at work today, things may be rough. It may not be what you want. But it isn't what others want, either. Someone else is having a really miserable day — worse than yours. You may never have a chance to say anything to that person, and you may not know why this day is awful for him. You may never know the person having the worst time of it — but he is near.

Today at work, remember life is about choices — even work life. We've all made bad choices in the past, but not today. This really is the day that our Lord has made. Why not choose to rejoice? Look around and think to yourself: **someone needs to see me** *be glad in it*.

PRAYER

Father, in the name of Jesus, I pray. I thank you for the new love, mercy and favor You give me at the beginning of each day. But so many others see only troubles today, troubles far beyond mine. Give me a heart to show them the miracle that You give today. Let us all be glad in it. Amen.

—Jimmy Davis, Jr.

Week 18, Day 1

WORKPLACE SEEDS

READING

Philippians 2:1-4 Is there any encouragement from belonging to Christ? Any comfort from his love? Any fellowship together in the Spirit? Are your hearts tender and compassionate? Then make me truly happy by agreeing whole-heartedly with each other, loving one another, and working together with one mind and purpose. Don't be selfish; don't try to impress others. Be humble, thinking of others as better than yourselves. Don't look out only for your own interests, but take an interest in others, too.

REFLECTION

What kind of **workplace seeds** are you planting today? Are you planting seeds of praise, encouragement, corrective assessment, and value? Are you using the tools of Christian critique, mentoring, and stewardship when planting those **workplace seeds**?

Or, are you planting seeds of belittlement, worry and insecurity? Are you using one of Satan's many tools, like selfish ambition, vein conceit, mean-spiritedness, manipulation, or dishonesty?

Yes, excellence is required in public service, and excellence requires hard work and bottom-line results. Yet the tools of Christian critique, assessment, and stewardship can be used constructively to plant **workplace seeds** that help others flourish and improve the agency.

Excellence grows from the value we place on coworkers. Advancing the agency does not emerge from selfish zero-sum competition. As *Christian* public servants, let's plant His **workplace seeds**.

PRAYER

Lord, You have given me the gifts of Christian compassion and kindness, as well as gifts of Christian critique, assessment and stewardship. Please aid me in my spiritual quest to sharpen and blend all these gifts and use them to the best of my abilities for Your glory. Let not my passion for success hinder me from being a light unto someone else's path. Restore in me a clean heart filled with love and concern for my fellow Christian servants. In Jesus' name, Amen.
　　　—Cassandra D. McLendon

Week 18, Day 2

CALL ON THE LORD

READING

1 Chronicles 16:8 Give thanks to the Lord and proclaim his greatness. Let the whole world know what he has done.

REFLECTION

Two of my MPA students just submitted a near complete draft of their Capstone project. In the acknowledgement page, both thanked the Lord for His presence and assistance throughout the process.

I am blessed to have students who know how to **call on the Lord** as they struggle to find their research question, develop their design, review the literature and contemplate comments from me. I am blessed to think that, perhaps someday, the offices in all government and nonprofit buildings will be filled with *Christian* public servants.

Today may we be inspired to **call on the Lord** in all we do!

PRAYER

Lord, Thank You for Your constant presence in my life. You are a source of our joy. In Your name, I pray. Amen.

  —Patricia M. Shields

Week 18, Day 3

WORK AT HARD WORK

READING

Acts 20:35 And I have been a constant example of how you can help those in need by working hard. You should remember the words of the Lord Jesus: "It is more blessed to give than to receive."

REFLECTION

The week's not nearly over, you might be growing tired of the work on your desk. You work hard, I know. I work hard. We all work hard. But do we **work at hard work**?

Scripture hints at an acceptable answer. For Christians, work should be "hard" because it means giving a piece of ourselves to someone else — a piece of ourselves that we can never take back. It is why we were called to public service, isn't it? We desire to serve the public because it is a selfless act — a sacrifice of ourselves to help someone who needs something.

Maybe your hard work is not overtly apostolic — like the men and women going into the leper camps providing for the needs of social outcasts. But as a *Christian* public servant, your work is sacrificial when done excellently and in accord with the will of God. It is indeed more blessed to give than receive because we give of ourselves as *imitators of Christ* who gave of himself for the work of salvation.

So as this week continues, **work at hard work**! Enjoy doing it as it is a selfless imitation of a God who is also sacrificial and self-giving.

PRAYER

Dear God, thank You for allowing me to **work at hard work**. You teach, through the example of Christ Your Son, to be sacrificial people. Help me to see my work as an act of self-giving worship in which all that I do benefits others more than myself. In this way, I heed the words of Jesus: "It is more blessed to give than to receive." It is in His name that I pray. Amen.
—Dominick D. Hankle

Week 18, Day 4

DON'T WORRY ABOUT IT

READING

Colossians 3:23 Work willingly at whatever you do, as though you were working for the Lord rather than for people.

REFLECTION

You work at it with all your heart for long hours, day after day, only to get more projects handed to you. Looking around, you see clutter. Some do things half-heartedly. They just kind of sit there, talk some, and basically watch others work. With seemingly less on their plates, they are more relaxed. They'll live to be 105, and the bets are you'll be lucky to make it another 5. You begin to wonder, is this fair?

Without even realizing it, your latest project is one that others covet — including those who bring clutter to the table. It wasn't given to them. It was given to you because your supervisor actually notices your hard work and devotion. She knows your work can be trusted as it comes from the heart. She knows she'll never have to hold you accountable because you will hold yourself accountable for both process and product.

But you know this new project is going to require extra-long hours without extra-big pay. You also know that the work will be done in spite of the clutter. So you still ask, *is this fair?*

Don't worry about it.

Besides your supervisor, be certain that God notices. Be absolutely certain about that fact. He is aware of everything you do, and He is proud of what you do when your heart is set at working for Him.

So forget about the clutter around you. Forget about, *is this fair?* Simply know that He is right there next to you - always.

Today as you head to work, remember for Whom you are really working. The clutter? Just **don't worry about it**.

PRAYER

Heavenly Father, I thank You for blessing me with one more day to work for You. I ask that You watch over me as I tackle my tasks in Your positive light. Grant me strength and motivation to keep going and ignore the clutter. In Your Son's name, I pray. Amen.

    —Meredith Pulsford

Week 18, Day 5

LONELINESS, STRANGENESS, AND DISCONNECTEDNESS

READING

2 Chronicles 16: 9 The eyes of the Lord search the whole earth in order to strengthen those whose hearts are fully committed to him. What a fool you have been! From now on you will be at war.

REFLECTION

All countries have people protecting their embassies. In the U.S., they are members of the Marine Corps Embassy Security Group and, like in all countries, these men and women (and their families) serve their nation and God in distant places around the world.

When I was a younger man, I traveled throughout Europe. I often assumed that no matter how I behaved, no one would ever know. I could tell anyone anything, and they would have no way to verify whether I was telling the truth. It was possible every day to wake up in a new place and be a "different person."

I could play this game without worrying about consequences, right?

Well no, *that's* wrong!

Scripture reminds us that there is no place on earth where the Lord cannot see. Wherever you serve the public — wherever your job takes you — God not only knows your location, but He knows *your heart, mind, and will.*

The simple truth: God knew exactly what I was doing. He even knew when I was *thinking* of doing bad. Years later looking back, I am thankful because God was watching over me. He was (and is) ever-watchful in order to *strengthen* me. His watchfulness will also *strengthen you*.

You may face the **loneliness, strangeness, and disconnectedness** of living away from friends and loved ones. Or, you may live and work in the same town or region all your life and still feel a **loneliness, strangeness, and disconnectedness**. Know that God sees where you are, and He has made it His purpose to *strengthen you* — especially in the face of temptation.

As you work today, let him strengthen you.

PRAYER

Father, meet me in my work space today. Remind me that You are ever watching in order to strengthen my character and make me more like Jesus. Help me to feel Your presence as comfort and not intrusion. Thank You for loving me despite all that You see. In Jesus' name I pray. Amen.

—Loren Crone

Week 19, Day 1

NOT GONNA FORSAKE YOU

READING

Deuteronomy 31:6 So be strong and courageous! Do not be afraid and do not panic before them. For the Lord your God will personally go ahead of you. He will neither fail you nor abandon you."

REFLECTION

It's Monday, and the workweek begins all over again. Preparing the children for school; making sure their homework is in their backpacks. Finding time for a simple good morning kiss with my spouse. Thinking about all that lies ahead. The unending meeting this morning. That audit in the afternoon. The report that needs to be in no later than five. As the coffee brews, I have only a handful of stand-up seconds to study God's Word before leaving for work.

Life and work can seem overwhelming, especially on Mondays.

But be strong and courageous. God understands better than you just how taxing this day really will be. He knows what you're going through. He's watching you right now, and will guide you every step throughout this day.

Yes, a lot to do. But remember, you are a *Christian* public servant. He goes with you on this Monday morning. He's **not gonna forsake you**.

PRAYER

Eternal Father, Creator of heaven and earth, I ask that You continue to strengthen Your servant as I execute Your will in my work life and in my whole life. I know You have called me to serve others — to be a Christian public servant. Guide me as I do Your work in my workplace this week. Give me strength to continue to press forward even when I feel like giving up. I know You will not leave me. In Your precious Son's name, I pray. Amen.

—Deyonta T. Johnson

Week 19, Day 2

TRULY GREAT FOR GOD

READING

Jonah 1:2 Get up and go to the great city of Nineveh. Announce my judgment against it because I have seen how wicked its people are.

REFLECTION

God knew Nineveh was a great city but, due to free will, He allowed its leaders to make some very wicked decisions. There came a time when God could no longer stand its wickedness. Something had to give. And even though He was thoroughly upset with the choices made, His unimaginable grace allowed this great city one more chance — and Jonah was the instrument He chose to convey this urgent message.

Sound familiar?

Like in the days of Jonah, we want to think we live and work in "great" cities — whether it is the largest city in the region or the smallest town on earth. And naturally, as public servants, we want to think we work for "great" agencies and departments within those "great" cities. But while we might think our workplace and community are truly great, scripture calls us to ask: are they **truly great for God**?

Just as in Jonah's time, God still allows us to make our own decisions — regardless of how beneficial or wicked the consequences may be for those whom we serve. Let's face it, the public and nonprofit sectors make their fair share of mistakes, and even faith-based agencies can commit the greatest errors. Truly in God's eyes, *something has to give*!

As *Christian* public servants, will you and I hear the same call that Jonah did? Will we be His instrument?

Today let's start to make our workplaces, agencies, and communities **truly great for God**.

PRAYER

Father, remind me that true greatness comes from submitting to You. Please give me the strength to make my agency and my city truly great for You. In Jesus' name, I pray. Amen.

—Michael J. Gordon

Week 19, Day 3

BUILDING FOR OUR SUCCESS

READING

Psalm 127:1 Unless the LORD builds a house, the work of the builders is wasted. Unless the LORD protects a city, guarding it with sentries will do no good.

REFLECTION

As public servants, we strive to lead and build the organizations we manage or direct. Goals are set, planning is implemented, budgets are adopted and professional staff members are hired. All is in place for success, or is it?

Unless God is with our activities, our efforts will be futile despite all of our best efforts.

An organization or city can crumble and collapse from corruption or mismanagement on the inside. We see this each day on the news.

Leaving God out of our professional lives is a mistake and will lead to frustration and disappointment. We need to make God our highest priority and guide, and then He will do the **building for our success**.

PRAYER

Lord, watch over all cities today. Let the public servant stand guard not in vain. In Your name, I pray. Amen.

    —Sam Gaston

Week 19, Day 4

PRAY AND THINK QUICKLY

READING

Nehemiah 2:4 The king asked, "Well, how can I help you?" With a prayer to the God of heaven.

Philippians 4:6 Don't worry about anything; instead, pray about everything. Tell God what you need, and thank him for all he has done.

REFLECTION

Nehemiah is one of my favorite characters of the Bible. He started out as a cup-bearer (a public servant) to the King of Babylon, during the exile period of Jewish history, and ended by being a leader (public manager) of the rebuilding of Jerusalem. The turning point in his life came in what appears to be a casual conversation with the king. It is what Nehemiah did in the middle of the conversation that I most admire about him.

He prayed to God.

I presume the conversation between Nehemiah and the king was at a normal pace — he was asked a question, he prayed and then he answered. This precludes the time to recite a long, memorized prayer. His was likely a basic call for help from the heart, or maybe it was a pleading for wisdom. Nevertheless, one of Nehemiah's public management skills was the ability to **pray and think quickly** on his feet.

You know, a public servant in the 21st century must have that very same skill. We're expected to "think fast on our feet" but, without prayer, thinking fast can get us into trouble. Conversations are extemporaneous — rarely rehearsed — and unfortunately I have never found the "redo" button for words that come out of my mouth.

The ability to **pray and think quickly** on our feet is one management skill that all *Christian* public servants should practice!

PRAYER

Lord, please help me to know I can rely on You in moments of trouble and moments of opportunity. I simply need to ask. Help me to be joyful and pray continually. In Your name, I pray. Amen.

—Larry Ketcham

Week 19, Day 5

WHEN THE SUN DOESN'T EVEN SHINE

READING

Matthew 5:16 In the same way, let your good deeds shine out for all to see, so that everyone will praise your heavenly Father.

REFLECTION

When I was in the free-world, I knew someone who worked late at night. He wasn't a gangster. No, he was an honest man. Had kids, a wife and was trying to keep his family together. He was a busboy on the midnight shift at a truck stop along the interstate in Aniston, Alabama. He'd work so hard for so little money — quickly cleaning up after everyone, soaking up spills with his hand-rag, getting their eaten food on his clothes — and to go through all that at a time of day **when the sun doesn't even shine**!

Back then, I didn't realize just how much light he really had. He treated everyone with respect and kindness and made very tired truck drivers feel like kings. It didn't matter if few saw him shine. Those who received his light, felt it — and so did our Lord.

Last Sunday in church we talked about people living in shame, fear and doubt. Regardless of what the clock says, they live and work in spiritual darkness. But that's not what I'm talking about here. I'm talking about people who actually work when the physical world is in darkness.

You may be a correctional officer on the swing shift, walking past a cell just like mine. You may be a police officer on night patrol, or an ambulance driver racing to a 2 a.m. accident involving teenagers, or a firefighter putting out a 4 a.m. house fire. You may be a janitor cleaning hard before everyone else wakes and shows up for work. You may actually be the brother from that truck stop, now working on the highways at night to make a better life for your family. And unlike others just going to work right now, you read this devotional on your way home.

You are a *Christian* public servant when you carry out Jesus' work plans — even if not too many are awake to see the light coming from your good works. Know that the light you so shine glorifies God a thousand-fold because you work **when the sun doesn't even shine**.

PRAYER

Father, in the name of Jesus, I pray. Thank You for using brothers and sisters, who work late nights and swing shifts, to shine their light before a few so that You can be glorified so brightly in heaven. Amen.

Jimmy Davis, Jr.

Week 20, Day 1

WHERE HELP COMES FROM

READING

Romans 8:26-27 And the Holy Spirit helps us in our weakness. For example, we don't know what God wants us to pray for. But the Holy Spirit prays for us with groanings that cannot be expressed in words. And the Father who knows all hearts knows what the Spirit is saying, for the Spirit pleads for us believers in harmony with God's own will.

REFLECTION

How many times at work do you see a citizen or client or coworker who just doesn't have a clue? It may be a not-yet-believer or a Christian who has temporarily gotten lost. Who knows, it could be you, right? Regardless, it is a person who, in the midst of a crisis, doesn't know **where help comes from**.

You know the type: he talks about "luck" or "the stars" as if this life is some kind of a casino in Vegas. She rubs a rabbit's foot — like that's really gonna do something. He has special numbers, and she crosses fingers to encourage good fortune. And both are always the ones who say "our thoughts are with you" when it comes to someone else's crisis.

But what do "thoughts" have to do with anything? What is luck?

As a Christian, you know **where help comes from** — the Holy Spirit. By seeking His help, you can serve as an interceder for that citizen or client or coworker — or yourself. You may not know the particulars of the crisis — shoot, that person (including yourself) may not even know what to pray for — but you *still* know **where help comes from** and so you seek the Holy Spirit.

(You don't even have to tell the person that the Holy Spirit is now in control, until perhaps an opportunity arises to testify over a cup of coffee or lunch!)

The Holy Spirit will plead *with groanings* — with *groanings*, mind you — for that citizen, that client, that coworker, or for you — in harmony with God's own will. So seek Him right now, this very moment, even before you get to work. Take a split second to close your eyes and bring Him into the workplace equation. As a *Christian* public servant, you're helping that person — perhaps helping yourself — in *ways unimaginable*!

Luck? The stars? Rabbit's foot? Special numbers? Crossing fingers? Whatever!

Seek help from **where help comes from**. Now that's the way to start the workweek!

PRAYER

Lord, I thank You for giving me personally the Holy Spirit to guide me as citizens, clients and coworkers — and me — have so many needs presented and

unpresented. Lord, as I start this workweek, I need to be sensitive to Your Holy Spirit, get in Your presence, and rely on Your guidance to show me how to be a servant. In Your Mighty name, Jesus, I pray! Amen.
—LaShonda Garnes

Week 20, Day 2

WHATEVER YOU DO

READING

Colossians 3:23-24 Work willingly at **whatever you do**, as though you were working for the Lord rather than for people. Remember that the Lord will give you an inheritance as your reward, and that the Master you are serving is Christ.

REFLECTION

It's easy to understand how a missionary can impact God's kingdom or how an author can write a distinctly Christian book. But do you view your time in the workplace as your *unique way of honoring God?*

Is there a *Christian* way to patrol streets, fight fires, be a receptionist, write job descriptions, hold meetings, keep records, write grant proposals or seek external funding? Is there a *Christian* way to case-manage or conduct audits and performance appraisals? Is there a *Christian* way to enact legislation and implement policy?

Is there a *Christian* way to be a public servant? Scripture suggests there is, and it happens when you serve the Lord in **whatever you do**.

Martin Luther echoes this by saying, "The Christian shoemaker does his Christian duty not by putting little crosses on the shoes, but by making good shoes, because God is interested in good craftsmanship."

While your work may look similar to that of an atheist, the difference lies in the *attitude toward the work*. For example, the Christian who works as cashier at a grocery store can serve his neighbor by going out of his way to provide excellent customer service. By affirming the value of each customer he helps, he is working to further God's kingdom.

How might a *Christian* public servant — in government, nonprofits, healthcare, education and more — use the workplace as a daily opportunity to serve the Lord? Do you see your faith and your work as separate, or are you dedicating your entire life to Christ's kingdom?

As a *Christian* public servant, use today to find ways to honor God in **whatever you do**.

PRAYER

Lord, thank You for the diverse set of gifts and talents that You have given us, as well as the opportunities we have to use them for Your glory and the good of others. Forgive me for the times that I have not done so. Today help me to see the connection between Your kingdom and my work so that I learn to serve You in all things. For I know that my reward ultimately comes from You and not from men. In Your name, I pray. Amen.
  —Hugh Whelchel

Week 20, Day 3

HUMP DAY IS DOABLE

READING

Genesis 1:16, 19 God made two great lights—the larger one to govern the day, and the smaller one to govern the night. He also made the stars... And evening passed and morning came, marking the fourth day.

Ephesians 6:10 A final word: Be strong in the Lord and in his mighty power.

1 *Corinthians* 15:58 So, my dear brothers and sisters, be strong and immovable. Always work enthusiastically for the Lord, for you know that nothing you do for the Lord is ever useless.

REFLECTION

Today is *hump day* — the fourth day in the Judeo-Christian week and the divider in the secular work-week. If I can only get over this "hump," weekend repose will be a lot closer. Yet as I start this morning, I am still less than half-way to that "promised land"!

Most Wednesdays make it very clear: public service is a tall order. Even the most committed public servant certainly experiences that *hump feeling* when the week's frustration and fatigue causes her to wonder whether the labor is in vain. Add to each week's "hump" is the constant state of red tape, budget constraints, and seemingly ungrateful citizens and clients expressing a sense of entitlement over what you do and even who you are. The sheer enormity of public service seems too much to conquer and, here we sit, just at the beginning of *hump day*!

Though it is my deepest desire to serve with neither frustration nor fatigue, I have come to realize that I *am* only human. In my human frailty, the job of public service is *not* doable. But because of God's almighty power, I *can* stand firm and press on to do the work — today and for the rest of the week. Through Him, *not me*, my work is of value. My labor is *not* in vain.

And just look at what God did on His hump day: He created the sun, the moon and all the stars! In Him, even *my* **hump day is doable**!

PRAYER

Dear God, thank You for the privilege to serve. Even on Wednesday, please help me to give myself fully to the work of public service, standing firm and unmovable. On this particular Wednesday, help me to remember that my labor is not in vain; regardless of circumstances and obstacles, it is *NOT* in vain. Bless the public service, today and every day, so that it will glorify You at all times. In Jesus' name, I pray. Amen.

—Dyteya Lewis

Week 20, Day 4

SEEK FIRST AND LAST HIS ADVICE

READING

Hebrews 12:11 No discipline is enjoyable while it is happening—it's painful! But afterward there will be a peaceful harvest of right living for those who are trained in this way.

REFLECTION

Workplace discipline is needed when there has been some kind of failing. Perhaps the supervisor is partly to blame for not catching misbehavior earlier but, for the most part, the failure rests squarely with the person making the bad decision. If you're like me, you don't like taking disciplinary action; yet we both know there are situations where it is necessary.

So, how are *Christian* public servants supposed to administer discipline? Do we rely on the employee handbook? Do we discuss the situation with our own supervisor or HR? Absolutely! But, as Christians — especially as Christians in a secular workplace — we need to **seek first and last His advice**. Have an extended conversation with God prior to making the decision. Offer silent bullet prayers as you sit across from the employee and render the consequence. Pray continually afterwards as you seek evidence of behavioral change.

Of all the workplace functions, discipline requires a Christian to **seek first and last His advice**. When we do not, so much can interfere with our thinking and actions. We might let our reading of rules pull the trigger of discipline too quickly, or we may permit our desires to give the benefit-of-doubt and avoid conflict to delay our primary task of steward leadership.

As this workday begins, I hope no one faces the possibility of conducting a disciplinary action. But if you are in that situation, **seek first and last His advice**.

PRAYER

Father, I give You thanks for Your commandments for they are the pathway to righteousness and order for my life. Help me to have the strength and wisdom necessary always to administer discipline in a manner that respects the dignity of the individual and restores order and peace. In Your Son Jesus' name, I pray. Amen.

    —Stephen Pincus

Week 20, Day 5

LET GOD BE IN CONTROL

READING

Matthew 6:25(a) That is why I tell you not to worry about everyday life

Romans 8:28(a) And we know that God causes everything to work together for the good of those who love God

REFLECTION

After a long day of work followed by school, I read an email that caused me great distress. Realizing it was late, and that I had to wake up very early the next morning, I decided to go to bed rather than concern myself with the troubling message.

Now, I'm one who usually falls asleep quickly. Yet that night, I could not. I tossed and turned as my brain raced with ominous thoughts about that e-mail. As I lay in my bed, stress overwhelmed me. Unfortunately, I listened to the voice of Satan as he whispered in my ear about unsettling issues -- not the least of which how exhausted I was going to be the next day!

Rather than heeding my ear, I turned to my heart. So I rose from my bed and fell to my knees in prayer. With the reassurance of God's care and plan for my life, I finally was able to rest.

As a *Christian* public servant, it's easy to get stressed over workplace issues. There is so much beyond your control. Just remember to **let God be in control**. Stress and worry accomplish nothing save fatigue and suffering.

At work today, let God be in control.

PRAYER

Dear Lord, please help me always remember that ultimately You are in control, and that Your perfect plan will prevail. In Your name, I pray. Amen.
  —Paul Theroux

Week 21, Day 1

ESTABLISH OUR HEARTS

READING

James 5:7-8 Be patient as you wait for the Lord's return. Consider the farmers who patiently wait for the rains in the fall and in the spring. They eagerly look for the valuable harvest to ripen. You, too, must be patient. Take courage, for the coming of the Lord is near.

REFLECTION

I don't know about you, but I'm not a patient person; I never have been. As I get older, I thought I would become more patient, but no. Waiting is hard to do, yet we all have to wait on one thing or another. Being patient while you wait is ever harder to do.

Academics wait a lot: appointments with tardy students; meetings delayed because a colleague thinks it's neat to be stylishly late; waiting on hearing from an editor about a manuscript.

As a public servant, you also wait a lot: supervisory approval to make a needed purchase; completion of paperwork concerning one of those mandatory rules. Perhaps you are waiting on a homeless client with mental issues that make it impossible for him to keep to a schedule. And the week is long, and this makes it particularly hard to sit back and be patient.

Yet, through *James*, God gives us a command, not a suggestion. We are to *be patient*. We are to **establish our hearts**.

That's easier said than done, but that is exactly how *Christian* public servants are to behave as we wait for the results of our proposals, paperwork; the outcome of our outreach, our daily interactions with both citizen and client. In too many instances — in every instance — we cannot produce results. *We can only produce efforts and diligence, while God produces the results.* And for that, we must be patient.

So today, take a deep breath and keep working to the best of your ability. Let's just **establish our hearts** upon Christ, upon His Word, upon His name. Be patient. His results draw near!

PRAYER

Dear God, help me be patient. Help me to keep my heart established upon You and Your Word. And above all else, Father, help me to know that You are returning soon, and that your labors in the field will not be in vain. In Your Son's name, I pray. Amen.
—Stephen M. King

Week 21, Day 2

WE ARE NOT OUR OWN

READING:

1 Timothy 6:12a Fight the good fight for the true faith.

REFLECTION

Having one of those workweeks? Too many concerns crossing your desk? Multiple tasks requiring simultaneous completion? Having to redo a project because, well, just because! *You've probably even sent or received a few e-mails that you wish didn't go out.* Seems like everything is running against you.

To be sure, it's a struggle. But, there is a cause. As *Christian* public servants, **we are not our own**. We are motivated by Christ. He is our cause. He is why we are here — at our workplaces — doing what we're doing — *even now*. Everything — including the struggle — has a reason. It's up to us to hear what He is saying according to His purpose and whom He desires to touch.

Yes, this workweek — it's clearly a struggle. But do not give up. Keep fighting the good fight for the true faith. Remember, **we are not our own**.

PRAYER

Lord, let me fight the good fight for You today. Throughout each crisis, let me learn Your meaning and purpose. In all that I do, let me glorify You. In Your name, I pray. Amen.
  —Chris Summers

Week 21, Day 3

PURSUIT OF GOOD WORK

READING

Colossians 3:23-24 Work willingly at whatever you do, as though you were working for the Lord rather than for people. Remember that the Lord will give you an inheritance as your reward, and that the Master you are serving is Christ.[

REFLECTION

Have you ever felt "excluded" or "cast out?" Given you're a public servant, such feelings are not uncommon. Perhaps some coworkers insist on belittling their own profession. Or, does the problem lie outside the workplace?

You hear a lot of negativity and jokes about public servants. *Bureaucrat bashing* abounds and, as a *Christian* public servant, you can feel "singled-out" and "cast out."

The desire to be liked is not necessarily wrong. The danger is when we make it an idol. Then, we might say or do things, or remain silent, just to make us feel included. Bashing your own profession takes place for the sake of fitting in.

Rather than working to find approval from others, be proud of doing *good and excellent work!* This may not lead to fame, fortune, influence, or even invitations to the coffee klatch — it may not stop jokes — but it will lead to respect from those who really know the field. More importantly, the **pursuit of good work** will be pleasing to the One who really counts.

As this workweek continues, don't let the desire to be liked or included compromise your spiritual effectiveness. Don't let the feeling of being "cast out" change your Christian workplace priorities. Pray for deliverance from that temptation.

Today, know your profession is important and needed by citizens and society. So focus on the **pursuit of good work**. Let God take care of everything else.

PRAYER

Lord, thank You for letting me work for the renewal of Your kingdom every single day of my life. Sometimes, it can be easy to lose sight of this in the workplace. Help me to focus my thoughts, motivations, and actions on pleasing You rather than on appeasing others. In Jesus' name, I pray. Amen.
  —Art Lindsley

Week 21, Day 4

LITTLE SPARK OF LIGHT

READING

John 8:12b I am the light of the world. If you follow me, you won't have to walk in darkness, because you will have the light that leads to life.

REFLECTION

I once worked in a setting where I was the only believer. Each morning a coworker insisted on having his radio tuned to a station where the songs had wicked language. He played the radio so loudly that no one could avoid hearing the music's immorality. Such lack of respect for others! My first thought each day, perhaps after the fantasy of throwing his radio out the window, was to get transferred out of there!

Then God, through His Spirit, spoke to me. He let me know He placed me in that workplace, at that moment, to bring His light. It was hard, and I took some abuse, and nothing changed overnight. But I watched as God began to speak to others in that workplace, including my supervisor and that particular coworker. The "radio guy" eventually quit tuning to that station — and he made that choice without me even complaining to anyone!

I witnessed the difference that **little spark of light**, with God's anointing, can make. In fact, I was sad when I finally was assigned away from that specific setting. That **little spark of light**, which God commanded me to shine on others, also reshaped my heart about all my coworkers, including the radio guy!

What is your workplace culture like? Does it seem gloomy and absent of His presence? You can be that **little spark of light** making a difference in that dark environment. I would even venture to say that God has placed you there specifically for that reason.

Or, has your light gone out? Have you lost that spark? At work, have you actually surrendered to the darkness? It's never too late to flip the switch and let the light shine again!

Today at work, become once again that **little spark of light**.

PRAYER

Father, thank You, for Your Son Jesus, who came to bring Your light into the darkness of this world. Thank You for lighting the way that I may know hope and peace. Use me, Father, to be that light to others. I ask this in Jesus' name. Amen.

—Bill Dudley

Week 21, Day 5

BUT YOU CAN CHOOSE FAITH

READING

Matthew 17:20 "You don't have enough faith," Jesus told them. "I tell you the truth, if you had faith even as small as a mustard seed, you could say to this mountain, 'Move from here to there,' and it would move. Nothing would be impossible."

REFLECTION

As public servants, we know that many mountains arise between us and the opportunity to serve the public effectively. Mountains come in a variety of forms throughout the world. In one setting, it may be a wayward leader making it harder for others to govern. In another, lack of transparency in one area of public service may raise citizen doubts about the entire public service. In still another, debate over finance and taxation may play havoc on programs needed by all citizens, or those especially needed by the most vulnerable. Naturally, there are internal mountains in every setting: a supervisor with her own agenda; a coworker unwilling to pull his own weight; a citizen or client refusing to do his part. Plus, in every setting, mountains take the form of training limitations, the postponed purchases of needed fire trucks or police cars, the threat of hiring freezes, the fear of furloughs, layoffs and the like.

In whatever country you serve the public, mountains are inevitable. But know that if you choose to walk by faith, in the how and not just the what, mountains can be moved — perhaps not as fast as you would like, but they will be moved with certainty. Even with faith the size of a mustard seed, mountains will be moved!

Yes, mountains are inevitable today. New ones will arise tomorrow. **But you can choose faith**. If you do so, "nothing would be impossible for you"!

PRAYER

Thank You, Lord, for the gift of faith. May I use this precious gift in my workplace. For Your glory, may I move mountains today! In Your Son's name, I pray. Amen.

— Lyse-Ann Lacourse

Week 22, Day 1

QUIET CORNER IN THE CAVE

READING

Psalm 103:13-18 The LORD is like a father to his children, tender and compassionate to those who fear him. For he knows how weak we are; he remembers we are only dust. Our days on earth are like grass; like wildflowers, we bloom and die. The wind blows, and we are gone—as though we had never been here. But the love of the LORD remains forever with those who fear him. His salvation extends to the children's children of those who are faithful to his covenant, of those who obey his commandments!

REFLECTION

Time. It's the one commonality of every workplace. Indeed, our lives seem to center on it. Time to wake up for work. Time to dress for work. Time to go to work. Time to work. Time to bring home work. Time to think about work. Time to enjoy the fruits of work. *Time.*

I am reaching the fastest part of my sprint for this workweek, and I am approaching the very peak of efficiency for the year. But now *God calls me to stop.* God wants me to be still for some time and find that **quiet corner in the cave** of my soul where there is no room for anything or anyone but .... Him and me.

In my quiet corner, I must stop and remember that all this is really temporary. Too much of my time is spent running away from death instead of making peace with it. Fact is, the only thing I am truly doing each day is drawing nearer to the certainty of earthly death. Does my life reflect this? Do I live as if my days are numbered? What should I do differently today at work — how might I better serve Him — if the remaining days on my work schedule number just one?

As a *Christian*, is your faith fitting into your life or is your life fitting into your faith? As a *Christian* public servant, what is the relationship between your faith and your work? There are times when God calls you to stop and turn to Him.

At work today, find time for only Him in that **quiet corner in the cave** of your soul.

PRAYER

Thank You, my Lord, for blessing me with time — so far — to work and live. Thank You for breaking the body of Your only Son, pouring out His pure blood just for my sins. I pray that today You will give me quiet pause to see my sins for what they are. I pray that You will grant me time and strength to correct them. In your Son's name, I pray. Amen.
—Stephanie van Straten

Week 22, Day 2

MORE DISCIPLINE THAN CHURNING

READING

Psalm 46:10a Be still, and know that I am God!

REFLECTION

I'm a churner. You know the type, I can't sit still. There's so much to do each day, and I don't like to tarry very long. Even talking to God seems to be done with the quick step. (That's right — I don't seem to have time to talk *with* Him, so I just talk to Him.) When I pray, I pray for intervention — quick intervention. My prayers are calls to God for help with an immediate problem. My prayers are efficient, as is my life. As a professional woman and mother, I try to build efficiency in everything I do — and this includes talking to God.

So this particular verse, calling for stillness and transformation, is a bit alarming. I'm struggling with it because the more I sit still, the more work I have to do. I mean, even during worship time — even in reading this very devotional this morning — my mind is running through my "to do" list. I'm racing toward those issues I need to resolve today, to what was left on my desk from last night. Even when He wants to tarry with *me*, my mind is churning away from the Eternal to the immediate.

So I'm trying to learn to be still. If you're like me, you know full well it's not an easy lesson. Stillness, after all, requires **more discipline than churning**.

Yet it's the only way to truly hear God. And if I cannot *hear* God, how can I truly hear the hearts and voices of those with whom I work? If I cannot *hear* God, how can I truly work in His efficiency? I need to know He is God, in my life and in my workplace, and that takes **more discipline than churning**.

PRAYER

Father God, I know how to be efficient, to be forceful, and to be directive. I do not know about stillness. Help me stop the churning! I need the chance to hear *You*. I need an opportunity to tarry with You so that I can truly hear others. Tarry with You so that I can truly do my work in Your efficient glory. Tarry with You so that I can know You *are* God. In Your Son's name, I pray. Amen.
—Stephanie L. Bellar

Week 22, Day 3

IN THE SHADOW

READING

Psalm 63:7-8 Because you are my helper, I sing for joy **in the shadow** of your wings. I cling to you; your strong right hand holds me securely.

REFLECTION

For as long as I can remember, I've wanted to *be* a mother. So I can't tell you how elated my husband and I were when we found out I was going to *be* one! Unfortunately, I miscarried that child. You see, as much as I wanted to *be* a mother, that wasn't going to happen — at least not right now.

I wondered, what was God trying to show me in the midst of such great pain and anguish? As I prayed, scripture came to me. Sitting **in the shadow** of the Lord's wing means I am protected. No matter what might come my way, God's hedge of protection continues to cover me.

You might ask, what does my story have to do with public service — or anything else in your life?

In your work, have you ever had a desire to achieve something to *be something*? Like wanting to *be* a mom, I also want to *be* a leader, *be* a manager, *be* significant, *to be something special*. But what happens when you can't *be* those things?

There are times in our careers when no matter what we do, we cannot *be* what we believe we should *be* in that moment. And so we struggle. We may cry, hang our heads, and lose heart. And then we are reminded of scripture. Even though we haven't become what we want to be, we remain **in the shadow** of the wing of the Lord.

Being **in the shadow** of God's wing is the greatest place to be. Even with lost opportunities and failure, we can take heart that we are **in the shadow**. There, we are safe. His will yet reigns over us. There is beauty of being there. His wing is with Him wherever he goes, so you see, you are also with Him. Despite failure, loss, pain and struggle, you remain and abide in Him, and you are protected. This also means that you will have the opportunity to *be something special* to Him. That you will *be* what He has called you to *be*.

Take refuge **in the shadow** of his wing. *Be* free to dream. *Be* reminded that it is the Lord who is your Help, and it is He who brings forth new life and renewed life. Allow new life and renewed life to be a testament to who God is, and what He desires to do in your life. Take all of that, and be constantly mindful that His Will is to bless you to serve others and, in that service, to *be* a blessing to those you serve.

At work or home, being **in the shadow** of His wing is the greatest place to *be!*

PRAYER

Dear Jesus, thank You for allowing me to be a blessing at work. Thank you for giving me such an awesome place to *be*! Thank You for protecting me **in the shadow** of your sweet and powerful wing. Thank You for encouraging me, even in the midst of loss and failure. At work today, and throughout all hours of the day and night, I am thankful that I remain in Your will. And I thank You that I can share You with those whom we surround at work today. In Your name, I pray. Amen.

    —Angelina Moyo

Week 22, Day 4

CHRONICALLY UNLOVABLE

READING

John 13:35 Your love for one another will prove to the world that you are my disciples.

REFLECTION

In the public service, we are often confronted with the **chronically unlovable**. I'm not referring to people being rude as a result of having a bad day. I mean citizens, clients and coworkers whose unpleasantness and anger might be a function of being chronically displaced, disrepaired, disappointed, disabled, discarded, or detached.

It's easy to love those we like or basically get along with. But it's much more difficult to love others under our own strength. Sometimes we mistakenly let our feelings and perceptions guide us instead of following the commandment of our Lord.

Yet the challenge remains : He commands us to love one another, even those who are **chronically unlovable**. And as *Christian* public servants, there is no better way to prove we are His disciples!

PRAYER

Father, let my love for others at work today be a witness to You. In Your Son's name, I pray. Amen.
  —Suzanne Denis

Week 22, Day 5

KNOW CHRIST IN YOUR WORKPLACE

READING

John 6:27 But don't be so concerned about perishable things like food. Spend your energy seeking the eternal life that the Son of Man can give you. For God the Father has given me the seal of his approval.

REFLECTION

In the end, all that we do in this life fades away and is never as enduring as we believe it will be. Thousands of years from now we will be nothing more than dust, and the fruit of our labor will be like forgotten leaves of last year's autumn.

If all we ever put our trust in is the results we can see now, we will lose that which God has prepared for us in eternity. Perishable things are vanity, money, fame, recognition from the powerful, and power itself. Food that endures for eternal life is character, virtue, love of Christ, and communion with God.

As this workday unfolds, we should perform our temporal duties well and with humility. Yet always look for the eternal nuggets of truth that break forth from the floods of temporal toil. *Know Christ in your labor.* **Know Christ in your workplace**! Know Christ in your daily schedules and meetings! To know Christ and to feed on Him is to have eternal life. This is what we have, the very presence of Christ in our lives, in our work, and in our daily routine. Anything that distracts us from that is spoiled meat. We must seek the *bread of life* even as we toil in the everydayness of temporal labor.

Know Christ in your labor. Know Christ in your workplace!

PRAYER

Dear God, I seek only You. While I work today, let me only find You. When I am distracted by my daily tasks, draw me closer to You through those activities. May I begin my day in Your presence, fulfill its duties with You next to me, and when I rest my head on my pillow this evening, let me rest in You. In Your Son's name, we pray. Amen.

—Dominick D. Hankle

Week 23, Day 1

MISFORTUNE INTO FORTUNE

READING

Jeremiah 29:14a "I will be found by you," says the LORD. "I will end your captivity and restore your fortunes."

REFLECTION

My workplace is one of misfortune. People come here because of it. They tried the *wrong ways* to turn their **misfortune into fortune**. Their efforts caused open wounds and, once here, many try to heal themselves.

I remind them that no man can heal himself. They must find God. No matter how long the process, only God can heal them from sin and misfortune, and restore them to Him, our Father.

Is your workplace any different from mine? Are there not people trying to heal themselves in some way? Do they not need to find God and His healing over some misfortune?

And what about you and me? Are we any different?

As your workday begins, remember: Only He can turn your **misfortune into fortune**.

PRAYER

Father God, no matter how long the process, You will heal me and restore me to You. In Your time, You will turn my **misfortune into fortune**. The right kind of fortune. No sinful fortune. Your fortune. Bless me today in knowing this to be true. In Jesus' name, I pray. Amen.

—Chris Summers

Week 23, Day 2

REALLY GOOD KNOCK-KNOCK JOKE

READING

John 15:11 I have told you these things so that you will be filled with my joy. Yes, your joy will overflow!

REFLECTION

Do you like a **really good knock-knock joke**? Are you a laugher? As a Marine Corps officer (now retired), I was often told I laughed way too much. That attribute is easily mistaken for being soft — contrary to the image of a *hard charging* Marine. (But all knew that, at the appropriate moments each day, I was *hard charging*!)

My tendency to be a laugher got me thinking about Jesus. Did He have that same attribute? You know, the bible never speaks of Him laughing or even smiling. Instead, it goes into detail about His weeping, instructing, healing, chastising and, ultimately, His suffering.

Yet scripture never claims that Jesus *didn't* like a joke. There must have been times when He enjoyed the first-century equivalent of a **really good knock-knock joke** — even while saving the world! Perhaps with His disciples? With the children? With the people on the streets? Jesus must have experienced laughter and just some good clean fun with those around Him. Maybe He was a laugher, but knew when to be *hard charging*.

Heading to work today, remember that your Walk with Christ does not preclude laughter. Far from it. Having good clean fun with coworkers can be part of showing to Whom you belong. Sharing a laugh with those you serve can be an attribute of being Christian.

As a *Christian* public servant, don't be afraid to laugh! Just know when to be *hard charging*.... Now, does anyone have a **really good knock-knock joke** to tell at work?

PRAYER

Dear Lord, please continue to ensure my heart is filled with the spirit of joy and laughter so that I may share these gifts with others crossing my path. When I set out to spread Your word to those in need of encouragement, when I do Your work in my workplace, let my *hard charging* be sprinkled with a hint of humor in order to soothe the soul and relax the mood. In Your name, I eternally pray. Amen.

—Steve Butler

Week 23, Day 3

PUT UP GUIDEPOSTS

READING

Jeremiah 31:21a Set up road signs; **put up guideposts.**

REFLECTION

Which way do we go? Right? Left? What is our agency's objective? Are we on the right path in terms of our mission statement? Above all, are we on the path to honor Jesus?

These are the questions I ask myself daily.

While I am ambitious, headstrong, determined and willing to fight for our residents, the Living Word of God tells me to **put up guideposts**. I must walk forward with the agency growing, but I must do so in *His* will and not in mine. If I proceed in *my* will, then I am lost and certainly not in service of Our Lord the way I seek to be. I must constantly **put up guideposts** so that I don't stray from His path.

Which direction is your agency going? East? West? North? South? You might work for a secular organization, but still you want to stay on His path, don't you? Regardless of where you work, you need to **put up guideposts**. Don't go astray.

PRAYER

Lord, thank You for paving the way for me. At work today, help me stay on Your path. In Jesus' name, I pray. Amen.

—Tajuan McCarty

Week 23, Day 4

ALWAYS HIS SEASON

READING

Ecclesiastes 3:1 For everything there is a season, a time for every activity under heaven.

1 Peter 5:7 Give all your worries and cares to God, for he cares about you.

REFLECTION

Typically I gauge a supervisor's mood and availability before interrupting him or her for a decision on something I feel is urgent. If the supervisor happens to be focused on another matter, my issue probably won't get the attention it deserves. It's better to choose a time when the person can concentrate fully on my issue so that I get a well-considered response. As the saying goes, "when you need an answer really bad right now, what you'll get is a really bad answer right now." So, wise public servants learn to *choose the right time*.

But that kind of workplace-smarts can create an unintended consequence for the *Christian* public servant. It may cause you and me to think that, at least at work, we have to *choose the right time* to be with God.

Of course, we know deep down that's not the case. We can approach God anytime, even in the midst of our work. After all, He already knows everything we're dealing with before we come to Him, and He is always fully available to each one of His children. But still, we sometimes get into the habit of not approaching Him at work, except perhaps on our own break time.

So at work today, break that habit! Don't wait for the lunch hour or, worse, until you've tried everything else. It is **always His season**. Seek His wisdom and guidance immediately and constantly. Each minute of the day, give Him your worries and concerns.

Save the "choosing" strategy for coworkers, colleagues, and supervisors. In your workplace, there's *no really bad time* to be with God! It is **always His season**.

PRAYER

Dear God, thank You for being accessible to me at work today. Thank You for caring about every detail of what I do and what I'm about to do. Thank You for taking from me the cares and worries that easily distract from the joy of serving You. In Your Son's name, I pray. Amen.

—Martha Smith

Week 23, Day 5

IT WILL HOLD ONTO YOU

READING

I Timothy 6:10 For the love of money is the root of all kinds of evil. And some people, craving money, have wandered from the true faith and pierced themselves with many sorrows..

REFLECTION

The life we live on this earth is short and fleeting, and all the riches we amass, all of the fame we claim, and all the recognition we accrue is nothing compared to what we will witness in our heavenly home.

In fact, if you hold onto the love of material wealth—or the love of fame or the love of recognition — **it will hold onto you**. You will be controlled by it. You will forever be bound to accumulating more and more — and not really know why you are doing it.

As public servants, we have a special calling: *our work must be of profit not just for ourselves, but for the betterment of the public good.* We all need good salaries, and we all need better raises. And recognition is a nice thing. But Paul tells you to flee from the love of such temptations.

Run as fast as you can away from that kind of love! If you don't, **it will hold onto you** and prevent you from being the *Christian* public servant *God has called you to be.*

PRAYER

Father, help me, as a faithful *Christian* public servant, not to love money, not to love fame, not to love recognition. Help me to humbly fulfill the calling and purpose You have given me. Enable me to work diligently on my tasks. Rewards will come in this lifetime, but I know they will certainly accumulate and overflow in the next. I praise You and thank You. In Jesus' name, I pray. Amen.
    —Stephen M. King.

Week 24, Day 1

DO YOUR JOB

READING

Exodus 32:10, 11(a), 14 Now leave me alone so my fierce anger can blaze against them, and I will destroy them. Then I will make you, Moses, into a great nation." [11] But Moses tried to pacify the LORD his God. "O LORD!" he said. "Why are you so angry with your own people ... ? So the LORD changed his mind about the terrible disaster he had threatened to bring on his people.

1 Timothy 1: 13 ...even though I used to blaspheme the name of Christ. In my insolence, I persecuted his people. But God had mercy on me because I did it in ignorance and unbelief.

Luke 12:47 And a servant who knows what the master wants, but isn't prepared and doesn't carry out those instructions, will be severely punished.

REFLECTION

It's difficult being a good supervisor, and it's extremely difficult being a good *Christian* supervisor. As a *servant leader*, we want to show mercy — just like when Moses pleaded with God to let His wrath die down or how Paul reminds us that even he was treated mercifully.

But as a *steward leader*, we must maintain accountability. After all, we are responsible to all of our employees, our supervisors and organizations, the citizens we serve, and, of course, our God. For the success of any public or non-profit organization, *steward leadership is as important as servant leadership*.

I bring this up because good supervisors are forced to engage in disciplinary actions. Yes, you cringe at the effort it takes dealing with those kinds of problems. *Bad apples* — who may be very nice people, even practicing Christians — can still easily drain 80% of your time and energy. And with bad or misguided supervisors, the tendency is simply to show mercy in the hope that the problem goes away.

Well, good supervisors know that personnel problems don't just disappear, and the principles of steward leadership tell us that they cannot be ignored. Yet, if God can get upset with the Israelites, *bad apples* can also cause good supervisors to act in anger.

You are called to accountability. When forced to discipline an employee, **do your job**. Remember the positive as well as the negative and, above all, first *let your wrath die down*. But, as a good supervisor and a *Christian* public servant, **do your job**.

PRAYER

Father, I thank You for Your divine mercy. Guide me today in being both a servant leader and a steward leader. When confronted with problems, first let my wrath die down. Then, give me the strength and courage *to do my job*. In Your Son's name, I pray. Amen.
    —Stephen Pincus

Week 24, Day 2

BEARER OF SECOND CHANCES

READING

Jonah 3:1 Then the LORD spoke to Jonah a second time.

REFLECTION

You know, there are times when some people frustrate *the Christianity right out of me*, and I don't want to give them another chance. It could be a staff member or a client or someone on the board. Doesn't matter. I'm just tired of being the **bearer of second chances**!

I know you feel this way, too. After all, as public servants, we're supposed to *get it right the first time*! Isn't this the common theme among those of us who lead? We know how to _____ (you fill in the blank). And if *we* know it should be done right the first time, then everyone must know that it should be done right the first time.

But wait a minute.

Isn't it our responsibility to lead and serve in the same manner God did with Jonah? Our staff, residents, clients and board members are not perfect, and neither are we. As *Christian* public servants, we must be the **bearer of second chances**. We must also give *ourselves* a second chance.

I mean, am I not to show the same grace, mercy and love to others that Jesus shows to me? I don't know about you, but Jesus gave *me* 1000 X 1000 chances (and still counting) today, so do I have any reason not to be the **bearer of second chances**?

OK, so as I was saying, there will be times when someone frustrates *the Christianity right out of me*, and I won't want to give him or her another chance. When this happens, Jesus gently reminds me of the way He is with me .... and the way God was with Jonah.

PRAYER

God, You know I get frustrated, impatient, tired and just plain angry and don't want to give others the second chance they need. During these moments, please continue to remind me of the "second chances" YOU gave me. The second chances You are giving me right now. Thank You for loving me so much that You continue to give me those second chances each day, and help me to remember to bestow the same grace and love to those I lead and serve. In Jesus' name, I pray. Amen.

—Tajuan McCarty

Week 24, Day 3

RUN THE RACE WITH
GREATER PURPOSE

READING

Hebrews 12: 1b-2a ... And let us run with endurance the race God has set before us. We do this by keeping our eyes on Jesus...

Luke 11: 9b Keep on seeking, and you will find.

REFLECTION

For many of us, there comes a point in our lives where we stop and reflect on how we have spent the first three, four, or five decades. Have we accomplished anything with a kingdom purpose? Or, have we spent our lives pursuing our own vainglorious desires. Maybe we call it a mid-life crisis or maybe it is something else. What really matters, is *how we respond*.

As I've pondered these issues lately, I can't help but wonder whether I am *jogging along gingerly* rather than *running with purpose*. And, if that be the case, is God's purpose for me still off in the distance because of my failure to **run the race with greater purpose**?

Sometimes contemplating such questions is uncomfortable, but none the less necessary. For me, at least, it is certainly time to spend more time in the Word. Time to ask for God's guidance, seek out his will for my life, and ask the Lord to open my eyes to his plan.

In terms of your work and career, are you at the same point?

PRAYER

Lord, you have a divine purpose for me. Please give me the strength to **run the race with greater purpose** and guide me through my growth as a *Christian* public servant. In Your name, I pray. Amen.

—Adam B. Lowther

Week 24, Day 4

THOUGHTS OF WISHING

READING

Romans 8:28 We know that God causes everything to work together for the good of those who love God and are called according to his purpose for them.

REFLECTION

I woke up this morning and looked outside just to see my car glossed over in frost. I instantly began to think how much I hate this weather, how I wish it was still summer, how I wish I lived somewhere warmer. Frankly, the **thoughts of wishing** just kept flowing.

Prepared for work, I was walking to my car, still grumbling, when I received a text message from a fellow Christian friend. A U.S. Marine, he is currently on field operation training and sleeping in a tent for 9 days. In his text message, my friend joked about how frost was forming inside His tent! Cold, but he thought it was funny!!

I was taken aback and my perspective instantly changed. I was no longer consumed by those **thoughts of wishing**. That little frost on my windshield is not a catastrophe. The late winter in southeastern Virginia is not that bad. I am thankful I am not sleeping in a frosted tent! I am thankful that my friend thinks it's funny!!

Things may not go your way today. Depending on where you live and work in the world, your car may either be buried in snow or boiling under the hot sun. You may get a flat tire on the way to work. You may even walk into a firestorm once you get to work. *Not a problem!*

As a *Christian* public servant, be thankful. Just like my friend — that *Christian* public servant in a frosted tent — allow God to fill fully your heart today with thanksgiving and praise rather than all the things you wish you had or all the things for which you could be unthankful. *Life doesn't have to be great in order for your heart to be filled fully with thanksgiving.*

The ups and downs at work and life bring unforeseen beauty in many ways. God is working for your good because you love Him and follow Him. *So stop complaining!* At work today, don't be consumed by those **thoughts of wishing**.

PRAYER

God, You are so awesome! My faith in You has the ability to restore me, even on my worst days. Help me use the right perspective at work today and remember that in ALL things (good or bad) it is for my good. You alone are almighty and powerful, not the circumstances I may face. In Your Son's name, I pray. Amen.

—Angela Arbitter

Week 24, Day 5

NOTHING MORE THAN HIS SCUM

READING

Matthew 9:10-13 Later Matthew invited Jesus and his disciples to his home as dinner guests, along with many tax collectors and other disreputable sinners. But when the Pharisees saw this, they asked his disciples, *why does your teacher eat with such scum?* When Jesus heard this he said, "Healthy people don't need a doctor, sick people do." Then he added, "Now, go and learn the meaning of this Scripture. I want you to show mercy, not offer sacrifice. For I have come to call not those who think they are righteous, but those who know they are sinners."

REFLECTION

Do you keep others from Jesus because of your self-righteousness?

Are you shocked that someone like me, *scum* sitting where I am, would ask someone like you that question? Here on Life Row, there is a lot of self-righteousness. So, what about where you live and work? *Do you keep others from Jesus because of your self-righteousness?*

I become self-righteous when I start thinking church belongs to me, or when I preach like I invented the Gospel. You, too? Or, is it when you sing in the choir as if you are the main attraction; or when you tithe as if He will fail without your money? Or, is it when you need to arrive early each week to Sunday school because only you know how to make coffee?

We carry our self-righteousness throughout the week. We become judgmental, and that makes us cruel when someone doesn't quite fit into our standard of being a Christian. We tend to charge others a fee for the same mercy that Jesus gives us freely.

I have no idea where you work or even what that might be like. But we are identical. God gives us a gift of mercy, not sacrifice. When you view what you are doing for Him as a sacrifice, that is when Jesus sees you as doing nothing more than questioning the *scum* around Him.

As you go to work today, remember the mercy you receive freely from Jesus — mercy neither you nor I deserve. Pour that mercy onto others throughout the day so that they too can be like us — nothing more than sinners following Christ — **nothing more than His scum.**

PRAYER

Father, in the name of Jesus, I pray. Continue to keep me humble so I can see, love, and have mercy on someone else today — just like You have mercy on me every day. Amen.
　　　　—Jimmy Davis, Jr.

Week 25, Day 1

PERFECT NUMBER OF WATTS

READING

John 9:5 But while I am here in the world, I am the light of the world.

Matthew 5:15 No one lights a lamp and then puts it under a basket. Instead, a lamp is placed on a stand, where it gives light to everyone in the house.

REFLECTION

What kind of light shines through you today at work?

As public servants, we know the day will be difficult. Meeting the needs of some citizens will be complicated (*can't find the right wattage — need a three-way bulb*); some encounters with coworkers will be demanding (*where are the higher watt bulbs?*); some situations with be frustrating (my client's *bulb burns out way too quickly*).

As a *Christian* Public Servant, remember that God has given us the *Ultimate Light* — Jesus. His light adjusts automatically with every situation, with every encounter, with every need. It will never grow dim. After all, it's a *name-brand* light with *superb consumer recognition* and carries an *eternal lifetime guarantee!* With Jesus, we always have the **perfect number of watts**!

As you serve the public today, will you shine the *Ultimate Light*? Or will you hide it under a basket and continue to "go at it alone"?? You may be the only light that someone sees. Make sure your light exhibits the love of Christ. Make sure the light you shine is the one with the **perfect number of watts**.

PRAYER

Lord, I pray that Your light shines brightly through me today. Lord, I pray for courage not to hide it under a basket. May all *Christian* public servants shine Your light and give Your children the brightest hope. In Jesus' name, Amen.

—LaShonda Garnes

Week 25, Day 2

THE WAY YOU DO YOUR WORK

READING

Matthew 5:13 You are the salt of the earth. But what good is salt if it has lost its flavor? Can you make it salty again? It will be thrown out and trampled underfoot as worthless.

REFLECTION

It's tempting to think that once we are saved, we just need to bide our time on earth until we can get to heaven. Sometimes we might want to disengage from the brokenness of the world, setting our sights on heaven and the future.

But this is not how the Bible tells us to act! At Christ's second coming, God will restore this earth to the way it was before the Fall. God has delivered each of us from darkness into light so that we take part in that restoration process as his servants, image-bearers, and children. This is why Jesus tells us not to disengage, but to be the salt and light of the earth.

As *Christian* public servants, we are in a special position to do this!

When we believe, repent, and enter into the kingdom in this age, our lives become a witness to the way things could be. Even **the way you do your work** becomes a signpost pointing to the way things will be in the new heaven and new earth.

PRAYER

Lord, thank You for Your promise to restore the earth to a perfect and complete state. Thank You for my part in advancing Your kingdom and bringing about that restoration. Help me to embrace my role as Your servant by being faithful in the work that You have for me in the here and now. It is in Jesus' name, I pray. Amen.

—Hugh Whelchel

Week 25, Day 3

HOLDING PATTERN

READING

Romans 5: 2-4 Because of our faith, Christ has brought us into this place of undeserved privilege where we now stand, and we confidently and joyfully look forward to sharing God's glory. We can rejoice, too, when we run into problems and trials, for we know that they help us develop endurance. And endurance develops strength of character, and character strengthens our confident hope.

REFLECTION

You're not moving forward in your career. You desire a promotion, a pay increase, or even a new challenge. With all your heart, you believe you deserve it. Yet, nothing seems to change. You remain suspended in the same position you've held for an endless time. Sometimes we desire change so badly. We pray for it. We're not willing to wait for it. We end up in that **holding pattern** — that nightmare of not being able to move forward or backward. Do you know someone who feels that way? Is it you?

As a *Christian* public servant, remember that God is sovereign in your life and in your workplace. He controls advancement and change. Not you, but Him. God allows you to experience that **holding pattern** so you can develop godly character and patience. And, as you know, public service desperately needs men and women with godly attributes to lead in this dispensation of time. Resist the temptation to consider your current position with frustration or anger. Instead, know that God is using your position to transform you into the *Christian* public servant He needs.

Today at work, know that **holding pattern** will last only as long as He needs it to last. And yet, know that you currently enjoy *undeserved privilege*. So rejoice and be exceedingly glad!

PRAYER

Heavenly Father, help me to have hope and patience as I wait for You to manifest change in my life and in my current work circumstances. Grant me the grace that I need to embrace change when it finally comes to pass. Help me to walk in total obedience regarding the change that takes place so that You will be glorified. In Jesus' name, I pray. Amen.

—Sabrina Wooten

Week 25, Day 4

CAUSE OTHERS TO WONDER

READING

Philippians 1:27-28(a) Above all, you must live as citizens of heaven, conducting yourselves in a manner worthy of the Good News about Christ. Then, whether I come and see you again or only hear about you, I will know that you are standing together with one spirit and one purpose, fighting together for the faith, which is the Good News. Don't be intimidated in any way by your enemies.

REFLECTION

It's easy to get wrapped up in <u>me</u>. At work and in my classes: my problem, my workload, my term paper, my lunch break, my deadline.... me, me, me. Others know I claim to be a Christian, so they must certainly wonder about me, my words, and my actions.

Christ is faithful in reminding me that life is about *Him* and glorifying <u>only</u> *Him*. Yet living as a citizen of heaven, in a manner worthy of the *Gospel* of Christ, isn't easy. Driving to work, I'm disheartened -- too often I **cause others to wonder** about me, not Him.

But in the parking lot, I realize I'm not alone. He gives me the Holy Spirit, His Word, and fellow believers. Walking into my building, I know there are enemies inside, on my floor, just down the hall, perhaps next to me. My workplace is part of a sinful world. So I need to follow the Holy Spirit, stand side by side with other believers in prayer, unite with them in the *Gospel*, and join them in the Hope of Christ. As I take the elevator, I understand I have to be worthy of His Good News and, if I am, I need not be afraid.

As this workday begins, others will oppose Christ in many ways. Fear not and stand firm. Have confidence in Christ, be a citizen of heaven, and strive to be worthy of His *Gospel*. As a *Christian* public servant, **cause others to wonder**.... about Him, not you.

PRAYER

Father, life is never about me. Convict me when I lose sight of Your purpose. Groom me to be more like Your Son and to live in a manner worthy of Your name. Strengthen my faith when I enter my workplace. Let my life cause others to wonder about You. In Your Son's name, I pray. Amen.
—Brooke Hollingsworth

Week 25, Day 5

NO VACATIONS

READING

1 Timothy 1:15-16 This is a trustworthy saying, and everyone should accept it: "Christ Jesus came into the world to save sinners"—and I am the worst of them all. But God had mercy on me so that Christ Jesus could use me as a prime example of his great patience with even the worst sinners. Then others will realize that they, too, can believe in him and receive eternal life.

REFLECTION

Have you ever had a selfish plan? I did about 6 months ago.

My plan was to lay back and simply "play church" for a while — just go to church, read my bible, and that was about it each week. Just take it all in for myself. I guess I just wanted a vacation.

A couple of weeks later, a friend walked up to me after church and said he'd been noticing exactly what I was doing — just going through the motions. He told me that, with God, there are **no vacations**.

He said there will be a long retirement package coming to each and every one of us once we get to heaven. But for now, count on it: there are **no vacations**.

What I had forgotten was made clear by my friend. God gives to me. He gives to me personally each and every day. If I just keep selfishly what He gives me, I will miss the real blessing of being used as a *prime example* of His great patience and the mercy He has for me — so others will realize that they can believe in Him and receive eternal life.

You don't have to be where I "work" to know this, too. So today where you work, put aside your selfish plan and allow Christ Jesus to use you as His *prime example*. If you do that, someone will have an opportunity to believe and receive eternal life.

At work today, put aside your desire to take a break and relax. Put aside your laziness. You will get that eternal retirement package. But for now, know that there are **no vacations**.

PRAYER

Father, in the name of Jesus, thank You for Your mercy and patience with me — especially when I try to place my selfish plans over Your plans — especially when my laziness hinders You in advancing Your kingdom in me and through me. Amen.

    —Jimmy Davis, Jr.

Week 26, Day 1

BIG DANCE

READING

1 *Corinthians 15:57* But thank God! He gives us victory over sin and death through our Lord Jesus Christ.

Matthew 25: 32-34 All the nations will be gathered in his presence, and he will separate the people as a shepherd separates the sheep from the goats. He will place the sheep at his right hand and the goats at his left. Then the King will say to those on his right, "Come, you who are blessed by my Father, inherit the Kingdom prepared for you."

REFLECTION

I don't know how popular the game of basketball is in your country, but I'm a big fan — especially college basketball. In my country, there's a tournament at the end of the season, and those invited to play call it the **Big Dance**. It begins with sixty-eight teams, but only one can become the national champion. For all the teams blessed enough to be in the **Big Dance**, everything ends with a single loss.

This year the losing coach in the championship game said "... it hurts to come so close." On the winning squad, an injured player who did not play in the championship game still received a national championship ring. You see, being on the winning team's roster is more important than individual contributions in any particular game.

While I'm a big fan, I must keep basketball in perspective. After all, it's just a game.

You know, there are days when work seems like a sporting tournament. Competition! All the work and preparation may be for a losing cause. You may come just so close to victory. Yet the stakes are much higher at work than in sports, and too often it is more than the "coach" who gets fired for failure.

In the midst of workplace competition, it's so easy to lose perspective. Yes, your job is not just a game — it's real important! But winning in your job is not the **Big Dance**.

Christ reminds us that, while there will be losers, *we* can be victorious. We just need to be on His team. And you don't want to be like that losing coach, saying "it hurts that I came so close." And like the injured player, remember that being on His roster — even when you sometimes lose or get injured for His sake — is more important than any particular success you will find at work today.

As you struggle over today's competition, keep it in perspective and take comfort in this: As a *Christian* public servant, you are already on the winning team! You already won the **Big Dance**!!

<u>PRAYER</u>

Lord, at work today remind me that I am on Your team. Help me to advance You, to recruit those who are in need of Your victory. Thank You for what You paid that I might have victory, despite all the worries I have about my job today. In Your Most Holy name, Amen.
  —Loren Crone

Week 26, Day 2

ALLOW GOD'S BEST

READING

Proverbs 10:12 Hatred stirs up quarrels, but love makes up for all offenses.

REFLECTION

As a U.S. federal employee, I am very aware of the bureaucratic blockages that can occur when trying to take the next logical step towards improvement. Forms must be filled out. Committee meetings attended. Cases made, positions defended.

It's easy to find lines drawn in the sand, rising enmity among coworkers, and "strife being stirred up." It is during such moments that the Holy Spirit's urging can lead us to a better path. *Listen to Him.* Consider all perspectives, pray for wisdom for both you and the other discussion participants.

As a public servant, remember that we are all *one team* working for the common good. As a *Christian* public servant, remember that our common good is actually His good for His people for His glory.

So don't let petty anger divide your purpose!

In all encounters today, let our Father's love cover your prejudices and preconceptions. Today, **allow God's best** to be the goal and prize.

PRAYER

Lord, please show me Your might today. Show me how Your power and love can cover my sins, my dislikes, and my selfishness—to open doors for Your best purposes. In Thy name, I pray. Amen.

    —Erika D. Doster

Week 26, Day 3

CAN'T AFFORD TO DAWDLE

READING

Proverbs 13:4 Lazy people want much but get little, but those who work hard will prosper. The soul of the sluggard craves and gets nothing, while the soul of the diligent is richly supplied.

Philippians 4:13 For I can do everything through Christ, who gives me strength.

REFLECTION

Don't know about you, but this workweek is really dragging. Plus, in the area of the world I live, the weather just won't cooperate. Best just to stay in bed this morning!

Ever dawdle? On days like this, I sometimes do. Am I the only one working or studying today who feels the temptation to dawdle? On a morning like this? *Oh, come on!*

But as a *Christian* public servant — as a student preparing to enhance my career — I know I really **can't afford to dawdle.** Can you?

Too much is at stake. Sure, my future is at stake, but there's more. There are citizens and clients, as well as coworkers and fellow students — all expect my very best. *But still there's more!*

Doesn't God expect His very best through my efforts? Doesn't He expect His very best through your efforts, too?

So even on a day like today, I really can do all things through Christ! You can, too! And, with His strength, we both know our very best can be presented — especially this day, particularly on a morning when the weather just won't cooperate.

So, for His sake, get up and get going! We both really **can't afford to dawdle**.

PRAYER

Dear God, thank You for the opportunity to work and to study — so that I may serve You better. On this morning, help me fight the temptation to put off for another day what can and should be done today. Through Christ, shower me with motivation today and warm me with a soul richly supplied. In Jesus' name, I pray. Amen.

—Adam Schenkel

Week 26, Day 4

PASSAGE THROUGH YOUR DESERT

READING

Exodus 14:13-14 But Moses told the people, "Don't be afraid. Just stand still and watch the LORD rescue you today. The Egyptians you see today will never be seen again. The LORD himself will fight for you. Just stay calm."

REFLECTION

As the Israelites began to face their giants, they questioned why they left the land of prosperity. They became so overwhelmed that they questioned their leader. They had given up and were ready to go back to where they'd been instead of trusting that God had a plan to take them through their desert.

Difficult times, struggles, and hardships are inevitable. They seem to come part-and-parcel with public service. At work, it is so easy to allow circumstances to affect our vision and question our purpose. And when today's troubles end, naivety wins if we think that, just because we commit ourselves to serve others, trials won't come again.

We know tomorrow's work may well find us in still another desert!

As a *Christian* public servant, remember that our Lord *will* fight for *you* — just as He did for the Israelites. You don't have to question that which you need not understand. All you need to do is to have faith. Today as tomorrow, He will give you **passage through your desert**.

PRAYER

Thank You, O God, for keeping Your hand over my life. Your plan and purpose always prevail. Forgive me for questioning what I need not understand, and remind me to place my trust in Your faithfulness, always. In Jesus' name. I pray. Amen.

—Christie Brown

Week 26, Day 5

HOW LONG TO WAIT

READING

Psalm 130:5 I am counting on the LORD; yes, I am counting on him. I have put my hope in his word.

REFLECTION

Counting on the Lord... I can attest to the wisdom of doing that. After all, as the old folks say, "He may not come when you want Him, but He's always on time." So I am counting on Him, but I am not sure just **how long to wait**.

There have been instances in my career when I thought I "missed the blessing" by either not waiting long enough or simply waving it off due to not knowing when it actually arrived. I admit that sometimes I wish I had taken advantage of an opportunity.

I am counting on Him; it's just tough not knowing **how long to wait**.

But if I continually seek a relationship with God, I can count on receiving the essential gifts with respect to His perfect plan. And, you know what? With the exception of my childhood dream of becoming a famous Hollywood actor, the Lord is doing an outstanding job of fulfilling my needs! I can count on Him!

Counting on the Lord... As this workday begins, understand that He knows what you want and how badly you want it. Know that He is always on time. So be patient and work on your relationship with Him.

Today, *place your hope in His word* and worry less about **how long to wait**.

PRAYER

Dear Lord, thank You for all the blessings You have bestowed upon me. It is only by Your grace that gifts come forth. As Your humble servant, I continue to wait for You. Eternally I pray in Your name. Amen.
— Steve Butler

Week 27, Day 1

NO REASON NOT TO TRUST GOD

READING

Hebrews 13:5-6 Don't love money; be satisfied with what you have. For God has said, "I will never fail you. I will never abandon you." So we can say with confidence, "The LORD is my helper, so I will have no fear. What can mere people do to me?"

REFLECTION

We all know someone who is trying to find another job. Perhaps he is staring at a RIF. Perhaps she is currently unemployed. Perhaps that person is you, or perhaps it is a loved one.

The public service is no different than the private sector when it comes to an unstable economy. In my country, there are spending cuts in government at all levels as well as belt-tightening across the nonprofits. Budget concerns? Got 'em! External funding? Harder to find by the minute! And, unemployment just doesn't want to go away.

It's easy to become afraid. Isn't it? Emotions run off the chart. Don't they? With all the anxiety, weekends seem to drag longer than the work-week. And it's hard to sleep at night.

Insecurity leads to fear, and fear leads to a lack of trust. We begin to sin because we use the situation as an excuse *not to trust God*. And that's a very big sin, one of the biggest, *not to trust God*.

I have to ask myself: "Who am I expecting to meet my needs - my employer or God? Who *really* provides for me — my agency or my Lord?"

Tough questions, but we know the answers. God meets my needs, in every way, each and every day. I rely on Him for my income; for my daily bread. He is *my helper*, no matter what instability or insanity hits my agency today, this week or this year.

While everything changes, nothing changes: the agency may leave me, but He will never leave me. I will have no fear. I have **no reason not to trust God**.

PRAYER

Dear Lord, I am sorry that I have not trusted You as my security in the past. I acknowledge that You are my provider, and that my work is done for You. Take charge of my feelings and my fears, and help me to stay in the security of Christ. Thank You for the peace that You give me in that security no matter what happens in the world's economy. No matter what happens with my job or with my career, thank You for the security of Christ You shower upon me. In Your name, I pray. Amen
—Lynne Marie Kohm

Week 27, Day 2

WHAT YOU DON'T DO

READING

Luke 12:25-26 Can all your worries add a single moment to your life? And if worry can't accomplish a little thing like that, what's the use of worrying over bigger things?

REFLECTION

Our work as public servants is never easy and, regardless, we know that life brings big worries as well as small worries. Serious and tragic events occur and minor frustrations abound. Things will happen today at work, as they will before you get to work and after you go home. You can count on some things going wrong, even if today is not one of your really bad days.

What matters is not what you do, but **what you don't do**. Do not allow yourself to drown in your own worries, either big or small. It's not going to add an hour to your life, but it will make the workday *seem like an eternity*!

As a *Christian* public servant, rely on your faith in God and His love to deliver you from worry. Give God your burdens, both large and small, so you can be freer from stress and discouragement.

Today will be long enough without you making it longer!

PRAYER

Dear God, hear my prayer. Lift my worries and burdens from my mind and shoulders. Give my heart peace that You are listening and know what is right. At work today, and throughout my day and night, renew my faith in You. In Your Son's name, I pray. Amen.

—Mary Anne King

Week 27, Day 3

LIKE THAT MAN IN THE SYNAGOGUE

READING

Matthew 12:9, 10a, 11 Then Jesus went over to their synagogue, where he noticed a man with a deformed hand... Then he said to the man, "Hold out your hand." So the man held out his hand, and it was restored, just like the other one!

REFLECTION

Part of my job entails interviewing prospective employees. And I can say, it's interesting to see how people react in this situation. Some are energetic and others are reserved. Whatever their posture, each applicant is required to: *describe a weaknesses*.

People seem reluctant to respond honestly. Perhaps they think their weaknesses, if fully disclosed, will cost them the job. But, as Christians, we find victory by our honesty — even when it means disclosing our shortcomings.

Just **like that man in the synagogue**, we have an opportunity to be honest through God about our inadequacies. It's risky business, I know. Sometimes we mistakenly keep our weaknesses hidden from prying earthly eyes, and yet sometimes we find the courage — **like that man in the synagogue** — to reveal our need and watch God work a miracle.

Honesty? Transparency?? At work??? On an interview???? It's always risky *taking a step of faith*, but He is also faithful! The miracle of truly good things happening never happens without faith in our Lord.

Whether you're employed or going on an interview, today you will be challenged to be honest and transparent. Gain strength from God and just *hold out your hand*. As a *Christian* public servant, have faith **like that man in the synagogue**.

PRAYER

Matchless Savior, I want to be totally honest through You today. I am not perfect, and only You can fix me. I know You are with me. I have faith in You. In Jesus' name, I pray. Amen.

—Courtney Christian

Week 27, Day 4

GOD'S INTENDED RESULTS

READING

Genesis 50:20 You intended to harm me, but God intended it all for good. He brought me to this position so I could save the lives of many people.

REFLECTION

You hold a public service position for one reason: to bring good to your neighborhood, community, country, humanity. This is true whether you hold an elected or appointed position, in government or the nonprofits. It remains true regardless if you're a governor or a custodian. Whatever position you hold, you do so to help your agency protect and improve the lives of many people.

At work today, remember why God put you in the position. Then, stop questioning why things are not working so perfectly. Stop waddling in the mire and be bold in your faith, remembering that only God can bring good out of a bad situation. We just need to be comfortable with God's will.

So, instead of getting angry, frustrated, or confused — be patient and allow **God's intended results** to prevail! You don't know the full plan, but you know you *are* a player! You are His player!!

So, wait for God's intended results!

PRAYER

Lord, as I serve You and Your people today, I will fully have faith in You! Regardless of confusion, uncertainty, or anguish, I will be bold enough to stand on Your Word! Lord, let me focus on the capacity You gave me as a *Christian* public servant. Let me not get distracted from Your power. In Your name, I pray. Amen.

—LaShonda Garnes

Week 27, Day 5

THAT OTHER KIND OF SWEET PERFUME

PRAYER

2 Corinthians 2:14b Now he uses us to spread the knowledge of Christ everywhere, like a sweet perfume.

REFLECTION

Are you wearing a fragrance right now? Inmates are not allowed to, but I remember the smell of my favorite after-shave. And, you know, I will never forget the sweet scent of my girlfriend's perfume. Now that's not to say I never smell it around here. Correctional officers and some ministry volunteers wear cologne and, oh, it does bring back memories. Plus, I still get to smell the scent of sweet perfume when my mother and sisters come to visit.

I bet you splash some on before you go to work, don't you?

But what about **that other kind of sweet perfume**? The sweet perfume of Christ? Do you splash that on, too? Do you wear it throughout your workday like you do that other stuff?

I bet it is easy to wear **that other kind of sweet perfume** when you go to comfortable places, like church or at home. But what about places not so comfortable? Christ wants you to wear it everywhere — even at your job.

I have friends here on Life Row who have the courage to wear His aroma each and every day. In such an uncomfortable place, only His scent can purify *our own smell* — what we have done and have not done in our lives, and everything we see and feel around us now. They know that only His aroma can lead them and others to *where we all want to be someday*.

So as you put on your favorite fragrance before you go to work today, do not forget **that other kind of sweet perfume**. It is the Scent even I can wear here on Life Row.

Let it purify *your own smell*. Let **that other kind of sweet perfume** lead you and others to where we all want to be someday.

PRAYER

Father, in the name of Jesus, I pray. Thank You for trusting me to spread the knowledge of Christ. Thank You for blessing me each day with that sweet Scent that draws others to Your Son, Jesus Christ. Amen.

—Jimmy Davis, Jr.

Week 28, Day 1

TEMPTATION IS SIMPLY AN INVITATION

READING

Philippians 3:13b Forgetting the past and looking forward to what lies ahead

REFLECTION

I am a former mayor and an ex-convict. I am a brother-in-Christ. This week I will tell you my story.

Although I campaigned and was elected, I really wasn't prepared to be mayor. In facing so many challenges, I often asked God, "Why me? Why do I have to make decisions when so much is at stake, when so many lives are affected?" Don't get me wrong, I wasn't blind. I knew what I was doing, and I frequently questioned my motives. Was I acting as a politician? Was I acting as a leader? Was I ever acting like Christ?

Each day I prayed that God would give me courage to do the right thing in the midst of so much stress and so much temptation. Well, God helped me with the stress, but He also allowed me to make my own choices concerning temptation. You see, **temptation is simply an invitation** *to live away from God.* In accepting that invitation, greed and lust become more important than Him.

Guess, what? I accepted that invitation. I accepted bribes.

The truth finally surfaced. I remember praying, "Oh dear God, why did I lose control and succumb to temptation?" I was sentenced to 2 years in a U.S. federal prison. I was naturally ashamed of what I had done to me and my wife. My life was shattered. I *lost hope* for the future.

Have you ever accepted an invitation to live away from God? Have you ever lost hope?

PRAYER

Father God, each day at work, I am tempted in one way or another. Bless me and give me Your hope to say "no!" to temptation. Let me not live away from You. In Your Son's name, I pray. Amen.

—David Krider

Week 28, Day 2

WHO AM I

READING

2 Corinthians 5:16a So we have stopped evaluating others from a human point of view.

REFLECTION

I am a former mayor and an ex-convict. I am a brother-in-Christ. This week I am telling you my story.

I plummeted from that mountain top as mayor down into the valley of the unknown. I was sentenced to two years in prison for accepting bribes. Lord Jesus, I thought, am I the same good person I was before all this happened? Am I different now, a bad person, as a result of what I did? As I entered prison, I had to ask, **who am I**?

Paul says not to frame a man by the outside, but the fact is we do that all the time. "He's that *white* guy" or "she's that *tall* lady". For me, I had to cope with, "He's that mayor going to prison!" "He's that *convict*!" My wife had to cope with that, too.

Like you, I am far more complicated than what you see according to the flesh. And the fact is, we all make mistakes - some serious enough that if your mistakes were exposed, trouble would certainly follow. Now I'm not saying I didn't do wrong, but does doing wrong mean I'm a bad person? When you make a mistake, are you a bad person?

Let me ask it another way: Is who you are determined by what you do, or is what you do determined by who you are? Now that's an important question, and only you can answer it about yourself. In my cell, that's what I thought about for 2 years, as I tried just to calm down and make the best of it. Funny thing about a cell: it can become a sanctuary that gives the inhabitant the luxury of time to think honestly about himself —about **who am I** — a luxury that seemed too expensive when I was back at city hall.

There are enough people in the world willing to paint you as a bad person when you do something wrong. They did it to me. Do they do that to you, too? They pile on, and it is way too easy for you to agree with them.

Today, ask yourself: **who am I**? Only you know the answer.

PRAYER

Father God, I pray that I will recognize myself by the inside and not from a human point of view. Help me to realize that the greatest service performed by my trials and tribulations is to reveal my wrong doing, not my wrong "being." I need You alone to define **who am I**. In Your Son's name, I pray. Amen.
—David Krider

Week 28, Day 3

LESSONS UNLEARNED AT CITY HALL

READING

Luke 11:9 And so I tell you, keep on asking, and you will receive what you ask for. Keep on seeking, and you will find. Keep on knocking, and the door will be opened to you.

Proverbs 3:5-6 Trust in the LORD with all your heart; do not depend on your own understanding. Seek his will in all you do, and he will show you which path to take.

REFLECTION

I am a former mayor and an ex-convict. I am a brother-in-Christ. This week I am telling you my story.

Your life may be great now, but what do you do when you start tumbling off that mountain top into the Valley of Despair? I tumbled, remember? I *really* tumbled. As I entered prison, my tumble wasn't complete. I slid face-first all the way down, got bruised and abused, ignored and ridiculed.

But in the midst of all that turmoil, being in prison was one of the *best* things that ever happened to me! Not realizing it at first, God was preparing me for my greatest adventure! All I had to do was knock and trust.

In prison and in the free world, perseverance is a great element of success. If you knock long and loud enough, someone is bound to answer. If it is the Lord's door, well, He's waiting to hear your tap-tap! (He's even answering *before* you even knock!) It wasn't easy for me to learn to knock, and my hubris did not let His door open so quickly. While I didn't fully trust Him at first, perseverance taught me **lessons unlearned at city hall**.

What did I learn about Christian perseverance in a world filled with Satan and secularism? I learned *what you and I need*. Needed is *spiritual food* so that we grow as Christians. Needed is knowing it takes a *full-time effort* to live a life of Grace. Needed is accepting we *cannot survive in a vacuum*, whether in prison or city hall or your own work setting. Needed is a *constant relationship* with God and with the Body of Christ. Needed is realizing the journey is life-long and can be achieved only through the *hard work* of remaining open to God's persistent love.

These are my **lessons unlearned at city hall**.

PRAYER

Lord, strengthen me today in the hard work of Christian persistence. Strengthen me in knowing that the power of my example will far exceed the authority of my status. In Your Holy name, I pray. Amen.

—David Krider

Week 28, Day 4

ONLY WAY TO STOP THE PAIN

READING

Mark 11:25 But when you are praying, first forgive anyone you are holding a grudge against, so that your Father in heaven will forgive your sins, too.

REFLECTION

I am a former mayor and an ex-convict. This week I am telling you my story.

In prison I had so much venom for two men, accomplices I thought were my good friends, who went to the FBI and turned state's evidence. I hated them without control. I just couldn't shake that feeling, and it was destroying me. Every day I would pray for God to help me forgive them, as I knew my hatred was wrong since I actually deserved to be in prison.

I took daily walks in the yard to be alone with God to seek His guidance. God has a funny way of working in all our lives to give us what we need to glorify Him, in ways that only He understands. Sometimes we think we recognize those ways and sometimes we don't. All in all, was it possible that I had to go through this forgiveness process in preparation for what God was planning for my life in the future?

I finally allowed God to step in, take control of my life, and use me to glorify Him. And yes, it took several years but I was finally able to approach both men and totally forgive each. I was even able to express my *gratitude* for what they had done as it had actually made me a better person than before this whole thing started.

And wow, what a relief I felt by truly forgiving them! That heavy weight was finally lifted and, once again, I could feel the *calmness* that had been vacant in my life for so long.

Have you been hurt by someone in your professional life? You may say, "I can't forgive him because he hurt me so badly." Yes, the pain is real and nobody really forgives anyone without acknowledging the hurt and the hatred that are felt. But until you forgive that person, he will continue to hurt you because you have not released yourself from the past. Forgiveness is hard work but, through Christ, it is the **only way to stop the pain**.

PRAYER

Father, let me stand praying today with an understanding that forgiving is not forgetting. If I try to forgive by simply "forgetting" offences, I will fail on both counts. With forgiveness that comes only from You, I can begin to think about my trespassers without anger or resentment. Lord, give me the power to begin the hard work of forgiveness today; the power of surrendering to You so that I can truly forgive *through* You. In Jesus' name, I pray. Amen.

—David Krider

Week 28, Day 5

GOOD NOVEL

READING

Joshua 1:9b Be strong and courageous! Do not be afraid or discouraged. For the LORD your God is with you wherever you go.

Psalm 29:11 The LORD gives his people strength. The LORD blesses them with peace

REFLECTION

I am a former mayor and an ex-convict. I am a brother-in-Christ. This week I have been telling you my story. I wrap it up today!

"Free at Last!" I'm out of prison, but what do I do now? Many things have changed in the free world over the last couple of years. What now, God? No job, mid 50's. Where do I go from here, and what should I do with the rest of my life? Lead me, oh Lord, whatever You wish for me is what I'll do.

Yes, leaving prison was just about as scary as entering it. Coping with freedom, just as hard as coping without it. It's the same for every paroled inmate. It's difficult to stop thinking about the past. Depression starts to set in, and I was stuck on what I had been through. I needed to focus on the *brighter tomorrow* promised by Christ.

God's plan can be compared to a **good novel** with many chapters. Some chapters are exciting and good, others are boring and difficult. Some we prefer not to have to read, but no chapter lasts forever.

Sometimes God puts us through the paces. He allows a certain amount of suffering in our lives. He seems to be able to work much more effectively in the lives of people who know that they can't make it on their own, especially those who acknowledge that they need God. And that's where I am at this point in time.

When you finally surrender to God, be aware that He will place you where He needs you! For me, He returns me to prison quite regularly to give my testimony and to give hope to inmates. He instructs me to let them know that there is a life after prison, and that God does still love them in spite of what brought them there. My wife and I have been blessed with opportunities to minister to paroled inmates and their wives, as well as be involved in a program that offers alternative sentencing to street crimes.

I no longer look for mountain tops because I know the foot of the Throne.

In your life and in your career, know that God forgives your sins, eliminates your shame, releases you from the chains of the past. His Grace allows you to move beyond it. When you go through unpleasant times, give Him thanks because He is preparing you for something else.

Be ready to read another chapter in a **good novel**!

<u>PRAYER</u>

Father, thank You for difficult times for, through them, You make me stronger and bring me closer to You. Let me never forget: "Not my will, but thine will be done." In Jesus' name, I pray. Amen.
 —David Krider

Week 29, Day 1

ALWAYS BRING HOPE

READING

Psalms 3:3 But you, O LORD, are a shield around me; you are my glory, the one who holds my head high.

Psalm 141:3 Take control of what I say, O LORD, and guard my lips.

REFLECTION

As public servants, we know that words have impact. Either verbally or in writing, we inform people about the many positive things we are doing. Through words, we learn about the many things that we still need to do better in order to improve the human condition. Yes, words bring good news, promising news, and challenging news for the sake of tomorrow. Our words can bring hope.

Yet earthly words also offer the potential for destruction. Our words can rob good news and raid the promise of tomorrow. Too many times, it seems like devastating words can tear down faster than loving words can build up.

During the last workweek, did you deal with a disgruntled citizen or client? How did you use words? I mean, did you say things you shouldn't have? Perhaps last week a colleague spoke words that smashed your day. Maybe you returned the favor before you went home on Friday. Did the words you used make you feel good over the weekend?

As this workweek begins, earthly words may try to destroy you. *Don't let them!* You may want to strike back with your own vicious words. *Don't do it!* Understand that His words promise He will lift up your head high. Realize that His words help keep guard over your lips this very workday.

As a *Christian* public servant, know that His words **always bring hope**.

PRAYER

Almighty King, thank You for the death and resurrection of Your Son! Your grace is so apparent every workday, but especially during this Most Holy week. Thank You for reassuring me of Your protection. I relinquish to Your will every task I do this day. I know all hope is in You. In Your precious Son's name, I pray. Amen.

—Courtney Christian

Week 29, Day 2

GROW, ADVANCE, AND SERVE

READING

Luke 5: 8-11 When Simon Peter realized what had happened, he fell to his knees before Jesus and said, "Oh, Lord, please leave me—I'm too much of a sinner to be around you." For he was awestruck by the number of fish they had caught, as were the others with him. His partners, James and John, the sons of Zebedee, were also amazed. Jesus replied to Simon, "Don't be afraid! From now on you'll be fishing for people!" And as soon as they landed, they left everything and followed Jesus.

REFLECTION

Jesus may have recruited people in an unconventional fashion, but He certainly was an effective leader. He recruited people who were willing to give up everything for Him and spread the Word of God.

As Christian public service *leaders*, we must be willing to give those who show dedication a chance to **grow, advance, and serve** - just as Jesus helped His disciples. As *Christian* public service *followers*, we must be able to sacrifice and show that we *are* dedicated to all moral and ethical values and missions of the agency. With help from God, supervisors will give subordinates every reason not to be afraid and every opportunity **grow, advance and serve** in their chosen career paths.

A number of doors have been opened to me because I showed dedication. But the most doors have opened because I worked for kind and compassionate leaders who wanted to see their followers **grow, advance, and serve**. I am thankful that these leaders have come into my life.

Whether you are a supervisor or coworker, today help someone **grow, advance, and serve**.

PRAYER

Dear God, help me to be a good follower and a good leader. Help me to give people a chance to **grow, advance and serve**. Help me to be dedicated to my work to Your glory. Let me never forget that I am working for You at all times. In Your Son's name, I pray. Amen.

—Christopher Sean Meconnahey

CHAPLAINS DO NOT CARRY RIFLES

READINGS

Leviticus 19:11b   Do not deceive ... one another

REFLECTION

A wise old minister once advised me, "When you visit a hospital following the birth of a new born baby, remember there is no such thing as an ugly baby, or at least you should never say so. And if you ever come across that nonexistent ugly baby, just say: 'Now *that's* a baby!'"

While life sometimes requires a bit of tact, civil society begins to deteriorate when it can no longer differentiate between dishonesty and veracity. Too often today, the norm of our discourse centers on small but growing untruths. The media may call it "spin," but why shouldn't we call it *deceit*?

It's not just people in the news that "spin". It's also public servants in their workplaces. For a while, my workplace was Afghanistan. One day my roommate was caught without his rifle. When a Marine corrected him on this carelessness, my roommate (a *physician's assistant*) said "**chaplains do not carry rifles**". The Marine, now under the impression that my physician's assistant friend was a chaplain, quickly apologized.

It's true that **chaplains do not carry rifles.** But by fooling the susceptible Marine, my friend was doing nothing to develop his own character. He forgot that *lying erodes our communion* with God and our fellowship with one another.

So yes, sometimes you should be tactful so not to offend a mother and her ugly baby. But as a *Christian* public servant, what are you saying today that reflects your own character? What are you saying that confirms your communion with God and your fellowship with coworkers and those you serve?

Do your words differentiate dishonesty from veracity?

Are you really in a position to make that claim, **"chaplains do not carry rifles"?**

PRAYER

Father, may my words always be true. At work today, help me to speak truth to power, and trust in Your grace that my communication might lead to building rather than demolishing. May truth always be my guide, and may I be willing to hear the truth as a sound source of encouragement. In Your Son's precious name, I pray. Amen.

—Loren Crone

Week 29, Day 4

FOR THE TOUGH TIMES

READING

Psalms 112:7 They do not fear bad news; they confidently trust the LORD to care for them.

Romans 12:15 Be happy with those who are happy, and weep with those who weep.

Esther 4:14b Who knows if perhaps you were made queen for just such a time as this?

REFLECTION

When I first entered public service, I imagined that one of the coolest parts of the job would be the role of *insider*. I loved the idea of getting the "inside scoop" before most citizens.

Perhaps you also are someone entrusted with knowing the nitty-gritty details of what's going on in your community. If so, you likely know that being an insider isn't all that it's cracked up to be. In fact, you've probably discovered that the "inside scoop" is rarely good news because word about good news runs crazy! If something is not immediately publicized, there's a good chance it's because someone is hurt or is suffering a loss. Being an insider means having the responsibility to respect confidentiality and show compassion to those who are in pain.

So, it can be very disheartening to be an insider. After a while, you wonder why you chose a career in public service in the first place.

But as a *Christian* public servant, you're called to deal with difficult events by showing the love of the Lord. In fact, you're blessed that your Father called you into public service precisely **for the tough times**. When the people you serve face tragedy, you can only truly serve them by first serving the God who blessed you with the opportunity to help. Perhaps being an insider allows you to be the first to intervene and find a solution, but it also allows you to be the first to pray for God's grace, love, and protection for those suffering.

Whether or not you are an insider, remember at work today that you are called not just to provide the help as required in your job description. As a *Christian* public servant, you are also called to show the love and assistance that Christ has to offer. This is especially true **for the tough times**.

PRAYER

Dear Lord, please bless the public servants You call to respond to tragedy and crisis. It is only through Your grace that the calling was issued, and it is only

through Your grace that one is best able to serve others. Grant grace and compassion, especially **for the tough times**, to reflect Your love for Your flock. I ask this in Your name and for Your sake. Amen.
—Martin Nohe

Week 29, Day 5

NO MATTER WHAT HAPPENS TODAY

READING

Jeremiah 29:11 For I know the plans I have for you, says the LORD. They are plans for good and not for disaster, to give you a future and a hope.

Romans 8:28 And we know that God causes everything to work together for the good of those who love God and are called according to his purpose for them.

REFLECTION

The diversity of our work puts us in many different situations that can test our walk with Christ. No matter the test — what our community or agency environment may be like, how much or little we agree with proposed remedies and policies — we still must stay true to who we are in Christ.

No matter what happens today, be the best *Christian* public servant for Him and for His people. Keep a humble heart and attitude. Be appreciative for all that you have today. Remain faithful that God is protecting you and preparing the way for what He has for you in the future. *He knows your path in His plan.*

No matter what happens today, hold on to your integrity and stand for what you believe to be God's will for you. The humility you exude, the godly character you demonstrate, and the peaceful spirit you share — all this will not only be a blessing to His people, but God surely will be pleased!

No matter what happens today, you will do great works for Him and His Kingdom and His people!

PRAYER

Lord, I pray that You will give me the tenacity to *serve You with a refreshed boldness.* Lord, I pray that you will increase my capacity to be selfless as I continue to act as a *Christian* Public Servant. Lord, when You see the fruit of my labor, I pray that You are pleased and receive all the glory. Lord, as I go forward in serving, go before me and show me my *path in Your plan.* Lord, I will be sure to give You the honor and praise. In Jesus' name, I pray. Amen.

—LaShonda Garnes

Week 30, Day 1

HANG ON TO THAT STRING

READING

Psalm 55:22 Give your burdens to the LORD, and he will take care of you. He will not permit the godly to slip and fall.

REFLECTION

Do you enjoy kite flying?

Kites fly because of the wind; an unseen force that does all the heavy work. The kite flyer is really only connected to that unseen force by a single, delicate string. With a good wind, all the kite flyer has to do is *hang on*!

As a child, I really enjoyed kite flying. Man, I thought there was *nothing better*! While I got away from it in college, today I'm rediscovering this wonderful hobby. For me, kite flying provides moments of solitude to think through the challenges I face. I envision all my problems loading up onto the kite. As the kite flies upward and outward, it appears smaller. Quite conveniently, my problems also seem smaller.

Now, I know kite flying does not fix problems. (After all, even the best kite comes crashing down to the ground each time!) It just gives me time to think and prioritize. And I also understand that this hobby is not for everyone. Besides: as the stress of the workday piles up, you probably don't have time to go fly a kite!!

But when we give our anxieties over to God, it's actually *better than kite flying*. If we truly think about it, God does the heavy lifting, just as the wind does in getting the kite off the ground. He makes our problems look pretty small as he lays out the solution. He is the Wind that leads us to where we need to be. And only when we pull away our problems from God do they ever come crashing back down to our own shoulders.

Your involvement is minimal — simply cast your cares to God, knowing that prayer represents *the delicate string* connecting you and your now-diminished challenges to His almighty will. Don't pull those challenges back to your world — your shoulders— or they will once again become too heavy. Just accept the direction of His Wind and **hang on to that string**!

Today at work, remember you have something *better than kite flying* to help you sort out things. You have the Lord. He will help place your problems in perspective. He will give you direction.

All you need to do is just **hang on to that string**!

PRAYER

Dear Lord, bless me with some of the innocence of a simpler time. Help me to freely give my cares to You, the Creator of the world, the Almighty, all powerful God who loves me. Lord, open my eyes to see Your hand in protecting and guiding me. Lord, grant me the wisdom to acknowledge that I can do nothing without You — but You can do miraculous things with me. In your Son's name, I pray. Amen.

—Larry Ketcham

Week 30, Day 2

ORIGINAL JOB DESCRIPTION

READING

Genesis 1:28 Then God blessed them and said, "Be fruitful and multiply. Fill the earth and govern it. Reign over the fish in the sea, the birds in the sky, and all the animals that scurry along the ground."

Romans 5:12 When Adam sinned, sin entered the world. Adam's sin brought death, so death spread to everyone, for everyone sinned.

Hebrews 2:8 You gave them authority over all things. Now when it says "all things," it means nothing is left out. But we have not yet seen all things put under their authority.

REFLECTION

Perhaps you haven't thought about it this way, but the *cultural mandate* from Genesis is really our **original job description**. Yet reading it alone, you would be hard pressed to understand why it's so easy to feel out of control. After all, God made us stewards of all that moves on the earth, and certainly that would include our own activities and actions as well as those of voters, policy makers, supervisors, coworkers and the citizens we serve. But sin and death were introduced, and this prevents us from fully carrying out the work God created for us to do.

Until Christ comes again and restores the earth to a sinless state, we can only imperfectly fulfill our **original job description**. Not this morning, but someday, we will be able to do so without the constraints of human flaw. In the meantime, as *Christian* public servants, we know we can still further His kingdom through our imperfect careers and in our imperfect workplaces and in our imperfect world.

As this workday begins, know this: striving to advance His kingdom, despite our imperfections, is certainly *worthy of great effort*.

PRAYER

Father God, thank You for giving me purpose and focus in my work through the *cultural mandate*. Sometimes I feel frustrated in my inability to do my work, or obey Your commands, perfectly. Thank You for giving me salvation in Your Son, Jesus Christ, and the hope that I will someday be able to fulfill our **original job description** completely and perfectly in Your restored kingdom. In Jesus' name, I pray. Amen.

—Hugh Whelchel

Week 30, Day 3

WORKING FOR THE LORD

READING

Colossians 3:23 Work willingly at whatever you do, as though you were **working for the Lord** rather than for people.

REFLECTION

It's Wednesday — hump day — and I just wish we were already over that hump! And this scripture is depressing; it makes work sound so harsh! Previous verses talk about slaves. You can almost get images of whips and chains. The work must be so hard that we must remember the reason we're doing it!

Perhaps that best describes your workplace — especially on a Wednesday!

In any event, this scripture offers a reminder: regardless of the task, regardless of where you work in public service, all things must be as if you are **working for the Lord.** At the end of the day, it really *is* about Him — not your supervisor, coworkers, agency, council, or legislature.

It's easy to get bogged down in the mundane particulars of each day, or the drama of "that" meeting or "that" encounter with a citizen or client. It's so easy to forget Whom we are really serving.

So, whether it is the smallest task or the largest project, those things that we do are a testament to who we are as *Christian* public servants. As you get over this week's hump, remember you are a picture of Christ to the world. Give Him your best and keep Him first.

Put yourself into it, and do it because you are **working for the Lord**!

PRAYER

Lord, my Master, please continuously remind me that all I do should be done as unto You. Despite the circumstances and surrounding issues, remind me to keep You first. Do not allow me to be overwhelmed by people or situations, but keep my eyes focused upon You. Remind me to give You my very best, and in so doing, I can give my very best to my community. Thank You for the opportunity to serve You and Your people. In Your name, I pray. Amen.

—Angelina Moyo

Week 30, Day 4

DIRECT YOUR PATH

READING

Proverbs 3:5-6 Trust in the Lord with all your heart; do not depend on your own understanding. Seek His will in all you do, and He will show you which path to take.

REFLECTION

A job opens, one that will substantially increase your salary. Looking at the criteria you are definitely qualified, but something just keeps nagging at you to stay where you are. In your mind, there is every reason to apply for that position. But wait a minute...

That little nagging in the back of your mind could very well be the Lord trying to lead you in the right direction — in His direction. Often we listen only when we are hearing what we want to hear. We disregard His voice when God tells us to do something uncomfortable or unpleasant or something that we just don't want to do. .

You have a source that can help you in your decision making at work today. Pray to God and ask for His guidance in all you do. He will never lead you wrong or astray. But you have to listen diligently when He speaks. Let *Him* **direct your path**.

Divine
Instruction
Regarding
Exact
Course
Travel

PRAYER

Dear God, help me to seek Your voice today in all decisions I make about work, my career, and my life. Let me not depend on the wisdom of my finite knowledge, or the whims of my ego, but only on Your word and Your direction. In Your Son's name, I pray. Amen.

—Joycelyn N. Biggs

Week 30, Day 5

A TONGUE WITH A FLAME OF FIRE

READING

James 3:5-6 In the same way, the tongue is a small thing that makes grand speeches. But a tiny spark can set a great forest on fire. And the tongue is a flame of fire. It is a whole world of wickedness, corrupting your entire body. It can set your whole life on fire, for it is set on fire by hell itself.

REFLECTION

I am an Explosive Ordnance Disposal (EOD) officer in the U.S. Navy. As an EOD officer, I would not send one of my divers into any action without an approved plan.

I have learned that *trust* is critical to combat effectiveness because *trust* must accompany any plan of action. Throughout a unit's training cycle, *trust* is tested in a variety of ways: among its members, its leadership, its procedures, and its equipment. Without *trust*, resiliency in the face of uncertainty and danger can be impaired.

I have also learned that *trust* can be damaged by what we say as much as by what we do. **A tongue with a flame of fire** damages the team's ability to follow its plan and operate effectively. Conversely, *words with purpose* actually bolster trust, reinforce the plan, and increase a unit's effectiveness.

Now, you don't need to have a job like mine to realize how damaging **a tongue with a flame of fire** can be. In fact, a tongue is probably the most powerful workplace equipment. But in the heat of any "battle," it can be used to help or it can be used to hinder.

Have you ever had one of those workdays when you just couldn't put a leash on your tongue? In the heat of "combat," you forgot what scripture says about **a tongue with a flame of fire**? As a *Christian* public servant, will you remember this scripture today?

PRAYER

Lord, only You can give my words purpose. I ask You to give me wisdom to help me use my words for Your purposes and plans and not my own. In Your Son's name, I pray. Amen.

—David Shultz

Week 31, Day 1

FOR GOD'S GLORY AND PRAISE

READING

Matthew 6:3 But when you give to someone in need, don't let your left hand know what your right hand is doing.

Romans 11:36 For everything comes from him and exists by his power and is intended for his glory. All glory to him forever! Amen.

REFLECTION

My father serves in a leadership position at his organization. When I was in high school, dozens of his subordinates were complaining that their office chairs were disgustingly filthy. However, the company with which his organization contracted its custodial service was not required to clean office chairs.

One evening dad asked me and some friends if we would be willing to help him with something. We shyly agreed not knowing what we were getting ourselves into. Turns out my dad had rented eight steam cleaner vacuums, and we went to his work unit at 8 pm on a Friday night. We finished cleaning all the office chairs by 4 am. (And let me tell you, steam cleaning chairs on a Friday night until 4 am was no fun for this teenager and her friends!)

When dad got home from work on the following Monday, I asked about the reaction of his employees. Were they grateful? Did they thank him?

He grinned a little bit and said, "Angela, it's all **for God's glory and praise**, not mine." I later learned he never said one word to anyone about personally steaming all the chairs. To this day, his employees believe the custodial company ended up doing the job.

What will you do for others at work today? Are you willing to invest long hours on tasks and remain content to be unthanked and unnoticed? Will everything you do be done **for God's glory and praise**?

Today, will you actually be a *Christian* public servant?

PRAYER

Lord, remind me to be humble in all my work. Remind me that nothing is for my own glory and that it is all for You — even when my work goes unnoticed and unappreciated. I'm Your servant, and my goal is not to live for myself, but to die to myself. In Your Son's name, I pray. Amen.

—Angela Arbitter

Week 31, Day 2

WHAT ARE YOU AFRAID OF

READING

2 Timothy 1:7 For God has not given us a spirit of fear and timidity, but of power, love, and self-discipline.

I Samuel 17:47b This is the Lord's battle.

REFLECTION

So, **what are you afraid of**?

Remember saying those words to dare a childhood friend on the playground? Or, maybe you heard them in a more daunting tone from a bully somewhere along the way home?

But when was the last time you heard these words from our Lord?

There may seem like a lot to be afraid of concerning your job and even your life. You fear the new boss and her new procedures. You fear the thought of downsizing and losing your job. You fear the doctor and his diagnosis. You fear your health insurance might not cover everything. You fear that, whatever is wrong with your body, it might prevent you from ever going back to work and living a normal life. You fear you're not saving enough for retirement or even to put your kids through college. You fear you may lose your home. Fear can paralyze us weak humans, and all too often it can completely destroy us.

So, **what are you afraid of**?

What if today you looked at the battles you face as if they were *the Lord's battles*? Pure and simply that: *the Lord's battles*. They really are, you know.

Well, I don't know about you but I think I'm ready to do a little downsizing myself — and *the first thing to be fired is fear*. When fear is removed from the equation, the enemy is disarmed.

So, **what are you afraid of**? There is no room for fear in my *Lord's battles*!

PRAYER

Dear God, thank You for loving me enough to desire a personal relationship with me. Please give me the eyes to see the battles in my life as Your battles, not mine. I claim the spirit of power, love and self-control, and I claim it today. In the precious name of Jesus, I pray. Amen.

—Debra Neal

Week 31, Day 3

WHAT ARE YOU WIRED FOR

READING

Ephesians 4:29b Let everything you say be good and helpful, so that your words will be an encouragement to those who hear them.

Philippians 4:8 Fix your thoughts on what is true, and honorable, and right, and pure, and lovely, and admirable. Think about things that are excellent and worthy of praise.

REFLECTION

I write and review technical data as part of my job. In hundreds of pages for which I am responsible in any project, people seldom takk note of the thousands of words and sentences I produce that are correct. What they notice is the misspelling on page 359, paragraph 2, line 3. Even in this devotional, your eyes probably caught the misspelling of "take" in the second sentence of this paragraph. You may think, "How could such a typo escape his review?"

We seem to be *wired only for the negative*. While I understand the need for excellence, we sometimes assume that critical analysis is the same as fixing strictly on what is wrong. I know I do. I can think of many instances in my career where, presented with the option to affirm or validate the efforts of others, I chose to provide just the opposite.

At work today, **what are you wired for**? Will you focus only on what your coworker does wrong, or will you also take note of all the worth she brings to the team? In the break room, will you only talk about the few stupid decisions your supervisor has made today? Or, will you affirm all the support he gives you every day? Will you see the citizen or client as an adversary, or someone you can help and encourage? While wiring your thoughts to find that which is excellent, you must also wire them to detect that which is true. And one truth is, your words can change the entire way someone may view their role and importance in your workplace.

What are you wired for? What words can you use to change this workday?

PRAYER

Lord Jesus, wire me to embrace what is true, honorable, right and pure today at work. Help me to see what is admirable along with what needs improvement. Help me to see the beauty around me, the blessings abounding, and the joy surrounding all that I do today. Help me to be a blessing to those I encounter on this workday. Use me to glorify You. It is in Your name that I pray. Amen.

—Bill Dudley

Week 31, Day 4

CLEAN AND LEAN HOUSE

READING

1 Corinthians 14:40 But be sure that everything is done properly and in order.

REFLECTION

This past week my family moved to a new home. It was a big job and, as anyone who has moved knows, it was no fun. It took sorting, cleaning, organizing, packing, wrapping, communicating, labeling, and throwing away *a lot of junk*. Sometimes moving is the only way to a **clean and lean house**!

Throughout the process, I began to understand what was really important. Initially I kept almost everything from my home office, thinking that a couple of boxes would do. But as I continued to need more and more boxes, I began to re-evaluate the situation. I started to only keep what I really needed.

If your agency was moving to a new building, and you were only allowed to take two boxes of stuff to the new location, what would you take?

Too often we hang onto material items that we no longer need. But worse, we do the same with conceptual items; we hang onto old ways of thinking. Worse of all, we may hang onto a *workplace routine with Christ* that is, well, too dusty, too predictable, or just way too comfortable; we discover it no longer does any good for anyone — not you, not your coworkers, not your client/citizens, and not even your Lord!

We hang onto many workplace habits when there are other ways — perhaps new and less comfortable ways — which would be more efficient, more effective, and more productive for everyone. There might also be other ways — perhaps new and less comfortable ways — which might better serve our Lord.

Today at work, keep a **clean and lean house** so that you have room to grow and find better ways to be productive and to glorify Him!

PRAYER

Heavenly Father, even though at times it is hard to let go of the old and comfortable things and routines, help me to remember that it is the only way to keep a **clean and lean house**. Just as I need to keep a clean and orderly environment, help me to first make it a priority to keep a *clean and orderly heart*. Continue to strengthen me and allow me to see where there may be any "junk" in my life. In Your Son's name, I pray. Amen.

—Jason David Graber

Week 31, Day 5

RIGHT FIELD AT THE RIGHT TIME

READING

Matthew 9:37-38 The harvest is great, but the workers are few. So pray to the Lord who is in charge of the harvest; ask him to send more workers into his field.

REFLECTION

Because of where I am, I used to think this scripture was not for me. Oh, but I was wrong! Each day I awake, I now ask God *where He needs me most*. Is it the field of my own cell? Is it the field with others when I go outside? Maybe it's the field in the law library. Or, perhaps it's the field in my own church.

I try my best to be that worker He can count on. The one who hears His call and obeys His command. Each day I awake, I now prepare myself to be sent to the **right field at the right time** — not the field I choose or when I choose, but *when and where He needs me most*.

As I once did, you might think that this passage is meant for someone else — perhaps only missionaries in Africa or maybe volunteers who come to visit places like where I live. Oh, you are wrong! It really does apply to you. His fields are many: your family, your hair salon or barbershop, your mall, your parks, your grocery store, your church. His fields even include your drive to work and especially the place where you work.

He will call you into different fields for different harvests. One field may be for harvesting *healing*, another for harvesting *restoration*, and still another for harvesting *encouragement*, or *building faith* or *spreading His truth* to others. On some days, He needs you in only one field. On other days, He needs you in many fields. Always for His reasons and always for His harvest.

As you awake and get ready for work today, also get ready to be sent to harvest *where He needs you most* — to the **right field at the right time**.

PRAYER

Father, in the name of Jesus, I pray. Thank You for all the fields you bless me to work in. Thank You for equipping me to help with Your harvest. Thank You for giving me the courage to stir the hearts of others so they may also go into the fields — when and where You need them most. Amen.

—Jimmy Davis, Jr.

Week 32, Day 1

SEEK TO SEE THE LORD AT WORK

READING

Ephesians 6:7 Work with enthusiasm, as though you were working for the Lord rather than for people.

REFLECTION

Stopped at a railroad crossing while coming into work. My mind began drifting away from the blinking lights and toward the meaning of this scripture.

If I truly were to take the mantel of serving others *as if I were working for the Lord*, how might this change my perspective on this Monday morning? How would it change my actions once I get to work? And what about that word, *enthusiasm*?

If I serve you today, and I **seek to see the Lord at work** in you, I am sure I would engage with you differently, speak with you differently, and ultimately serve you differently.

And if I **seek to see the Lord at work** in you today, I must serve you with *enthusiasm* rather than faintheartedly.

Well, the railroad crossing is clear now, and I must continue on my way.

As you continue on your way to work this morning, ask: will I approach today's tasks with *enthusiasm*? Ask: do I plan to **seek to see the Lord at work** in those I serve? Ask: will I remember to serve others as if I am *really serving the Lord*?

Now, go and have a tremendously blessed day!

PRAYER

Dear Lord, help me to serve with my whole heart, to be all in for You! Help me to serve others as if I am serving You. Give me this strength. In Your name, I pray. Amen.

—Kathleen Patterson

Week 32, Day 2

WHAT TRUE RELIGION IS ALL ABOUT

READING

James 1:27 Pure and genuine religion in the sight of God the Father means caring for orphans and widows in their distress and refusing to let the world corrupt you.

REFLECTION

In today's secular society, the word "religion" so often has a negative connotation. Those who want to remove religion from the public square mainly talk about Christians as being judgmental, haters of everything that isn't within a tiny box, and just no fun!

How wrong can anyone be?!

Think about it, though. As *Christian* public servants, we have an unparalleled opportunity to demonstrate **what true religion is all about** — the outward expression of the internal change that occurs when we accept Jesus Christ as the living, loving light of the world. Yes, we have to operate within a set of boundaries established by constitutions and regulations, but sharing the Good News of Christ has never been about giving up when faced with Man's rules. Rather, it remains always about demonstrating the love of God in our lives.

At work today, you might encounter the distress of a client struggling with the loss of a loved-one in a week when the secular world cares less. You might be confronted with a citizen not understanding his property tax bill. You might even be faced with an irate elected official wanting the rules stretched just a bit to accommodate a constituent. Or, you might see a coworker depressed after goodbyes to visiting adult children who live most of their lives someplace else.

You can respond haphazardly like most people living in their tiny box called postmodernism. Or, you can respond deliberately in God-like fashion — engaging in the doing of the Word. A soft comment to the grieving; a patient explanation to the confused; a thoughtful but consistent application of rules in the face of pressure; a shared moment of fun with a coworker — all of these deliberate actions demonstrate **what true religion is all about**.

We may never know, at least in this life, the impact that quiet faith uncorrupted by the world will have on either a fellow Christian-in-need or a nonbeliever-in-search. As *Christian* public servants, though, it is our duty and blessing to demonstrate in our lives that, although we obey the rules of work in the public arena, we still follow the rules set in place by the One who we serve.

Throughout this workday, show the world **what true religion is all about**!

PRAYER

Father, as I go through this workday, help me remember that You are in charge of everything. Do not let frustrations or worries about the world around me, or the tasks before me, prevent me from deliberately showing others that You are God. Guide me to the right decisions today, and show me how I may further Your kingdom in my daily work-life. In Jesus' name, I pray. Amen.

—Anne-Marie Amiel

Week 32, Day 3

FIRST SET ABLAZE THE FIRE INSIDE

READING

Luke 12:49 I have come to set the world on fire, and I wish it were already burning!

REFLECTION

As I drove into work this morning, the sky appeared to be blazing. Brilliant colors of crimson, red, and orange beautifully colored the clouds. Immediately, my mind turned to what Jesus said in Luke's gospel — about setting the world on fire.

You see, in my field of public service, fire is a negative thing: always having a devastating effect on people and property. But fire also serves useful purposes: various kinds of controlled-burning can end wild fires, dispel darkness, bring warmth, and enable cooking.

So, the beauty of that blazing sunrise got me thinking. What does our Lord want you and me — *Christian* public servants — to do about *setting the world on fire*? Certainly we must be the *fire for Christ*; His instrument in lighting the dark places of our own tumultuous world — especially at work with coworkers and supervisors, people we serve, and the neighborhoods we protect.

Yes, but is that all? Mustn't we **first set ablaze the fire inside** ourselves; a controlled-burn to rid everything keeping us from lighting the outside: our fear, indifference, intimidation, anger, impatience, and all of our excuses?

A tough task on a mid-week morning, I know. But as you drive to work today, think about what He wants you to do in regards to *setting the world on fire* at your workplace. Then, think about what you must do to **first set ablaze the fire inside**.

Now, enjoy that sunrise!

PRAYER

Lord Jesus, thank You for Your fire. Let it cleanse and purify my life. Help me spread your fire each day as I perform my job in your workplace. Let me become Your instrument of transformation in this corner of the world where You have placed me. Let me start first with transforming the inside of me. In Your Son's name, I pray. Amen.

—Stephen Pincus

Week 32, Day 4

SECRET OF LIVING IN EVERY SITUATION

READING

Philippians 4:11-13 Not that I was ever in need, for I have learned *how to be content* with whatever I have. I know how to live on almost nothing or with everything. I have learned the **secret of living in every situation**, whether it is with a full stomach or empty, with plenty or little. For I can do everything through Christ, who gives me strength.

REFLECTION

You often hear people say: "You need to be *content* with what you have." But what exactly does it mean to be content? Frankly, I don't want to be content because it seems like the whole world is speeding right by me. Should I not try to get that raise? Should I not improve my current situation? Should I not look for a better job? Be content?? At this point in my career??? Really????

Look, I know scripture says I *should* be content, but what is the **secret of living in every situation**?

I believe Paul would tell you this: contentment has nothing to do with being satisfied with what you have or where you are in life. Yet it might also mean not searching this very moment for a better workplace or a higher position in that workplace or some way to advance in your career. If Paul were having coffee with you this morning, he would say that the secret lies in using all the gifts and talents God gives you, through your personal calling as a *Christian* public servant, in order to bring *the maximum return for the Master.*

The **secret of living in every situation** is found in working diligently to glorify God, serve the common good, and further the kingdom of God in everything you do. Once you have done that, He will guide you to meet other needs.

It has everything to do with your relationship with God, not your career. And that, my friend, is the **secret of living in every situation**.

PRAYER

Lord, it's so hard not to be on the move these days. Help me learn and live the **secret of living in every situation** by striving toward the goals to which You call me so that I can better serve You and understand when I have completed a job well done. I pray in Your Son's name. Amen.

—Hugh Whelchel

Week 32, Day 5

MORE MEASURED RESPONSE

READING

Proverbs 15:1 A gentle answer deflects anger, but harsh words make tempers flare.

REFLECTION

For any public servant, calmness and self-control are virtues to be practiced when dealing with coworkers and the public. This is especially important to remember when you are a *Christian* public servant.

Career stresses, family issues, tensions in dealing with unhappy citizens — a lot of factors can trigger our own anger and flare our tempers. And keep in mind: when you are the recipient of angry words or posturing, the natural inclination is to respond in kind.

It is not easy being a public servant, that's for sure. But *Christian* public servants have a higher obligation to find a better way to defuse situations. Today, let's find a **more measured response** for His sake.

PRAYER

Dear Lord, today at work let me keep my temper in check. I know that You will be glorified through a **more measured response** and acts of kindness. In Your name, I pray. Amen.
　　—R. Keith Jordan

Week 33, Day 1

WORRY GET IN THE WAY

READING

Matthew 6:32-33 These things dominate the thoughts of unbelievers, but your heavenly Father already knows all your needs. Seek the Kingdom of God above all else, and live righteously, and he will give you everything you need.

Matthew 11:28b Come to me, all of you who are weary and carry heavy burdens, and I will give you rest.

REFLECTION

If you're a student preparing to enter public service, this is the time of the semester when you're also worried about exams or papers. Even if it's been a while since your school days, I bet you still remember the tension and anxiety over grades.

You might be a full-time student, or you might be juggling school, family and a job — doesn't matter. Right now, there just isn't enough hours in the day. While I know it won't be any less stressful with that fresh diploma on my wall, today it's just too easy to let **worry get in the way**.

Worry can lead to mental fatigue and physical exhaustion. And if I'm not careful, *worry* can lead to something far worse: it can damage my spiritual life. If I let **worry get in the way**, I might be *too tired to pray* and *too anxious to worship*.

Whether you're a student like me, or the kind of *Christian* public servant I wish to become, worrying will not give you rest. God knows everything you need this week. Yet He doesn't want you in a state of mind and body where you can't seek first His kingdom. He doesn't want you so tired and stressed-out that you're unable to glorify Him today. He wants you well rested.

Either studying for exams or actually changing the world as a *Christian* public servant, He will give you rest. All you need do is seek Him first.

So as this workweek begins, don't let **worry get in the way**. Seek Him first.

PRAYER

Dear God, You know my worries and anxieties. Give me emotional and physical rest, Lord. Give me spiritual rest right now so that I may seek You first today in preparation for Your tomorrow. In Your Son's name, I pray. Amen.
—Logan Dickens

Week 33, Day 2

GO WITH THEM TWO MILES

READING

Titus 1:7-8 An elder is a manager of God's household, so he must live a blameless life. He must not be arrogant or quick-tempered; he must not be a heavy drinker, violent, or dishonest with money. Rather, he must enjoy having guests in his home, and he must love what is good. He must live wisely and be just. He must live a devout and disciplined life.

Matthew 5:41 If a soldier demands that you carry his gear for a mile, carry it two miles.

REFLECTION

It's shortly after 8 a.m., and our office is abuzz with phones ringing. We are a small municipality, so the majority of constituent calls are funneled through the administration office. One can expect anything and everything from these calls: water payments, requests for mayoral meetings, complaints about streets and parks, even wanting to know the correct time of day.

Our receptionist customarily greets the caller and asks, "How may I help you?" Granted, this is common practice in most enterprises. "How may I help you?" is a fairly universal statement in service-related endeavors.

But, it struck me this morning: When I use that phrase, just how sincere am I? Is my daily goal to assist people to the fullest extent or simply respond with a satisfactory effort?

In other words, am I willing to **go with them two miles** or merely settle on a *first mile mentality*?

As a manager, I understand I cannot expect more from my staff than the dedication they see in my work ethic. Sure, the *first mile mentality* gets the job done. But, to **go with them two miles** inspires a mindset in workers to do more than a job. It encourages them to be public servants, and not just public employees.

As a *Christian* public servant, I want them to see me exemplify what Jesus said to do: **go with them two miles** especially when a *first mile mentality* is all that is expected.

Today, will you promise to **go with them two miles**?

PRAYER

Heavenly Father, thank You for the opportunity to serve others. Please grant me wisdom in speaking with people. Help me demonstrate an attitude of graciousness and courtesy in my work. Allow me to glorify Your name through a servant-like heart. In Jesus' name, I pray. Amen.

—Courtney Christian

Week 33, Day 3

WHAT NATURE

READING

Colossians 3:9-10 Don't lie to each other, for you have stripped off your old sinful nature and all its wicked deeds. Put on your new nature, and be renewed as you learn to know your Creator and become like him.

REFLECTION

Boy sister, what a meeting! We got what we wanted, but we had to fight for it.

Now, I won't say I *lied* outright, but I did shave a bit off the truth.

And for what? A bigger budget? Permission to fill those open positions? That special project? An advancement? Greater bureaucratic lebensraum?

Was it worth it?

No one really knew I "shaved the truth." Besides, everyone at that meeting did the same, I just bet. They all understood "the game."

So it was OK, right?

Wait a minute. I'm a *Christian*. I *surrendered* my life to Christ. I'm supposed to cast off the "old sinful nature" and forever put on that "new nature."

I am commanded to do so. Aren't you?

There's another meeting tomorrow. Another bureaucratic battle!

What nature will I put on?

What nature will you put on?

PRAYER

Father God, it's never easy following You! You expect so little and yet I have to do so much. Help me to forget even where I placed that "old nature." At work today, help me, Lord, to wear my "new nature." In Jesus' name, I pray. Amen.

—James D. Slack

Week 33, Day 4

IN THE FRYING PAN

READING

Psalm 37:7b Wait patiently for him to act.

Proverbs 14:30 A peaceful heart leads to a healthy body; jealousy is like cancer in the bones.

REFLECTION

Have you ever been "stuck" in a position for a while? Have you ever wondered, "Doesn't God have more planned for me than this?"

Undoubtedly, there are times when we aspire to do more, take a leadership role, accept new challenges, or just make a move to a new position. However, our desire often goes unfulfilled. At such points, we pray and ask the Lord to assist us in our quest. Sometimes He gives us what we ask for. All too often, at least for me, He does not.

Perhaps He has something better planned down the road. Perhaps a bit more patience will keep me **in the frying pan** and out of the fire—protecting me from making a change that will ultimately be unhealthy. Or, perhaps I am not finished growing in my current position.

Whatever the case, you or I should be at peace and know that we are children of the Almighty. This job, this career and this life — it is all only temporary. And, while we should attempt to make the most of it, we should always stay **in the frying pan** and never lose sight of *our kingdom purpose*.

PRAYER

Lord, as I anxiously pursue bigger and better endeavors, give me the wisdom to stay within Your Divine Will and the clarity to stay **in the frying pan** and out of the fire. I cannot walk this road alone. You know that. There are so many twists and turns that must be maneuvered. You know that, too. Help me to always be sensitive to Your council as I pursue Your will and not my own. In Your name, I pray. Amen.
  —Adam B. Lowther

Week 33, Day 5

ONLY TO BLESS, NOT TO CURSE

READING:

James 3:9 Sometimes it praises our Lord and Father, and sometimes it curses those who have been made in the image of God.

REFLECTION

The weather is warm where I am, and that is a good thing. But a few wise guys here choose to keep the windows closed, and this makes it stuffier and hotter. They do just the opposite when it's cold, keeping the windows open to make it colder inside. Hot or cold, summer or winter, brothers lose control of their tongues. They shout curses. I would shout the most awful words. Everyone would forget that even wise guys are made in His image.

But then two years ago I asked God to help me with my tongue. I wanted to use it to praise Him more and curse at His image a lot less. Where I live and "work," that is a big request. It has been challenging at times — wise guys try everything to provoke you — but the more I pray about it, the more God is faithful to my request.

Have you ever had to put up with wise guys? When you see wrong, do you *speak wrong*?

As you go to work today, ask God to help you use your tongue **only to bless, not to curse** — no matter what wise guys do or say to you. At work — when you see wrong, do not *speak wrong*. God gave you that tongue **only to bless, not to curse**.

PRAYER

Father, in the name of Jesus, I pray. Heal my heart so my tongue can and will bless those who are made in Your image. Let me show others how to speak right. Amen.
　　　—Jimmy Davis, Jr.

Week 34, Day 1

DREADFUL MORNING

READING

Mark 1:35 Before daybreak the next morning, Jesus got up and went out to an isolated place to pray.

REFLECTION

My Monday mornings are dreadful. They start off slow as I push the snooze button and try to catch those last few minutes of sleep. The buzzer goes off again and, still not quite awake, I journey back to happier times: sleeping-in on Saturday and worshiping at the late service so I could do the same on Sunday. Sleep-in: *why can't I do that today??* Then, my consciousness quickens and I jump to thoughts about that never-ending merry-go-round I call my job: I have to get out of bed just to return to the same old work routine with the same old people with the same old problems? The buzzer sounds again, and now I'm gonna be late. I go from zero to sixty in a few seconds. I'm not ready, but I have no choice. I must greet this **dreadful morning**.

The beginning of the workweek may be inevitable, but what if the day could start better? Heck, what if every workday could start better?

What if I start each workday like Jesus started His workday? Rather than lingering in bed, mourning the memories of the weekend lost and grieving the expectations of the newborn day — what if I got up and prayed — *very early in the morning, while it is still dark?*

Come to think of it, isn't Jesus the *Christian* public servant you and I try to imitate?

If so, then let's start the workday differently, like He did: with prayer — *very early in the morning, before daybreak.* This **dreadful morning** won't be nearly as bad!

PRAYER

Heavenly Father, thank You for the opportunity to see another day! There are times when I choose to complain about the same old things but, Lord, help me to remember that a little time with You can carry me a very long way. In Jesus' name, I pray. Amen.

—Crystal Featherston

Week 34, Day 2

WEIGHTS AND MEASURES

READING

Proverbs 11:1 The LORD detests the use of dishonest scales, but he delights in accurate weights.

Proverbs 3:27 Do not withhold good from those who deserve it when it's in your power to help them.

REFLECTION

Every time I go to the gas station, I see messages pasted all over the pump: *Cash Only - Emergency Button here — free carwash with fill-up - $1.00 hotdogs inside.*

Despite the variety, there is always one important label on the pump: the seal of the last government **weights and measures** inspection. Why is this important? Because it is in the public interest for everyone to be treated fairly — for those buying fuel to never get more or less than they pay for.

The concept of *honest* **weights and measures** is *biblical*, and something that we can, and should, use in our work — especially when dealing with other people. When we evaluate others, we size them up and form an opinion. That opinion, for better or worse, not only helps shape who they will become in the workplace, but also the value of their work.

Lavish an employee with undue compliments, or withhold deserved praises, and you will do the organization an injustice. Overrate an employee's work, and the opportunity for genuine improvement is lost. Shortchange the employee on a good appraisal, and you may lose that genuinely good employee.

Scripture tells us that God detests the use of *dishonest scales*. Our Lord is *delighted with accurate weights*. Scripture instructs us *not to withhold good* from the deserving when we have the power to act. As *Christian* public servants, we do have the power to act.

Our **weights and measures** must be accurate and pure, and only then do we glorify Him.

PRAYER

Dear God, please give me the calm reassurance of Your presence when I evaluate others, reminding me to be fair in my assessments, and to act when it is justly within my power to do so. Please bless the decisions I make in my work, so that they serve as a testament to Your character. In Your Son's name, I pray. Amen.

—Deanna Alexander

Week 34, Day 3

THINK OF OUR EXAMPLE

READING

John 13:5 ...and poured water into a basin. Then he began to wash the disciples' feet, drying them with the towel he had around him.

REFLECTION

Taking initiative to physically assist those we serve requires a fair amount of courage. As a health care professional at a VA hospital, I know this all too well. I often have opportunities to work with people who need help with basic activities of daily living, but doing so can be embarrassing as well as technically challenging.

Sometimes your job can also take you to unpleasant situations, performing unpleasant tasks. Sometimes dealing with the people you are supposed to serve can be quite unsavory. This doesn't just happen in *doing* public service, but also in *learning* public service. If you are a student preparing for a career serving or teaching or ministering to others, perhaps some course assignments and even internship experiences can be unsavory. We are all in this together.

Jesus laid aside his position, took courage, and began an unsavory and lowly job to show us how to love each other. This is a lesson worth learning well. Any time you are saddled with something you reactively think is unpleasant —**think of our Example**. As *Christian* public servants, do as He did.

PRAYER

Lord, today in my work, give me courage to view my least favorite tasks in a new way — Your way. Help me do for others as You did for others. Help me do the things I need to do in the same spirit as You did the things You needed to do. Let all public servants think of You — **think of our Example** — and then realize what a privilege it is for us to perform each and every task, savory or unsavory, because we do them for You. In Your name, I pray. Amen.

— Erika D. Doster

Week 34, Day 4

WITHOUT MEMORY

READING

Deuteronomy 31:6 So be strong and courageous! Do not be afraid and do not panic before them. For the LORD your God will personally go ahead of you. He will neither fail you nor abandon you.

Luke 6:31 Do to others as you would like them to do to you.

REFLECTION

We've all "been there" at one time or another: the newest person in the agency. How frightened and uncomfortable were you during that probationary period? How you lacked confidence — so much that your words were carefully guarded and earmarked.

I remember. Do you?

Yet in too many workplaces, there seems to be at least one senior person **without memory**. They've forgotten how it felt to be the youngest or newest. They don't remember how condescension riddled all pretense of self-esteem. They've forgotten how polite joking was a poor camouflage for the intent of ridicule.

Do you know someone **without memory** in your workplace?

If you are the youngest or the newest at your agency, hang in there! Drive to work today knowing God's promise: *He is there for you.* Throughout the workday, know *He will not let you fail.* As this workweek begins, be *determined and confident in Him!*

If you are senior, change the work culture just a bit! Driving to work today, think how you might nurture that newest team member. Throughout the workday, keep God's commandment: the Golden Rule. As this workweek begins, don't be **without memory**.

PRAYER:

Eternal Father, I seek You when it appears that I am alone at work. I seek You when I forget how it used to be when I was new. I ask You, O father, to bless Your public servant with the courage to stand on Your promise, accept Your commandment, aid Your people, and do Your work. In Jesus' name, I pray. Amen.

—Deyonta T. Johnson

Week 34, Day 5

STEEL DOOR SLAMMING SHUT

READING

Mark 9:48 ...where the maggots never die and the fire never goes out.

Revelation 20:15 And anyone whose name was not found recorded in the Book of Life was thrown into the lake of fire.

REFLECTION

Recently we had a fire/evacuation drill at my middle school. I had an extremely difficult time due to some major health issues, but when the alarm rang my *only charge* was getting my students safely out of the building!

I'm a survivor of a fire. In that building, there was a steel door that closed and locked immediately. The fire protruded through the roof and out the windows, but never through the steel door. I still recall that **steel door slamming shut**. Life was sealed on one side and fire sealed on the other. Once it slammed shut, there was no turning back.

You know, our eternity is *sealed this side of death*, and once death occurs there is no turning back. Someday soon, we will all hear that **steel door slamming shut.** Because I was not a practicing Christian at the time of the fire, if I had died, I would've spent eternity on the *wrong side of that steel door*, in a real Hell where the fire never goes out and the maggots never die!

You probably already have a personal relationship with Jesus Christ. If so, your name is written in the Book of Life. But what about your colleagues & coworkers? Your Students? Your boss?

At work and elsewhere, my mission is that of a *gospel firefighter* — get people away from the fire and into Glory. Won't you please join me? We're running out of time.

The fire/evacuation drill at my school was a test. I pray that a real fire will never invade my students' lives. But today someone around us may experience another kind of fire that is eternally very real.

At work and elsewhere, find a way to be a *gospel firefighter*. Do so today because, once someone hears that **steel door slamming shut,** there's no turning back.

PRAYER

Dear God, thank You for saving me from hell where the maggots never die and the fire is not quenched. Please equip me today as Your firefighter to rescue one soul from entering eternity separated from You. Give me the boldness and the strength to reach just one more for Your kingdom. In the name of Jesus, I pray! Amen.

—Debra Neal

Week 35, Day 1

BRAVE ENOUGH

READING

Matthew 5:16 In the same way, let your good deeds shine out for all to see, so that everyone will praise your heavenly Father.

Psalm 23:4 Even when I walk through the darkest valley, I will not be afraid, for you are close beside me. Your rod and your staff protect and comfort me.

REFLECTION

Are you **brave enough** to be *a good representative* of Christ?

There is a very real skepticism aimed toward those **brave enough** to be *openly Christian* in a fallen world, especially in a fallen workplace. Some people wait to catch any misstep of a Christian and, by exposing our fallen nature, seek to turn others away from God. They don't understand: Christians are sinners, and the fact that we know this is why we are Christians!

This workday, I'm really going to be **brave enough** — not only because I am called to imitate Him, but also because *wherever one Christian goes, so too goes the perception of all Christians.*

This workday, will you be **brave enough**, too?

PRAYER

Lord, at work today, as I serve community and citizen, help me be **brave enough** to be *a good representative* of Your body. Give me strength knowing You walk with me. Give me courage to let my light shine through every doorway I pass. Let my example blot out those who seek to turn others away from Your promise of everlasting life. If I fall, help me to draw attention to Your holy presence as You give me reason to rise again. If I stumble, help me to recover with a grace that calls others to You. Lord, I humbly beseech You. Help me be **brave enough** to be a good example, to do no harm, and to reflect Your goodness in this fallen world and in my fallen workplace. In Jesus' name, I pray. Amen.

—Glenn Lyvers

Week 35, Day 2

WORK DEEPLY MATTERS

<u>READING</u>

Colossians 3:17 And whatever you do or say, do it as a representative of the Lord Jesus, giving thanks through him to God the Father.

<u>REFLECTION</u>

God calls His people to do everything as His representative. This means every single aspect of our daily lives, no matter how mundane. Because all of our **work deeply matters** to God, we cannot separate the "sacred" and the "secular" parts of our day — all hours and all tasks belong to him.

What does this mean for *Christian* public servants, especially those of us who serve in the so-called "secular" sphere of the workplace?

Our work Monday through Friday has *no less significance* than when we serve on Sundays at church. We must resist the temptation of believing that He is pleased only when we share the Gospel in our workplace or when we earn money to give to the church. We must, instead, trust that *God is pleased* whenever we are working diligently using the gifts he has graciously given us. This includes our work on Sundays, but it also includes our work throughout the week. In His eyes, all of our **work deeply matters**.

How does this change how you approach your work on this Wednesday?

Will you trust that your **work deeply matters** to God?

<u>PRAYER</u>

Lord, I trust that You have been gracious to give me specific gifts and talents and that You desire for me to use them daily. I pray that I would be a diligent and faithful steward of these gifts today and every day. I know that, in Your eyes, my **work deeply matters**. In Your name, I pray. Amen.

—Hugh Whelchel

Week 35, Day 3

SOMEPLACE ELSE

READING

Isaiah 43:1b I have called you by name; you are mine.

Luke 12:7 And the very hairs on your head are all numbered. So don't be afraid; you are more valuable to God than a whole flock of sparrows.

REFLECTION

Roll call is a staple agenda item during City Council meetings. At the beginning of every session, our City Clerk calls the names of each Council member. The roll call establishes which ones are in the room to represent their constituents and which ones are, well, **someplace else**. It's an important activity, but roll calls are pretty mundane. Because they are usually making last-minute preparations for the meeting, one or another member may not even hear their name called out.

You know, as Christians, we participate each day in the most important roll call — the one conducted by God. He identifies us as His children in this process, and He establishes our future with Him. We become His representatives — He is our Constituent — because of this calling.

Yet just like at city council meetings, it can be mundane to hear God's calling renewed in each day of our lives. But in His case, we should not be shuffling our thoughts, preparing to get out of bed for work, or pretending that something — anything — is more important than listening to *His roll call*. And above all, we should not be **someplace else** when He calls out our names.

So listen up! As you prepare to start your workday, hear your name and be thankful you are on *His roll call*. You are important to Him — so precious that He counts the number of hairs on your head. As you go to work this morning, realize you really are worth a great deal to Him — much more than the birds and animals you see along the way — so much that He continues to summon you by name until you answer His call. At work today, realize that you are His representative — He is your Constituent — and He has work for you to do in His district. So listen up! Be in the room. Do not be, well, **someplace else**.

PRAYER

Precious Father, thank You for calling me. I want You to know that I am listening to You. I am in the room. I am not **someplace else**. I want to be a good representative for You today. I am blessed that I am Yours, and I promise to *shout out* my name for You. I know You have my destiny in Your hands. Remind me this very moment of Your great love for me, and help me to demonstrate that love to someone else at work today. In Jesus' name, I pray. Amen.
—Courtney Christian

Week 35, Day 4

WHY DID I DOUBT

READING

Matthew 14:31 Jesus immediately reached out and grabbed him. "You have so little faith," Jesus said. "Why did you doubt me?"

REFLECTION

Yesterday I drove to a public function, only to learn that I had the wrong day due to my own calendar faux pas. Frustrated and disappointed in myself, I was preparing to leave the venue when I met a person that God placed in my path. We not only clarified the correct future date, but committed to getting together to discuss a strategic partnership.

Why did I doubt You, Lord? Why did I fail to remember that You are sovereign and in control?

Why did I doubt?

PRAYER

Lord, at work, You have placed me where You want me to be. I accept this mission cheerfully and gratefully. I seek Your divine grace to keep me from *doubting You*, especially when You invariably and faithfully cover my mistakes in Your service. Thank You, Father. In Jesus' name, I pray. Amen.

  —David Boisselle

Week 35, Day 5

ENTERTAINING AN ANGEL

READING

Hebrews 13:2 Don't forget to show hospitality to strangers, for some who have done this have entertained angels without realizing it!

REFLECTION

In doing my job as a public servant, I sometimes get bogged down with the mechanics of the workday. You know what I'm talking about. You might get overwhelmed with public sector policies and procedures. In the nonprofits, you may be consumed with keeping the doors open.

It is so easy to forget the true mission: to help, to serve, to protect and defend.

But in the course of the workday, *Christian* public servants might also forget that *our spiritual mission* includes *encouraging others*. Sure the budget is imperative to success. Following procedures will keep us out of court. But from God's point of view, equally important is *a simple hello* to the cleaning lady you whisk past each morning. The sincere *"How are you doing today?"* asked of the cafeteria worker. Or the simple but daring words, *"God loves you"* to a stranger you pass on your way into the office.

Today let's not only remember the professional mechanics, but also *our spiritual mission*. A simple word of kindness or encouragement to someone you have overlooked in the past. As the Word says, you may be **entertaining an angel**. For that, you will be duly blessed.

PRAYER

Dear God, keep in my heart a spirit of kindness to all mankind, regardless of position, title, rank or affiliation. Help me to remember to keep kind encouraging words on my lips. In Your Son's name, I pray. Amen.

—Joycelyn N. Biggs

Week 36, Day 1

JUST ANOTHER MONDAY

READING

Isaiah 40:31 But those who trust in the LORD will find new strength. They will soar high on wings like eagles. They will run and not grow weary. They will walk and not faint.

REFLECTION

Is today **just another Monday**?

Sometimes we feel like hamsters running on the wheel of a mundane work-life. We go to our jobs, thankful we have them, but we have become complacent and bored. Once we *loved* the public service; helping people and doing good for society. Once we thought in terms of *career*. But, sadly, no longer. We think only in terms of job, and getting that job over with as quickly as possible so we can go home and try to forget.

Increasingly, we ask God when He will make a better way for us, open new doors, give us more opportunity — whether in this workplace or the next. And when God doesn't seem to answer, we go it alone. The cycle of boredom and complacency continues.

Truth is, God has us exactly where He wants us. He makes no mistakes, He orchestrates everything perfectly. I might be bored with my job, but God sees the bigger purpose for me being here. He knows what lay beyond this desk, this phone, all these emails, today's staff meeting, all those clients and citizens. He wants me to trust Him, to wait for His very best. He wants me to fulfill the purposes He has given me in this day, at this time, and this place.

At work today, don't move ahead by yourself. You will only drop out or lag behind. You are not alone. Wait on Him, and He will give you *fresh strength*. Today you will not grow weary. You will soar high on the wings like eagles!

Just another Monday? For His sake, don't make it so.

PRAYER

Oh Lord, that I would wait upon You, that I can soar like an eagle with the strength that comes from You. I don't know why You have me here, Lord, but every time I have waited on You and trusted You, You have brought something much better to me than I could have ever imagined. Give me fresh strength to fulfill Your purposes in this season of my life, for Your glory. In Your name, I pray. Amen.

—Sarah Majeske

Week 36, Day 2

FAITH TRUMPS ANYTHING

READING

II Samuel 11:15 The letter instructed Joab, "Station Uriah on the front lines where the battle is fiercest. Then pull back so that he will be killed."

Romans 8:28b God causes everything to work together for the good of those who love God and are called according to his purpose for them.

REFLECTION

As we go about our daily work, we can face betrayal - just like Uriah did. When I was president of a Christian professional association, I often heard from members who had their careers sabotaged because of their faith. Non-Christians betrayed most, but I know one colleague whose career was sabotaged by a fellow Christian!

Well, the wound of being betrayed by a believer damaged this scholar in a much greater way than had it come from a non-believer. She lost faith and, sadly, she never recovered.

Your workplace is no different. Yes, *bad things will happen*, right? There's always a chance that very bad things might happen. They may even happen today. There really are evil people out there ready to do evil things, and you may just work for one or with one.

But if you have *faith*, you just might see how God turns evil into good.

Yes, bad things may happen today at work, but one thing is certain: **faith trumps anything**.

PRAYER

Lord, I know something bad may happen to me on this workday. Grant me faith to trust You. Give me courage to surrender to Your divine providence. Bless me with strength to accept that which I cannot change — knowing that You are unchangeable in Your love for me and Your calling on my life. In Your name, I pray. Amen.

　　—Kevin Cooney

Week 36, Day 3

YOU WORK FOR CHRIST

READING

Colossians 3:22-24 Slaves, obey your earthly masters in everything you do. Try to please them all the time, not just when they are watching you. Serve them sincerely because of your reverent fear of the Lord. Work willingly at whatever you do, as though you were working for the Lord rather than for people. Remember that the Lord will give you an inheritance as your reward, and that the Master you are serving is Christ.

REFLECTION

In the public service, how many times do you hear: "Do more with less!" No one in the private sector would put up with having to do the work of three people with half the resources and a third of the salary, but we seem to do it every day.

What does that say about us? Public servants truly are servants of the public. We care about our communities, and our efforts add a tremendous value to the human condition.

Christian public servants even take it a step further. We demonstrate our dedication, not only to our earthly masters the taxpayers, but also to the ultimate Master. Even when we're tired of media insults and lack of public appreciation, even when we feel crushed by the pressure of unreasonable demands and lack of resources, and even when it seems the light at the end of the tunnel is just not there — we are commanded to give our very best, to do it with a joyful heart, and to glorify God at all times.

I know that's a tough order. I, too, get tired and frustrated. When that happens, just imagine the impact you have on coworkers and citizens by serving them with a smile and extra effort. Think about the seeds you plant when they realize **you work for Christ**!

So give it your best at work today. You won't regret it — not in this life and not in Heaven. You are a public servant, but much more than that. You are blessed to be a *Christian* public servant — **you work for Christ**!

PRAYER

Father, You alone know how hard public service work really is. I sometimes forget that You are beside me, guiding and encouraging me, and gently reminding me that everything I do is for Your glory. Please help me remember that I work for You, dear Jesus, at each turn of this workday. I pray that I will do and say the right things to bring relief to those I serve and joy to You, my ultimate Master. In Your name, I pray. Amen.

—Anne-Marie Amiel

Week 36, Day 4

RIDING RIGHT NEXT TO YOU

READING

Joshua 1:9 This is my command—be strong and courageous! Do not be afraid or discouraged. For the LORD your God is with you wherever you go.

REFLECTION

I've always had, well, mixed feelings about roller coasters. So last weekend I decided to brave one that rose 205 feet. The first drop was 90 degrees straight down at 75 mph. But before that first drop, the ride stopped just over the edge and dangled me there: face down toward all the people looking up at me! (*What did I look like to all those people?*) Oh, and I admit that, as the ride climbed to the top, my heart pounded. I prayed this would not be the time something went wrong with the ride. Didn't matter if I were crazy, it was too late to get off and too late to turn back. Then *woosssshhhh!* It dropped and twisted, flipped and turned!!

Was I crazy? Well, I learned the ride was over faster than what I imagined. Afterwards, I felt alive with excitement. But I also felt peace. I had taken the ride and conquered my fears.

Now, I'm not suggesting a roller coaster ride is a fix for all fears. And, the choices I had with that ride, they don't exist in your workplace. Some rides are real with very real consequences.

Still, *what ride do you fear* today? A meeting? An encounter? A deadline? An expectation? Like on my roller coaster, your ride could end up being more imagination than substance. All those fears of embarrassment or shame or persecution — well, they may come true. But then again, the ride might not be as bad as you think.

Remember, you are a *Christian* public servant. Wherever today's ride takes you, He is with you. Show others how a Christian takes the ride, and you will show them the Gospel. Regardless of outcome, you will receive His peace after the ride is over. You will learn (again) that you can withstand the twists and turns of any ride because He's **riding right next to you**!

So, *what ride do you fear* today? Know He's **riding right next to you**!

PRAYER

Father, in the name of Jesus Your Son, I pray. Bless me with courage to face the trials of this workday. Bless me with strength to endure the ride, and the confidence to be Your Word in the midst of it all. On this particular workday, may I glorify You in all I do. Amen.

—Bill Dudley

Week 36, Day 5

REJOICE IN THE MIDST OF THE CHAOS

READING

Romans 8:28, 31b And we know that God causes everything to work together for the good of those who love God and are called according to his purpose for them... If God is for us, who can ever be against us?

REFLECTION

Yesterday was one of those days when my agency was in an uproar. As a major deadline approached, managers became frustrated, coworkers felt pressure, and staff — don't even get me talking!

Does chaos ever hit your workplace? How do you handle it?

Well, it may sound funny, but you really should **rejoice in the midst of the chaos**.

As a *Christian* public servant, handle stress by knowing God is for you. Meet chaos with faith because He causes everything to work together for your good. Do the deadline with the attitude that you are glorifying Him.

Workplace chaos gives you a chance to shine for Him!

So it was hard for me to get to sleep last night — not because of the pressure, but because of joyful anticipation. And this morning, I can't wait to get back to the office! I know chaos didn't leave town last night, and deadlines don't take vacations. And, yes, the uproar will resume as soon as everyone arrives.

But if He is on my side, what workplace problem can be against me? Certainly, my Lord will give me another chance to glorify Him and, in the process, **rejoice in the midst of the chaos**!

PRAYER

Lord, I rejoice in knowing You are by my side each minute of this workday. I rejoice in knowing You will give me wisdom and strength to handle each situation that arises. I rejoice in knowing everything will work to my favor — in Your time, of course, not mine. In the process, may my work and leadership be pleasing and acceptable to You. In Your name, I pray. Amen.

—LaShonda Garnes

Week 37, Day 1

BECOME PROUD

READING

1 Timothy 3:1, 2b, 3, 6 This is a trustworthy saying: "If someone aspires to be an overseer, he desires an honorable position."…. He must exercise self-control, live wisely, and have a good reputation. He must not be a heavy drinker or be violent. He must be gentle, not quarrelsome, and not love money. An overseer must not be a new believer, because he might **become proud**, and the devil would cause him to fall.

REFLECTION

As *Christian* public servants — *overseers of the public trust* — we must live up to Paul's qualifications. The power that we attain can be a trap if we **become proud** at "our" accomplishments and, hence, fail to realize it is by God's providence that we are placed in the position of overseer.

Last workweek, what was it like? Did you enjoy a good reputation with coworkers and the citizens you served? Or, did people regard you with reproach? Did you **become proud**?

This workweek, what kind of overseer will you be?

PRAYER

Lord, You have placed me where You want me to be. I accept this mission cheerfully and gratefully. I seek Your divine grace; I don't want to **become proud**, for I am thankful and blessed that it is by Your divine providence that I serve as an overseer of the public trust. In Your name, I pray. Amen.

—David Boisselle

Week 37, Day 2

SELF-MADE

READING

Matthew 23:12 But those who exalt themselves will be humbled, and those who humble themselves will be exalted.

REFLECTION

When I bought my first new car, I was very proud of myself. There I was — in a fancy suit, signing the papers and getting ready to drive it home. *"Look at me,"* I thought, "I'm a **self-made** man!"

Then I recalled all the hard work others invested just so someday I might purchase this car. The sacrifices of my widowed mom. The unending support of my loving wife. People in my career who gave me a break.

As I drove off in that shiny new car, I was humbled. Rather than exalting my accomplishments that led to the purchase of that car, I exalted everyone who actually got me to that showroom.

It's so easy at work to take credit for everything we do. Sometimes we're afraid that others will not remember our contributions, and other times we're just plain selfish in wanting to take all the glory.

As a *Christian* public servant, remember Who ultimately deserves exaltation. Then, recall others who helped get you where you are today and where you want to go tomorrow.

Then — and only then — will your ride home from work tonight be as humbling as my ride from that showroom. The blessings are many in knowing you are not **self-made**!

PRAYER

Dear God, at work today please help me to be humble and exalt others and, most importantly, exalt You. In Jesus' name, I pray. Amen.
  —Matt Whitman

Week 37, Day 3

NO OPTION BUT TO STAND

READING

Ephesians 6:11-15 Put on all of God's armor so that you will be able to stand firm against all strategies of the devil. For we are not fighting against flesh-and-blood enemies, but against ... against mighty powers in this dark world, and against evil spirits in the heavenly places. Therefore, put on every piece of God's armor so you will be able to resist the enemy in the time of evil. Then after the battle you will still be standing firm. Stand your ground, putting on the belt of truth and the body armor of God's righteousness. For shoes, put on the peace that comes from the Good News so that you will be fully prepared.

REFLECTION

"Stand" is an action verb, and it is central to understanding this scripture. Paul tries to get his point across. He's emphatic. As if talking to teenagers, his words are repetitive in the hope that they sink in. Paul is worried about us. Be very careful in this fallen world — there is much more going on than earthly crime and injustice. Can he be any clearer about the evil out there? He knows what Satan can do, camouflaging his actions under the flesh-and-blood of the captured human. So Paul tells us to be upright. We have **no option but to stand**.

This is an important message for public servants, especially those involved with the processes of protecting, rescuing, healing, or rehabilitation. *Christian* public servants understand Paul's counsel. It's not just the random consequences of bad luck. For the *Christian* public servant, Paul's warning about evil is right on point.

And so, today you will help someone stand up again and regain pride. With feet fitted with readiness, you will teach that standing is the first step in escaping a bad situation, and escaping is the first process in the defeat of evil. With His armor, you will protect, rescue, heal, counsel, or rehabilitate so that feet may rise after being knocked down so severely. With God's guidance, you will show that *spiritual standing* is required to take God's chosen plan.

Yes, stand is an action verb. Stand is what we do as *Christian* public servants, and it is what we help others do. *Stand.*

Today at work, you and I have **no option but to stand**.

PRAYER

Dear Jesus, help me to stand for You. At work today, let me not shirk my responsibilities. In Your name, I pray. Amen.
　　—Tajuan McCarty

Week 37, Day 4

ALL-STARS

READING

Romans 12:6-8 In his grace, God has given us different gifts for doing certain things well. So if God has given you the ability to prophesy, speak out with as much faith as God has given you. If your gift is serving others, serve them well. If you are a teacher, teach well. If your gift is to encourage others, be encouraging. If it is giving, give generously. If God has given you leadership ability, take the responsibility seriously. And if you have a gift for showing kindness to others, do it gladly.

REFLECTION

It was a casual conversation in the break room. "My daughter just tested into the gifted class in grammar school, and my Son's is accepted into the honors program for college next year. Both have all A's," Jamela shared. "Wow," Ruth replied, "I wish my grandchildren did better in school. Serena can draw anything but has trouble with math. Mitchell is wonderful in science, but struggles with English."

We all want our children to be academic stars in everything and, secretly, we wish we too were **all-stars**. We see coworkers with skills we don't have and wish we could be like them. We see others lacking our best skills and wish they could be more like us. Work would go so much better if only everyone could be **all-stars!**

Really? Paul tells us that we are different by design and that it is a very good thing that we are not all alike. Now, I'm not suggesting we should not learn and advance from one position to another in the workplace. We should in every way strive to excel. But God has given each of us the gifts that fit into who He needs us to become and where He wants us to be. A big part of growing in Christ is learning to trust our gifts and learning to acknowledge and appreciate the gifts of others.

In the workplace, as in the classroom and life, we are not built to be **all-stars**.

Which coworker has gifts different than yours? Is someone better in time-management? Can someone apply regs quicker than you, or perhaps has a cooler hand with disgruntled citizens or clients? Who may be more advanced in a skill that God is developing in you? Is there anyone whose gifts can mature and bear fruit with your help? Can you find the giftedness in the citizen, client, coworker or boss who has been driving you crazy?

Folk wisdom says, "To the person who is good with a hammer, everything looks like a nail." Could it be that your Father's creation and plan is bigger and bolder and better than you have realized? Pay attention and you may find some new stars to appreciate at work today! Just as in those casual break room conversations about our kids, we must remember it is gift, not a penalty, that we ourselves may not be **all-stars** when we exit that same break room.

Prayer

Gracious Father, forgive me for my self-centeredness and tunnel vision. I am grateful for the gifts You have given me and I want to use them for Your glory. Lord, I also want to learn to see and appreciate the gifts You have given those around me. Today at work, I will share my gifts generously and accept gratefully the gifts available through others. As Your child, I want You to be as pleased with me as I truly am pleased with my children. In You Son's name, I pray. Amen.

    —Jim Stephens

Week 37, Day 5

GIVE THAT LIGHT TO EVERYONE

READING

Matthew 5:15 No one lights a lamp and then puts it under a basket. Instead, a lamp is placed on a stand, where it gives light to everyone in the house.

REFLECTION

A friend once told me about his new building at the college where he worked. When it first opened, he liked it except for one thing. The lights would automatically turn off in the classrooms at precisely 9 p.m. That was fine if you taught in the daytime, but my friend taught until 9:30 pm. For that last half-hour, he would search for a way to turn those lights back on.

Funny, the world is so different but we are all the same. Like my friend's building, the lights on Life Row also turn off at the same time but not by me. Like my friend, the lights of this world are beyond my control.

I do not like losing light because, without it, there is only darkness. In my old way, before I met Jesus, darkness ruled me. I would hide from light. I would search for darkness. You know, it is sorrowful what you can do when you are not in the light. But I have since learned that darkness is not the place to be — not in my world and not in yours.

So others can turn off the lights of this world too easily. And we never know when the light of this life will be turned off forever. Yet too many times, we brothers- and sisters-in-Christ hide the only Light we control — *His Light*. We choose not to **give that Light to everyone** in the house. We are afraid of it getting in the way of friendship or being accepted. Sometimes it is just easier living in the dark when His Light brings on so many responsibilities for others.

Perhaps you do not control the lights in your workplace. But you do *control the Light you give* to your workplace. Today at work, shine it freely. Do not put it under a basket beneath your desk. Do not file it under "later" or "maybe." Do not be afraid to sit His Light high on a stand.

Today, **give that Light to everyone** in the house where you work.

PRAYER

Father, in the name of Jesus, thank You for trusting me to shine Your Light every day. Give me courage not to hide it. Give me strength to raise Your Light so high that all may see it, and they will know that this is a house where You dwell. Amen.

—Jimmy Davis, Jr.

Week 38, Day 1

HIS PUBLIC SERVANT

READING

Matthew 11:28b Come to me, all of you who are weary and carry heavy burdens, and I will give you rest.

Ephesians 2:8-9 God saved you by his grace when you believed. And you can't take credit for this; it is a gift from God. Salvation is not a reward for the good things we have done, so none of us can boast about it.

REFLECTION

For about a year, I dealt with an overwhelming sense of underwhelming achievement, and that led to a lot of guilt. I never could seem to get everything done I believed I needed to do. I beat myself to a pulp.

You know full well how easy it is to beat yourself up in the public service. There may be days when citizens give you nothing but complaints. There may be months when some citizens and a few elected officials use the media to blast your agency. Budget cutbacks make it particularly easy to feel like hamsters running on a wheel. No matter how hard you work or how fast you move, you fail to get anywhere. Naturally you take work and work-worries home, but then you start to lag behind on family joys and responsibilities. Guilt rises because you feel ineffective in everything you think God expects you to do.

Well, I've prayed, studied scripture and even read a book by a guy named Tullian Tchividjian. I've prayed some more. Call me foolish, but I've concluded that God doesn't expect us to be mavericks — taking charge of our own lives and claiming not to need Him desperately to make it through each work minute. In fact, He rejoices when we find ourselves imperfect. It makes His day when we own up to that fact.

Now, I'm not suggesting it's OK for me to be lazy or that you should care not about the quality and quantity of your work. God loves us but still, not just anything goes with Him. But once we admit we're *imperfect public servants*, He takes over and gives us rest from stress and guilt. That's right, He takes over!

Yes, God wants you to be a good public servant. But more than anything, He wants you to be **His public servant** — a follower who is loved so dearly by Him that you rely on Him fanatically in every choice you take. This is why He offers us unending grace so that we can get over our mistakes and failures, take corrective action, and then move on with the work He has before us. So you see, you and I don't have to beat ourselves to a pulp. *He has already taken that beating on our behalf!*

Still feel like you're on that hamster wheel? Still overwhelmed? Still feel like a failure?

Accept the grace God is offering you, right this very moment, and revel in it. He's not expecting you to be a perfect public servant — just **His public servant** seeking His help and His grace in doing His work in His workplace.

PRAYER

Lord, help me stop trying to be one of those imaginary perfect people. (You know I can't even come close to being perfect.) I'm no maverick, Lord. I can't go it alone. I'm so tired and feel so guilty when I fail. I need rest. I need Your rest. Help me accept Your help and Your grace unconditionally and work within Your protective borders. Help me feel that precious peace You intend for Your followers in Your workplace. In Jesus' name, I pray. Amen.
    —Jennifer Jones

Week 38, Day 2

WALK AWAY FROM THAT TOMB

READING

Luke 24:5 The women were terrified and bowed with their faces to the ground. Then the men asked, "Why are you looking among the dead for someone who is alive?"

REFLECTION

Each day you hope to serve the public in significant ways. You also hope your career is going in the right direction. But maybe it seems you have little impact on the lives of others. And maybe you think you hold a dead-end position in an agency that really can't matter. Now, I bet you didn't enter the public service just to mourn each night its demise. Did you ever think you would someday mourn the seemingly dead idea of your career?

So much can go wrong when you *mourn the workplace*. You're filled with negativity as you leave home and, when you get to work, everything seems just plain awful. You gravitate to like-minded coworkers. You know who they are — in the break room, their talk always centers on how good it used to be or how it is supposed to be. Such mourning should make you feel better, but it does not. You are simply *seeking the living among the dead*.

Luke shows that it's just human nature to want to go back to that tomb to mourn what is lost. We want to return to what is dead because it's what we know. But we should also know that the tomb is nothing but a dark place. It lacks the light of the risen Christ.

Everyone has some workdays filled with despair. But if you sense being drawn down into a "death pit," stop and remind yourself that *God desires life for you* — even at your workplace. **Walk away from that tomb** and find the risen Lord. That tomb is empty. You will not find hope there. Christ can transform your difficult times and give old situations new life. Embrace Him, and He will shed new light on your job and your career.

Today at work, just **walk away from that tomb**!

PRAYER

Dear God, transform me by Your resurrection so that what I perceive as dead at work may be revisited with new life. I pray this in Your Holy name. Amen.
—Dominick D. Hankle

Week 38, Day 3

GOOD TO BE HIS DOG

READINGS

Revelation 22:15a Outside the city are the dogs—the sorcerers, the sexually immoral...

Proverbs 26:11a ...as a dog returns to its vomit.

Matthew 15:27b Dogs are allowed to eat the scraps that fall beneath their masters' table.

REFLECTION

Why do dogs get a bad rap? The "dog-eat-dog" workplace is blamed on "dirty dogs" who throw the agency "to the dogs." Even scripture is unkind when it comes to "man's best friend."

The negative connotation of "dog" reminds me of the condescending words used to describe Christians in many public and secular settings — including some workplaces. Perhaps abetted by Hollywood images, labels are whispered: "He's a holy roller," "she's a Jesus freak," "they're Bible thumpers," "they're all rabid with religion." This kind of ridicule is nothing new. While flesh, even Jesus was judged *less than a dog* by His many adversaries.

But you know, *it's actually neat to be called a dog*. Many dogs are tremendous public servants. They serve with distinction in the military, fire departments, with the disabled, and in law enforcement. They are loyal and obedient to their masters.

Now, I'm not suggesting that our Savior be referred to as a dog. Lord, no! But maybe we should embrace such insults and respond by confirming it's **good to be His dog**.

Given who our Master is, our workplaces should *go to the dogs*. After all, we get the scraps from beneath His table! And maybe, just maybe, those who use condescending labels might hunger for those scraps!

So at work today, when you hear negative descriptions about your brothers and sisters — and about you — just smile and confirm that it's **good to be His dog**!

PRAYER

Lord, at work allow me to show my obedience and loyalty to You. Let me share those miraculous scraps from beneath Your table. In Your name, I pray. Amen.
    —Steve Butler

Week 38, Day 4

RULE OVER OTHERS RIGHTEOUSLY

READING

II Samuel 23:3b-4 The one who rules righteously, who rules in the fear of God, is like the light of morning at sunrise, like a morning without clouds, like the gleaming of the sun on new grass after rain.

REFLECTION

I know someone who works in a government permit office. She brags that no one uttering a harsh word to the staff ever gets a permit in a timely fashion. "We have the power, and they don't!"

In my own academic work, I've met many global leaders. Most take their responsibilities seriously in service to the people who put them in power. But some are like my friend in that permit office. They place their own needs ahead of those who entrust them with the position.

Regardless of where you work in public service, you rule over those you serve. On a daily basis, you affect lives in countless ways through actions or inactions. Ruling over others is an awesome responsibility. The work is significant because of the power it offers.

Yet there is an old saying: the value of a leader is directly proportional to the leader's values. So it is with public servants. And, as *Christian* public servants, we share *core values* that require us to **rule over others righteously** — not with selfishness or power. We **rule over others righteously** because we rule in fear of the God who loves us.

As you go to work today, it's something to remember. **Rule over others righteously** knowing God is watching you.

PRAYER

Lord, bless me with the wisdom to make righteous decisions today that, above all, reflects my reverent and loving fear of You. Let my decisions give glory to Your influence on my life. In Your name, I pray. Amen.
　　—Kevin Cooney

Week 38, Day 5

MOST IMPORTANT TOOL

READING

Romans 12:2 Don't copy the behavior and customs of this world, but let God transform you into a new person by changing the way you think. Then you will learn to know God's will for you, which is good and pleasing and perfect.

REFLECTION

The problems you face on this particular Friday might seem insurmountable, whether you are a public servant or someone studying to become a public servant. Every MPA student learns that problem-solving requires a search for solutions using all the *tools-of-the-trade* — professional studies, workplace documents, career and job experience, interpersonal relations, and knowing the reality of the human condition.

However, if you only seek answers from worldly sources, you may become captured by cynicism and miss tremendous opportunity. Yes, we learn from all those around us and ourselves, but we also *learn from God.* In fact, He is the **most important tool** you can carry throughout the day.

Don't let today's problems overwhelm you. Use all the *tools-of-the-trade* — including the **most important tool**. Learn from God, the workplace is His classroom, and you are His student. Use His wisdom as part of your problem solving strategy.

Particularly in these times, we must all be good students of His. We must not neglect that **most important tool**.

PRAYER

Dear God, let me be Your student today. Teach me how to use all the tools needed to solve the problems facing me. You are the *Great Tutor*, and I confess I need You most. At work today, let me not neglect my **most important tool**. In Jesus' name, I pray. Amen.

— Christopher Meconnahey

Week 39, Day 1

GOD OF MONDAY MIRACLES

READING

Genesis 1:5 God called the light "day" and the darkness "night." And evening passed and morning came, marking the first day.
Colossians 3:24b The Master you are serving is Christ.

REFLECTION

It's Monday morning, but I'm actually pretty excited about going to work today! I mean it. After all, God works on Mondays, so why shouldn't I? And it's incredible, the kind of work God does on Mondays. Just look at what He did on that *first Monday*. He created light, separated it from darkness, and then He named it "day" and "night" — *day* and *night*, can you believe it!

I can't wait to see the miracles He will perform on this particular Monday!

So it's because He is the **God of Monday miracles** that I'm absolutely thrilled about working on this particular Monday! Because He is the **God of Monday miracles**, I bet you're also getting real excited about going to work today!!

As this workweek begins, let's remember Whom we serve and rejoice in our service to Him. Do your best, but remember it's not your job to perform miracles. He doesn't expect you or me to do anything nearly as spectacular as creating *day* and *night*! So when things get frantic today, as you know they will, just take a deep breath and have faith in our **God of Monday miracles**.

Hey, I wonder what miracles He does on Tuesdays? I can't wait!

PRAYER

Dear Heavenly Father, thank You for being the God of miracles. Thank You for the miracle of letting me awake and serve You for another day. Help me not to grumble or complain, or to become frantic over the miracles needed in my workplace. Give me strength just to do my job as I have faith You are always doing your job. Enable me to walk the walk that is worthy of Your name and the miracles You are performing right now. It is in Your Son's name that I pray. Amen.

—Stephen M. King

Week 39, Day 2

FALLEN FIRE FIGHTERS AND
POLICE OFFICERS

READING

1 *Thessalonians 4:13* And now, dear brothers and sisters, we want you to know what will happen to the believers who have died so you will not grieve like people who have no hope.

REFLECTION

Firefighters and police officers are part of that *special breed* of public servants. They risk everything to protect our life and property. They do so for little pay and even less recognition. So many, like my cousin Wade, lose their lives each year around the world in the process of protecting us.

As public servants, we all know our duty, and this places some of us directly in harm's way. But as *Christian* public servants, we know we serve a mighty God who gives us hope — the deepest kind of hope that others do not have. We trust Him, and we don't ask "why" when tragedies happen and the lives of some of our best public servants are taken. We don't ask because we know where they have gone. We don't ask because we have hope.

Today, regardless of the kind of public or nonprofit work you do or where worldwide you may do it, remember the **fallen fire fighters and police officers** in your community or region. Public servants who served us so readily and bravely.

PRAYER

Lord Jesus, I do not understand horrific situations in life, but my hope is placed in You. I therefore do not ask why. Instead, I ask that You welcome home the **fallen fire fighters and police officers**, and comfort their families. In Christ's name, I pray. Amen.
—Savanna Faith Cornibe

Week 39, Day 3

GO BEYOND THE TECHNICALITIES

READINGS

Micah 6:8b To do what is right, to love mercy, and to walk humbly with your God.

Colossians 4:1 Masters, be just and fair to your slaves. Remember that you also have a Master—in heaven.

REFLECTION

As a manager for an IT area in a university system, part of my job is to hire and fire. When hiring, I look not only for technical expertise, but also for ability to be a team player. When faced with a possible termination, I apply the same criteria. I don't take the firing task lightly because it affects the staff, the department, and the product this IT area delivers.

Recently I faced a termination situation. The employee's performance was consistently substandard. This hindered the team atmosphere and adversely affected the product. I tried to save him by utilizing every resource available. HR provided guidance, and we all hoped he would become a productive part of the IT team.

I also prayed a lot — for guidance throughout the process, and in making the final decision. I prayed that my anger and disappointment would not cloud my judgment. I prayed that the final decision would be best for all involved, including this employee. Prayer was central to building an exit package that made the process less painful and more dignified for him.

Terminations are difficult, and being Christian makes it more taxing. Any time you have to terminate, **go beyond the technicalities** and turn to God. Are you doing what is right? Is it done with the love of mercy? Are you walking humbly with God? Are you remembering that everyone involved reports to a higher Boss — in heaven?

As a *Christian* public manager, make sure your decisions are just and fair in His eyes. Today at work, **go beyond the technicalities** and turn to God.

PRAYER

Most gracious Heavenly Father, I pray that decisions regarding termination are made with humility, kindness, and love. With Your guidance, I pray You look kindly upon all who suffer in hearts and souls when difficult decisions are carried out. In Your Son's name, I pray. Amen.
    —Janis Dunn Slack

Week 39, Day 4

CHRIST'S SERVANT

READING

Galatians 1:10 Obviously, I'm not trying to win the approval of people, but of God. If pleasing people were my goal, I would not be **Christ's servant**.

REFLECTION

The public workplace has never been an easy setting for **Christ's servant**. And that's what you are, right? A Christian public servant, after all, is **Christ's servant**.

It seems we often find ourselves in situations involving controversial issues that do not comply with God's word. It may be an off-color joke in the coffee room; it may be a seemingly innocuous comment in a meeting; or it may be a hate-laden accusation about another person or another group or another race made by a client or citizen you are trying to help. For those studying public administration at some secular universities, it may be the ideology that is too-often preached as truth.

We are often challenged. Do we take a stand for God's commands or simply agree with the secular worldview? We fear taking a stand. People will look at us differently, won't they? It's easier just to slip under the radar and avoid all possible confrontations.

Yes, I am still in graduate school — preparing to become what you already are — a public servant. You may think my views are a bit naïve. But I really want to be like *you* — more than a public servant. Like you, I want to be a *Christian* public servant — **Christ's servant**.

As the challenges of this workday begin, do not be afraid to choose our Lord. Do not fear being **Christ's servant**.

PRAYER

Dear God, thank You for allowing me to be Your servant. Let me stand out in the workplace today as a light of You, for You. Help me to be strong and courageous in situations that need and await Your disarming influence. Let me serve as Your disarming influence. For You are my only Master, and I am Your hands and feet in this world and, especially today, in this workplace. In Jesus' name, I pray. Amen.
—Angela Arbitter

Week 39, Day 5

COST OF DOING SOMETHING

READING

Mark 6:37 But Jesus said, "You feed them." "With what?" they asked. "We'd have to work for months to earn enough money to buy food for all these people!"

REFLECTION

It seems that this year the Lord is really taking me out of my comfort zone and, like His disciples, asking me to do the impossible. Most recently, here on Life Row, He placed me in the middle of a bad situation involving a family member. I was clueless to do anything, and I was fearful of having to do a lot. But I decided to go into the situation and not worry about the **cost of doing something**. I knew that Jesus would pour into me the something He needed, and I would pour that same something into my family.

When we worry about the **cost of doing something**, we never do it. We stay in our comfort zone because the costs may be too high — the cost of our time, our peace, or the cost of God's money we are blessed with. We even worry about the cost of our love. *The real cost of worrying about such things is that we never see the great power of Jesus in anything!*

Today at work, let the Lord break you out of *the death row you call your comfort zone.* Let Him place you where He needs you. Help Him do the impossible for others. "You feed them."

Don't worry about the **cost of doing something**. He has already paid the bill.

PRAYER

Father, in the name of Jesus, I pray. Thank You for showing up for me in all of my impossible situations so I can witness Your great power and build my faith in Your Son. Thank You for allowing Your Son to pay my bill on His cross. Amen.

—Jimmy Davis, Jr.

Week 40, Day 1

NOT OUR CHOICE

READING

II Corinthians 5:20 So we are Christ's ambassadors; God is making his appeal through us. We speak for Christ when we plead, "Come back to God!"

REFLECTION

For *Christian* public servants, it is always a challenging issue. How should we relate to the particular culture in which we serve and live? One answer is found in this particular scripture. It offers the concept of "ambassador" as a means to describe our Christian relationship to the specific context in which we are placed.

Over the next five days, let's reflect on the office of an ambassador and what it suggests to us, as *Christian* public servants, in terms of how we go about serving our Lord when we serve others in our careers, in our workplaces, and in our life-places.

As this work-week begins, let's first recognize that, in the political realm, the office of an ambassador is *not an elected office*. One does not choose to run for election to serve as an ambassador. Rather, ambassadors are appointed.

As *Christians* who happen to engage in public service, guess what? We have already been appointed to be His ambassadors! It is **not our choice**; it is *our office*.

PRAYER

Lord, in my workplace and in my life, You have appointed me to serve as Your ambassador. In serving You in this capacity, grant that I may make wise decisions, exercise proper judgment, and exhibit needed sensitivities when interacting with all those I serve — especially those who presently do not know You as their Lord and Savior. In Your name, I pray. Amen.
—Corwin Smidt

Week 40, Day 2

HIGHEST CALLING

READING

II Corinthians 5:20 So we are Christ's ambassadors; God is making his appeal through us. We speak for Christ when we plead, "Come back to God!"

REFLECTION

All ambassadors are appointed, not elected. Since they serve as very unique official representatives, ambassadors also reflect a *very high calling*.

We, too, have been appointed as ambassadors — ambassadors for Christ. And as *Christian* public servants, our positions must reflect that **highest calling.**

Whatever your job in public service — school teacher or manager, police officer or budget officer, prime minister or building custodian — today reflect that **highest calling**. More than an employee, you are a *servant*. More than a public servant, you are a *Christian* public servant.

We have that **highest calling** to represent Christ as we work with others and as we serve others. So on this workday, let us understand and interpret the true meaning of our routine tasks. Serving, protecting and advancing others well — citizens, clients, students, coworkers — becomes a means by which we may well serve, represent and glorify Christ.

`Today, do not forget you are His ambassador. My friend, do not neglect that **highest calling**.

PRAYER

Lord, in the detail and substance of my job this day, enable me to serve You in all that I do and say. Let even the opportunities of "good morning" and "good afternoon" convey the joy that I experience in representing You. Remind me all day of that **highest calling**, YOU! In Your name, I pray. Amen.

—Corwin Smidt

Week 40, Day 3

GO

READING

II Corinthians 5:20 So we are Christ's ambassadors; God is making his appeal through us. We speak for Christ when we plead, "Come back to God!"

Matthew 28:19a Therefore, **go** and make disciples of all the nations

REFLECTION

Ambassadors are appointed, and they reflect a very high calling. Ambassadors serve the person who has appointed them. They are sent to serve in foreign territories. They do not seek the comfort and safety of their homeland. As *Christian* public servants, we are appointed, reflecting that highest calling, as ambassadors for Christ. We *serve and are sent*.

There is nothing comfortable about serving Christ in the workplace. By its very nature, it is a foreign land. Unlike our families and church communities, there is no safety or assurance in that foreign land. *Yet He sends us there anyway, and so we serve*.

In the final words of our Savior Jesus Christ, prior to his ascension, He commanded His disciples to "**go**" — not to linger nor to stay in the relief of one's safe and comfortable territory — but to **go** — **go** and make disciples.

We are ambassadors for Christ. We *serve and are sent*.

Go.

PRAYER

Lord, You have sent me into "foreign lands" outside my family and church community. Today as I interact with "foreigners" — those who do not know You or choose not to follow You — help me to measure my words and actions in ways that serve You and not myself. At work today, help me to show You in my service to others. In Your name, I pray. Amen.

— Corwin Smidt

Week 40, Day 4

SPREAD THAT MESSAGE

READING

II Corinthians 5:20 So we are Christ's ambassadors; God is making his appeal through us. We speak for Christ when we plead, "Come back to God!"

REFLECTION

So far this week, we have noted that ambassadors are appointed, reflect a very high calling, and are sent to serve in foreign territories. But not all foreign territories are the same—some may be allies, others adversaries, and still others may be neutral. The context, however, does not alter what ambassadors fundamentally do — ambassadors represent. They *spread the message* of the nation that sent them. *Christian* public servants — whether in government, nonprofits, education, healthcare, public safety or defense — are also ambassadors — *ambassadors for Christ*. We are appointed by Christ, reflect that highest calling of Christ, and are sent by Christ into that foreign territory known as the public service workplace.

And while each workplace is quite different, He has committed to each of us the message of reconciliation. In my own workplace — today — I must **spread that message**.

But wait a minute.

Note first, that it is *God* who engages in reconciling the world to Himself in Christ. *Our office—our task—is not to serve as reconcilers; only God can reconcile.* Rather, what we as ambassadors have been commanded to do is to *communicate the message of reconciliation*. God through Jesus Christ has reconciled us to Him, not counting our sins against us. And, in turn, He has committed each of us to **spread that message** of reconciliation.

This very day at work, is it possible for me to **spread that message**? Do I really have a choice? How about you?

PRAYER

Lord, as St. Francis of Assisi prayed, so do I. In my workplace today — right this very moment — make me an instrument of Your reconciliation (and peace). With coworker and citizen and client whom I serve — where there is hatred, let me sow love. Where there is injury, pardon. Where there is doubt, faith. Where there is despair, hope. Where there is darkness, light. Where there is sadness, joy. In Your name, I pray. Amen.
—Corwin Smidt

Week 40, Day 5

YOUR WORDS AND ACTIONS

READING

II Corinthians 5:18-20   And all of this is a gift from God, who brought us back to himself through Christ. And God has given us this task of reconciling people to him. For God was in Christ, reconciling the world to himself, no longer counting people's sins against them. And he gave us this wonderful message of reconciliation. So we are Christ's ambassadors; God is making his appeal through us. We speak for Christ when we plead, "Come back to God!"

REFLECTION

This week, we have noted that ambassadors are appointed, reflect a very high calling, and are sent to serve in foreign territories to spread the message of the nation that sent them. In order to do this, ambassadors must be knowledgeable of the culture to which they have been sent, sensitive to its particular customs and folkways, and have an appreciation, even a *love*, for the people of that culture. Only then can an ambassador *foster* understanding of the message. As *Christian* public servants, we are also ambassadors — *ambassadors for Christ*. We are appointed by Christ, reflect that highest calling of Christ, and are sent by Christ into that foreign territory known as the public service workplace to spread His message of reconciliation.

Today and every workday, your mission is to *foster understanding* of that message of reconciliation through **your words and actions.**

Now, I don't mean *regal words* and *pious actions*. Have you ever noticed? Some self-appointed ambassadors for Christ can be a bit pretentious, not understanding — certainly not loving — the culture of the "foreign territory". You sometimes see them at work, don't you? They emit a false sense of piety. They are condescending, not even knowing how to "kid around." You know, the "holier than thou" type.

They are poor representatives of Christ because their words and actions distract from the message of reconciliation. Everyone secretly waits for that kind of ambassador to sin, fall from grace, get caught doing something "human." Everyone secretly hopes to witness that person failing to practice what they preach. And boy, when that day comes, well .... !!

You are not that kind of ambassador! Are you? You love your profession, workplace, and the people with whom you work and serve. Don't you? Right??

If so, others see that **your words and actions** are different. When you slip up — and you admittedly do slip up — people see you not as a hypocrite but rather as a sinner who struggles daily to follow Christ. You are someone they can appreciate because, guess what, they too are sinners who, perhaps because of **your words and actions**, are also struggling to follow Christ.

So go forth, ambassador, and use **your words and actions** for Him today. Be assured that the Holy Spirit is present as you serve Him through **your words and actions** in that "foreign territory" called the workplace.

Prayer

Lord, as St. Francis of Assisi prayed, so do I now. At work today, make me an instrument of your reconciliation (and peace). At work today, grant that I may not so much seek to be consoled, as to console; to be understood, as to understand; to be loved, as to love. For it is in giving that we receive. It is in pardoning that we are pardoned, and it is in dying that we are born to Eternal Life. In Your name, I pray. Amen.

—Corwin Smidt

Week 41, Day 1

NO PAIN ON GOD'S WATCH

READING

1 Chronicles 4:9-10 There was a man named Jabez who was more honorable than any of his brothers. His mother named him Jabez because his birth had been so painful. He was the one who prayed to the God of Israel, "Oh, that you would bless me and expand my territory! Please be with me in all that I do, and keep me from all trouble and pain!" And God granted him his request.

Philippians 2:3-4 Don't be selfish; don't try to impress others. Be humble, thinking of others as better than yourselves. Don't look out only for your own interests, but take an interest in others, too.

REFLECTION

Jabez was a wonderful public servant! Born into the tribe of Judah, he was a man aspiring toward leadership. Yet unlike the meaning of his name, Jabez wanted to fulfill his destiny without causing pain to anyone. He did not want to ride roughshod over others as his territory was enlarged. Jabez wanted to cause **no pain on God's watch**.

Today some aspiring civic leaders, as they climb the bureaucratic ladders of the public service, care little if their colleagues or citizens suffer "pain" due to their administration. They think nothing of even the simple 'evil' of being inconsiderate toward others. Unlike Jabez, too many simply seek power and do not ask God to fulfill their destinies *without causing pain*.

As *Christian* public servants, let us emulate the spirit of Jabez! As this work-week begins, let us be of that honorable sort — tempering ambition with due honour for our colleagues, and serving all citizens and clients with the humility of servant-leaders. After all, the greatest leader ever to emerge from the tribe of Judah was also the greatest servant who ever lived — Jesus, our Messiah. We have His New Covenant example, which Jabez never had; and we have the Holy Spirit's indwelling, which Jabez never had.

So let us respond rightly, as the story of that humble Old Testament man, Jabez, calls us into honorable 21st century public service! Today, let us cause **no pain on God's watch**.

PRAYER

Father, today as I work with my colleagues to serve the public, please help me not to act out of selfish ambition, but to be considerate of the interests of others. And I thank You, Lord, for Your blessing on me as a *Christian* public servant. May my service bring You glory. In Jesus' name, I pray. Amen.
    —M. Evangeline Anderson

Week 41, Day 2

WILLING VESSEL

READING

Proverbs 16:3 Commit your actions to the LORD, and your plans will succeed.

REFLECTION

If you want to make God laugh, just tell Him your plans!

You might think you have a mission. You might even think you have a vision. And you may, but one thing's for sure. It MUST be fueled by your desire to glorify God and to make an eternity-difference in His world. When He puts something in your heart to do, He goes to work behind the scenes to ensure that it happens. All you need do is to be a **willing vessel**.

My pastor once told me, "missing out on God's plan for our lives must be the greatest tragedy this side of eternity." He's right.

Today at work, be His **willing vessel**.

PRAYER

Father, thank You for the gifts and talents You have given me. I realize You have a reason for giving them to me, so help me build my plans around You. Give me courage to commit all my actions to You and for Your glory. Lord, help me be Your **willing vessel**. In Your Son's name, I pray. Amen.

—Tammy Esteves

Week 41, Day 3

AS CHRIST SERVES US

READING

Ephesians 5:21b Submit to one another out of reverence for Christ.

REFLECTION

Even among the shy, a lot of our modern world seems to be built on the bricks of self-boasting. Resume books give us a clue, and the internet is filled with opportunities to web-lodge our self-proclamations. Even our promotions and advancements, we must admit, are based a bit on reputational hype. It may be convenient for others to accept that hype, but it is way too easy for us to believe it about ourselves. We end up anchoring our work thoughts and actions selfishly on ourselves and on our own careers.

In the fray of the workday battle, it's commonplace to forget that we are all sinners saved by grace. The sooner we remember this Good News, the sooner we can start practicing it and get pride out of our way; the sooner we can really get down to serving others **as Christ serves us**.

Your work tasks today may be daunting, and there may be a lot on the line with deadlines that just won't budge. But the people you work with are actually God's gift to help complete the job. Remember, lead and teach them with the godly example of submitting to them, and they too will want to serve even you **as Christ serves us**.

PRAYER

Lord, I am nothing without you. Filled with your sweet Spirit, I can do all things. Today at work help me to stay humble and submit to others so that I may serve and teach them faithfully out of reverence for You. In Your Holy name, I pray. Amen.

—Stan Best

Week 41, Day 4

NEED TO HEAR HIS VOICE

READING

Psalm 83:1a   O God, do not be silent!

REFLECTION

I am told (and most of the time I believe) God's timing is perfect. On some workdays, and this is one of them, I need to be reassured. I **need to hear His voice**.

I grow increasingly frustrated by people and events where it seems there is no effort to seek truth. Some leaders appear not to understand the issues encountered by those in the "trenches" of public service, and many in the trenches often appear incapable or unwilling to guide and enlighten those leaders. Career progression and agency success are impeded by people not seeking out the truth or, worse yet, knowing the truth but allowing others to bully them onto a different pathway.

You ever see this happening in your workplace?

As *Christian* public servants, we believe life in God's will is the best path; but there are days when so many of us watch in agony as the careers of others are advanced or the agency mission is altered, in part, because of some people never taking a principled stand. Like David and other psalmists, we see those who do not wish us well and, yes, we do want a feast before our enemies.

Do you sometimes feel this way, too?

On those workdays, we need to know we are living the life He wants for us. On those workdays, we really **need to hear His voice**.

And for some of us, that workday is today.

PRAYER

God, today I really need to hear Your voice today. I need to know my life is where You would have it be. There is so much I yearn for, both personally and professionally, including a stronger sense that my work actually contributes to the public good. I trust You but I really need to hear Your voice. Today speak to me, Lord, and tell me *Your* plans for *me*. In Jesus' name, I pray. Amen.

—Stephanie L. Bellar

Week 41, Day 5

WAKE UP AND LOOK AROUND

READING

John 4:35 You know the saying, "Four months between planting and harvest." But I say, wake up and look around! The fields are already ripe for harvest.

REFLECTION

During my hour outside in the yard, I sometimes like to run on the dirt path for exercise. As I started to run yesterday, my eye caught one of the officers. He clearly looked sad and discouraged. Something was wrong. So I stopped running when I got to his station, and I asked if he were OK. He said, "No." We talked a bit, and then he asked if I had a scripture that would help him. For the life of me, I couldn't think of one.

But then I felt the Holy Spirit. He whispered, give that officer the Word I gave you last night. So I did, and it blessed that officer as well as another officer standing nearby.

Scripture says that we need not wait until Sunday. There are fields already ripe for harvest. All we need do is to **wake up and look around** to find them. Yesterday those two officers became my field, and the one officer's sad heart was already ripe for the harvest. All I did was to allow the Word of God to speak through me to show them Jesus.

You might wonder what field God will have you working in today. And just what in that field will already be ripe for the harvest? Like me, you won't know until you see it.

So today at work, please make sure you **wake up and look around**!

PRAYER

Father, in the name of Jesus, I pray. Continue to clear my eyes so that I can see that particular someone today who is ripe to receive the Word that You give me to give to him. Amen.

—Jimmy Davis, Jr.

Week 42, Day 1

WORKPLACE PRAYER GROUP

READING

Psalm 103:2-4 Let all that I am praise the LORD; may I never forget the good things he does for me. He forgives all my sins and heals all my diseases. He redeems me from death and crowns me with love and tender mercies.

REFLECTION

A friend was terrified. Her husband had a life-threatening heart problem that required immediate surgery. Our **workplace prayer group** began to raise his name to our Lord. *Prayers were flying like rockets!* You could just feel the Holy Spirit at work!

Then we got the good news: suddenly our friend's husband no longer needed surgery. His cardiologist never saw anything like this in his entire career.

Secularists may claim it was just a coincidence, having nothing to do with our prayers. Members of our **workplace prayer group** know different. It has *everything* to do with our Lord!

Truly, we serve an awesome God! Scripture promises that the Lord pardons all our iniquities, heals all our diseases, redeems our lives from the pit, and then crowns us with loving kindness and compassion. Such repair comes only in God's time, not ours, and it sometimes occurs only in heaven. But God never reneges on His promises!

By the way, do you have a **workplace prayer group**? You should!

Involvement in a **workplace prayer group** takes no time away from your job, yet it might just be the most important thing you do at work!

PRAYER

Dear heavenly Father, thank You for healing our diseases, forgiving all our iniquities and for redeeming our lives from the pit. Help us to be your ambassadors at work and to pray at work for victory in health and victory over eternal death. In Jesus' name, I pray. Amen.

—Lyse-Ann Lacourse

Week 42, Day 2

MAKE OUR EFFORTS SUCCESSFUL

READING

Psalm 90:17 And may the Lord our God show us his approval and make our efforts successful. Yes, make our efforts successful!

REFLECTION

My grandmother once told me about "Alice," who worked with her at a company that made curtains. There was a daily quota, and all the seamstresses had to make the expected number of curtains. Alice was good at it, and she enjoyed her work. She always surpassed the quota and, in fact, made more curtains than anyone else. Some coworkers viewed her as a "rate-buster," and they would hide or damage her sewing tools in order to reduce her productivity.

When my grandmother expressed concern over what was happening, Alice told her not to worry. She said that God was in charge of her productivity, and that He makes *her efforts successful*. No one could stop Alice from doing her best.

As *Christian* public servants, we might not do a whole lot of sewing at work! Nevertheless, God is in charge of our productivity. Just like Alice did in the face of adversity, let us each day ask our Lord to **make our efforts successful**.

Yes, make our efforts successful!

PRAYER

Heavenly Father, I thank You for work. I ask that you make my efforts successful and be glorified in my work today and every day. In Jesus' name, I pray. Amen.

—TaQuesha Brandon

Week 42, Day 3

PLAYING BY HIS RULES

READING

Joshua 1:8 Study this Book of Instruction continually. Meditate on it day and night so you will be sure to obey everything written in it. Only then will you prosper and succeed in all you do.

REFLECTION

I love golf — all aspects of the game, especially its traditions and rules that all experienced golfers play by. A novice golfer (like my wife) may not worry so much about some of the smaller rules of the game. As her "coach," I say: "Honey, don't talk when someone is getting ready to hit." She replies, "Why? Does it stop them from *seeing* the ball?" Or, "Honey, once we finish putting, we need to clear the green so others can hit." Her reply again "Why? Are they in a *hurry?*"

With a novice, some rules may not mean much. For an experienced golfer, all rules are important. Playing by all the rules, formal or informal, can bring many kinds of success. Circumventing or not knowing the rules can bring all kinds of disaster.

The same is true with God's word and the principles He gives us to bring success in our lives. For public servants, **playing by His rules** brings success to our jobs and careers. After all, when was the last time a public figure was indicted when he was actually **playing by His rules**?

There are always new people joining the workplace — novices. We can help them know the agency rules, but we can also teach them how to apply God's concrete set of rules. Not by preaching (as perhaps a certain golf coach may lovingly do), but by showing and doing. Just like the novice golfer, those who see you **playing by His rules** will eventually catch on to your kind of success.

And they will want to have the same kind of success!

PRAYER

Lord, I pray for the ability to practice Your rules today at work so that I may be truly successful and bring honor and glory to You. In Your name, I pray. Amen.
    —Bill Dudley,

Week 42, Day 4

SEE THE PICTURE DIFFERENTLY

READING

Proverbs 15:31 If you listen to constructive criticism, you will be at home among the wise.

Proverbs 16:18 Pride goes before destruction, and haughtiness before a fall.

REFLECTION

Although no one currently alive is all-knowing, you encounter some people at work who think they are. You know the type. They may reveal themselves perhaps by developing a fundraising campaign without consulting other members in the department. Or, it may be a manager who restructures without input from the employees who actually do the job. Their actions reflect the fact that they value neither the agency itself nor the opinions and ideas of coworkers.

Constructive criticism and exchange of ideas are vital elements for nonprofit and public servants. There is never one way to accomplish a goal or task. Someone might have a more efficient way, or a more effective way, or a more compassionate way. Someone may have a better grasp on the "obvious". While it is important to speak up in times of opportunity and disagreement, it is essential to listen to the views and opinions of others.

As public servants, we must continuously learn new methods and techniques to better support our causes and serve the public. As *Christian* public servants, let not our pride, or lust for attention or credit, keep us from seeking and hearing the perspectives of others who just might know a little more than we do — others who just might **see the picture differently**.

PRAYER

Lord, help me to remain humble today at work. Bestow upon me the skills needed to remain on a path of peace and understanding with those with whom I work so that we can accomplish the goals You have set before us. Let me do my work in a way that glorifies You and only You. In Your name, I pray. Amen.
    —Cassandra D. McLendon

Week 42, Day 5

CHRISTIAN CORD TO BRAID

READING

Ecclesiastes 4:9-12 Two people are better off than one, for they can help each other succeed. If one person falls, the other can reach out and help. But, someone who falls alone is in real trouble. Likewise, two people lying close can keep each other warm. But how can one be warm alone? A person standing alone can be attacked and defeated, but two can stand back-to-back and conquer. Three are even better, for a triple-braided cord is not easily broken.

REFLECTION

When the stress of the workplace seems to get a step-ahead, it's so easy to be overwhelmed and deal with situations in solitude — an instance of taking on yet one more problem or task by yourself. You may be part of a work team, and that's important. But that's not what I'm talking about because work teams often add stress.

When it comes to stress, we are often like a *single cord* — at best, weak and unbraided but, at worst, braided with nothing but our own worry.

While we know God is always with us, how awesome it is to be able to confide in, lean on, and draw strength from the encouragement of a God-given relationship at work! You know, an informal group of Christians who act as a prayer/support/accountability team.

We know that He tells us "where two or three are gathered" and similarly, the wisdom in *Ecclesiastes* speaks to the strength found in two or three. My best friend and I share this passage often as a reminder that two are always stronger and, when He is in the center, there is nothing that can prevail against us.

At work today, start an informal Christian support group. Think about which coworker can be that 2nd **Christian cord to braid**. Then find a 3rd **Christian cord to braid**. At work or elsewhere, *a triple braided cord is not easily broken!*

PRAYER

God help me to recognize when others at work may need my spiritual support, and help me to realize that there's nothing wrong with asking for it myself. I'm thankful for the people you've placed in my life who surround me with prayer and encouragement, and I pray that You would help me to take time to be a source for those who need it as well. In Your Son's name, I pray. Amen.

—Christie Brown

Week 43, Day 1

PLAINLY ON TABLETS

READING

Habakkuk 2:2(b)-3 Write my answer **plainly on tablets**...This vision is for a future time. It describes the end, and it will be fulfilled. If it seems slow in coming, wait patiently, for it will surely take place. It will not be delayed.

Jeremiah 29:11 For I know the plans I have for you," says the LORD. "They are plans for good and not for disaster, to give you a future and a hope."

REFLECTION

My friend had an interview last week. Don't know if she got the job, but the process was interesting. The final question was, "What do you want to do in 10 years?" It led to a conversation about whether her career-dreams are compatible with the agency's mission and capacity. When the interview was over, my friend was told that too many people have <u>no</u> dreams at all.

I wonder what it might be like having no dreams. I mean, visions are one of the greatest gifts God bestows on us -- regardless of one's age and point-in-career. Yes, there are foolhardy ideas and unrealistic pipedreams. And Lucifer certainly can do his best to make every good vision and dream seem so far away. But to have <u>no</u> dreams ... *at all*?

Pray about your *career-dreams*. Be certain <u>your vision</u> is linked to <u>His plans</u>. Then, write them **plainly on tablets.** Put them in your wallet or purse, and pull them out when you get lost. Be patient and continue to invest much energy in accomplishing them.

Today, whether you are at work or on an interview -- know that He sees your *career-dreams*. After all, you have them written **plainly on tablets**! In His time and in His way, they will surely take place.

PRAYER

Heavenly Father, thank You for inspiring my life. Give me strength and wisdom to continue pushing for Your approved career-dreams. Thank You for giving me patience in the process as I strive each day to sort things out. In Your Son's name, I pray. Amen.
—Rachael Monnin

Week 43, Day 2

NO SURER SAFETY NET

READING

Proverbs 30:8b-9 . . . [G]ive me neither poverty nor riches, but give me only my daily bread. Otherwise, I may have too much and disown you and say, 'Who is the Lord?' or I may become poor and steal, and so dishonor the name of my God.

Luke 11:3 Give us each day our daily bread.

REFLECTION

Do you worry about *job security*?

Job security? You'd have to be nuts not to worry in this global economy.

I grew up in a poor family in the American "Deep South". I know what it's like to watch blue-collar parents struggle paycheck-to-paycheck, sometimes not knowing from where our next meal will appear, or how they will decide which overdue bill to pay.

But even in those circumstances, I do not recall anything but love, joy and peace. You see, in addition to hard work, my parents taught their children to *trust in God alone*. This would help later on in my life as my husband and I sometimes had no jobs in hand.

I thank God for my *seemingly* no-safety-net experiences. Whether I am employed or unemployed, whether my pay is minimum wage or much more — I learned to trust that there is **no surer safety net** than God.

In most parts of the world, these are not the best economic times. Underemployment, real and potential RIF's — all bring on a spirit of panic. Too often we allow this fear to take root and grow, robbing us of peace and robbing our workplace of our own productivity.

Too often we turn away from God and, in doing so, dishonor the name of God.

We think we live increasingly without safety nets, but actually nothing has changed since I was a child. In fact, nothing has changed throughout the ages: We still live in a world of God's *kept promises*. Because of that, there really is **no surer safety net** than God.

In the face of job insecurity, take peace in knowing that God puts us where He wants and needs us. He will take care of our needs as long as we keep focused on doing His will, following His calling, and serving Him one day at a time. While it may be difficult to see, He has always done so. His *kept promises* remain: Among them, He will always *give us each day our daily bread*.

Worried about *job security*? Sure. But there is **no surer safety net** than God.

<u>Prayer</u>

Dear God, I thank You for creating me for a purpose, equipped with unique talents and abilities to accomplish more in life than merely finding food, shelter and clothing. Help me to keep my eyes on You, my heart lifted up to Heaven, and my thoughts and efforts focused on doing Your will. Help me to serve others as You provide opportunities to do so. Do not let worry and fear weaken me and prevent me from doing the work You set before me each day. Help me to rest in the abundance of Your timely and sufficient provision for each of my human needs, as I follow Your calling and fulfill Your purposes. In Jesus' name, I pray. Amen.

    —Martha Smith

Week 43, Day 3

DESPISED WORK NEIGHBOR

READING

Luke 10: 29 -37 The man wanted to justify his actions, so he asked Jesus, "And who is my neighbor?" Jesus replied with a story: "A Jewish man was traveling from Jerusalem down to Jericho, and he was attacked by bandits. They stripped him of his clothes, beat him up, and left him half dead beside the road. By chance a priest came along. But when he saw the man lying there, he crossed to the other side of the road and passed him by. A Temple assistant walked over and looked at him lying there, but he also passed by on the other side. Then a despised Samaritan came along, and when he saw the man, he felt compassion for him. Going over to him, the Samaritan soothed his wounds with olive oil and wine and bandaged them. Then he put the man on his own donkey and took him to an inn, where he took care of him. The next day he handed the innkeeper two silver coins, telling him, 'Take care of this man. If his bill runs higher than this, I'll pay you the next time I'm here.' Now which of these three would you say was a neighbor to the man who was attacked by bandits?" Jesus asked. The man replied, "The one who showed him mercy." Then Jesus said, "Yes, now go and do the same."

REFLECTION

Wow! I love how Jesus really takes us to new levels. It's not enough to love the easy ones — nonbelievers are capable of doing that. We are to love all of our neighbors, and this includes those who aren't so easy. It includes those who we despise.

Now, you're probably not commuting to work today from Jerusalem down to Jericho. Nor are you doing roadwork between those two municipalities. But what about at your own workplace? What about your **despised work neighbor**? You know the one. The person who is sabotaging your work life. That coworker who talks about you behind your back. That underling who covets your position. Your supervisor who wants you out. That one person who views you as his **despised work neighbor**. Can you really love that person?

Sorry, but there's no way out on this one. Jesus offers us an ultimatum. We must love all of our neighbors — especially that **despised work neighbor**.

As you go to work this morning, remember He says, "now go and do the same." He doesn't exempt your **despised work neighbor**.

PRAYER

Dear Lord, You amaze me. Your love is so great, so big and so vast—that it infuses me. Please fill me with all that You are so that I can be like You today at work. Let me truly love all of my work neighbors. In Your name, I pray. Amen.
  —Kathleen Patterson

Week 43, Day 4

READING THE BIBLE CAN PUT YOU TO SLEEP

READING

Psalm 77:2, 11-12 When I was in deep trouble, I searched for the Lord. All night long I prayed, with hands lifted toward heaven, but my soul was not comforted... But then I recall all you have done, O LORD; I remember your wonderful deeds of long ago. They are constantly in my thoughts. I cannot stop thinking about your mighty works.

REFLECTION

We've made it past hump day, but everything is piling up. Worry begins to build up, too. Sound familiar?

The public service workplace really can lead to sleepless nights. It might be your mind replaying a meeting that resulted in more work and less budget, or finding safe space for a trafficked woman, or getting that homeless veteran to comply with needed treatment. It could be just too many juveniles needing your counseling, or a class with twice the students you can really teach. Who knows, you might have a capital case in your courtroom. Your mind could just be racing through every possible nightmare of an upcoming project.

For me, this is one crazy week in the engineer's office, and last night I laid awake. One similar night years ago, I switched on my bed light, grabbed my Bible and randomly opened it. Amazingly Psalm 77 appeared, and the psalmist wrote about sleepless nights! God has a way of getting my attention!

I say this without fear or shame, **reading the bible can put you to sleep**. Really! It helps you to calmly refocus and quietly place into perspective your frustrations. It clarifies what is really important for tomorrow's agenda. It relaxes you.

The next time you lay awake worrying, do like I did last night: switch on that bed light and open up your Bible. Cheaper than a trip to the pharmacy, **reading the bible can put you to sleep**!

PRAYER

Heavenly Father, thank You for taking control of my life. Thank You for showing that conditions plaguing me today are no different than what the authors of the Old Testament went through. And You still make applicable today the solutions offered in Old Testament times! When I feel stressed, weak, and all tied up in knots — help me to meditate on Your works. You are my God, please watch over me. In Jesus' name, I pray for a good sleep tonight. Amen.

—Larry Ketcham

Week 43, Day 5

HEAVINESS OF THE IMPERSONAL

READING

Isaiah 46:4 I will be your God throughout your lifetime—until your hair is white with age. I made you, and I will care for you. I will carry you along and save you.

REFLECTION

Working in a bureaucratic "market place" — permeated with rules, regulations, policies and philosophies of law — tends to obscure the ideals of biblical faithfulness. This is true whether you are a *Christian* public servant in government, nonprofits, health care, the military or education. There is always a constant **heaviness of the impersonal**.

God's faithful compassion, however, supports us in seasons of the impersonal assaults of non-relational necessities. In work such as ours, *Christian* public servants must be reminded: God's faithfulness is for a *life time* and extends *beyond the grave*. Human rules, regulations, policies and laws will change. God is faithful now and forever.

PRAYER

Father God, I praise You for Your faithfulness to me. You are my redeemer. You support and protect me with Your unfailing love. In the seasons of life when I feel the **heaviness of the impersonal**, including this last workday of the week, help me know and feel Your faithful love. Strengthen me to praise You all the days of my life! In Your Son's name, I pray. Amen.
  —Chris Summers

Week 44, Day 1

GUARD OUR HEARTS AND TONGUES

READING

Ephesians 4:29, 31-32 Don't use foul or abusive language. Let everything you say be good and helpful, so that your words will be an encouragement to those who hear them... . Get rid of all bitterness, rage, anger, harsh words, and slander, as well as all types of evil behavior. Instead, be kind to each other, tenderhearted, forgiving one another, just as God through Christ has forgiven you.

REFLECTION

I know what you're thinking. You read this scripture and thought, "I don't talk *that* way at home, work, church, or anywhere else! I am a *civilized* public servant! Nothing foul or abusive comes out of my mouth."

But then, you thought about it with an eye on the words: *kind...tender hearted...forgiving...*

Oops. Now you think, "Oh yeah...*those words, too.*"

If I catch my tongue from speaking foul or abusive words, yet my mind still considers words of bitterness, rage, anger — am I better for that? If I am rough with my coworkers because they've gotten on my nerves for "the last time" — am I showing Christ's love? If I am, once again, annoyed by that obnoxious citizen/client who asks the same questions every week, or that persistent constituent who insists on e-mailing me every day — am I as forgiving as Christ is forgiving with me?

Difficult decisions and honest appraisals must be rendered in the public service workplace. No way getting around that. But remember: whatever is in the heart comes out of the mouth. As *Christian* public servants, let's **guard our hearts and tongues** at work today.

PRAYER

Lord, please help me be mindful of what's in my heart and on my tongue as I go about my workday. Let no words form that would dismay You. Guard my speech as I complete the work You would have me do today. In Jesus' name, I pray. Amen.

—Sarah Majeske

Week 44, Day 2

HARMONY, RELATIONSHIP
AND COMMUNITY

READING

2 Corinthians 13:14 May the grace of the Lord Jesus Christ, the love of God, and the fellowship of the Holy Spirit be with you all.

1 John 5:7-8 So we have these three witnesses — the Spirit, the water, and the blood—and all three agree.

REFLECTION

Reading these verses always reminds me that — while each person of the Trinity has His own role to play in God's relationship with each of us and the world — *God remains One.*

    God as three-in-one is beyond our comprehension, but it is instructive to consider that through the Trinity, **harmony, relationship and community** lie at the heart of creation and form the foundation of the universe.

    What does that mean for public servants?

    Perhaps, as God's Trinitarian Being is one of **harmony, relationship and community**, so our role calls us to work for harmony and peace, and to act as *agents of "we, the people."*

    Christian public servants are called to find ways to ease the tensions caused by differing values. We are called to find ways to bridge divides. We are called to find ways to turn swords into plowshares, and to help people talk *with* (rather than past) each other.

    Contemplating the Trinity and its meaning is a lifetime's vocation, but as *Christian* public servants, its example of **harmony, relationship and community** can be very instructive in our professional and personal lives.

PRAYER

Lord God, I pray for discernment, through the example of Three-In-One, to finding the path of **harmony, relationship and community** in all aspects of my life — including in my workplace and with those I serve from that workplace. Grant me the wisdom to find the path, and the courage to walk upon it. May I walk hand-in-hand with coworkers and citizens — all coworkers and citizens — to achieve **harmony, relationship and community** that will glorify You. It is in Your Son's name, that I pray. Amen

—Allen Stout

Week 44, Day 3

ALL THE MOTIVATION

READING

1 *Thessalonians 5:16-18* Always be joyful. Never stop praying. Be thankful in all circumstances, for this is God's will for you who belong to Christ Jesus.

REFLECTION

Motivational speakers are everywhere. We so often turn to them — their quotes, stories, and illustrations — not only to inspire our teammates and volunteers, but ourselves as well. But in this short passage, we're given three concise steps: (1) always be joyful, (2) never stop praying, and (3) be thankful in everything.

The recipe for our success in public service is what's given to us in His word. So as *Christian* public servants, why should we look anywhere else? He is **all the motivation** we need!

PRAYER

Lord, help me to be conscious of my attitude each and every day. Help me to maintain a joyful and prayerful spirit throughout the workday. Let me be thankful in the ups and the downs at work so that I may be a light unto others. In Your name, I pray. Amen.
— Christi Brown

Week 44, Day 4

ON TROUBLED SEAS

READING

Matthew 8:23-27 Then Jesus got into the boat and started across the lake with his disciples. Suddenly, a fierce storm struck the lake, with waves breaking into the boat. But Jesus was sleeping. The disciples went and woke him up, shouting, "Lord, save us! We're going to drown!" Jesus responded, "Why are you afraid? You have so little faith!" Then he got up and rebuked the wind and waves, and suddenly there was a great calm. The disciples were amazed. "Who is this man?" they asked. "Even the winds and waves obey him!"

REFLECTION

Working in the public and nonprofit sectors can feel like being **on troubled seas** with waves and storms battering your boat. In the midst of changing policies, political agendas, and a multitude of other crisis, one wonders how organizations function effectively. The reality of sinful human nature is never clearer than when watching two leading figures battle in a public forum or boardroom. Debate is healthy, but "politics" is simply depressing to watch.

How many times have you thought the "ship" you are on is sinking? How often have you felt you need another job because you believe something different has to be better?

Even worse, are you just willing to sink into despair like so many around you?

As *Christian* public servants, our first response to difficult situations should be neither complete despair nor to flee as quickly as possible. We must remember that Jesus is with us in these difficult situations. While things look tough and the storms look devastating, we must first go to our Lord and cry out to Him. He is in *the struggles we face* every day. He may appear to be asleep, but that's only because we lack faith. He is always ready to embrace us and make the struggles we face *a grace-filled moment* to walk with him more closely.

I know things can be bad. But before you leave the ship, first fix your eyes on Christ. Ask Him what He desires. Perhaps you are to stay and ride out the storm. Maybe you're supposed to be the solution to your organization's problems. If it is God's will that you move on, it's better to do so as Peter did with his eyes fixed on the Lord keeping him from sinking into the sea.

Remember, you have this promise. "Even the winds and waves obey him." Christ is with you **on troubled seas.**

PRAYER

Dear God, let me always discern the vocation You give me in this life so I may more perfectly prepare myself for the next. May I serve my brothers and sisters with Christian virtue and vigor, allowing the world to see it is You working through me bringing forth Your kingdom which the human heart longs to know. All of this I ask in Your Holy name. Amen.
    —Dominick D. Hankle

Week 44, Day 5

SPEAK THE TRUTH

READING

Ephesians 5:8-9 For once you were full of darkness, but now you have light from the Lord. So live as people of light! For this light within you produces only what is good and right and true.

Job 33:3 I speak with all sincerity; I **speak the truth**.

REFLECTION

As public servants, there are times when we face uncertainty. In fact, uncertainty seems to be the norm nowadays. The economy in my country, the U.S., has not recovered sufficiently to provide funding stability. In my country's federal system, the consequences of insufficiencies seem particularly pronounced in local governance.

Last week my city government distributed preliminary instructions for the next fiscal year. Budgets are to be reduced. In conjunction with this, property assessments would again decline, providing further strain on city revenues and city services.

Does this happen in your agency? Make do with less; find a way to make reductions yet again.

As public servants, we crunch numbers and dollars to get to the "bottom line." And, "bottom lines" are important in the stewardship of the people's money — don't get me wrong.

But as *Christian* public servants, we must not only present the "bottom line." We must **speak the truth**. Appointed *Christian* public servants must not sugarcoat truthful consequences just to keep coworkers from searching for jobs elsewhere. Elected *Christian* public servants must not soft-sell the obvious for the sake of future campaigns.

No, all *Christian* public servants have a godly obligation to **speak the truth** to both coworker and citizen. Surely we are the *children of light*, and light produces every kind of truth.

With the Holy Spirit's help, **speak the truth** — regardless of how good or bad that truth be. Especially in this economy, coworkers and citizens deserve it. And, after all, that same light will also bring forth every kind of goodness and justice.

PRAYER

Heavenly Father, thank You for being the Great Provider of all my needs. As our leaders begin to plan for the next fiscal year, send forth Your Spirit upon them so that they may truly discern Your will. Help me and others to **speak**

the truth and live as *children of light* — sharing the reality of sacrificial conse-
quences, as well as the certainty that goodness and justice will come forth. In
Jesus' name, we pray. Amen.
  —Stephen Pincus

Week 45, Day 1

DO WELL

READING

Ecclesiastes 9:10a Whatever you do, **do well**. For when you go to the grave, there will be no work...

REFLECTION

We wouldn't have chosen public service as a career path if we did not hear a calling to serve others in some capacity — government, nonprofits, education, public safety, defense — you name it. Normally we are excited about that calling.

But each faces times when we are tempted to become complacent or to give less than our best effort. Political and bureaucratic frustrations can be burdensome. Balancing work and family obligations is a constant struggle. In the lives of people we serve, perhaps we only are involved with the planting of seeds and not so much with the harvesting of fruit. In the routine of daily work life, it is so easy to get lost among the trees of "what must be done" and forget about the forest of "why it's needed".

As *Christian* public servants, it is important to remember that our public missions, and the people whom we serve, deserve our very best efforts. Taxing as today may be, take comfort in God's word and pride in your performance.

As this work week begins, everything that you do — **do well**!

PRAYER

Dear Lord, give me strength and patience to withstand life's trials and put forth my very best effort in work and everything I do. In Your name, I pray. Amen.

—Mary Anne King

Week 45, Day 2

I AM COMFORTABLE

READING

2 Corinthians 5:17 This means that anyone who belongs to Christ has become a new person. The old life is gone; a new life has begun!

REFLECTION

I do not like change, even if it is for my benefit. For instance, my favorite work-out shirt is black with a big "LORD'S GYM" printed across the top in gold lettering. Pictured below is a cross with Jesus and, under it, the slogan "no pain, no gain."

I *loved* that shirt! But my wife did not share my obsession. See, the shirt had turned dirty grey, the gold was now mustard brown, the stencil was cracking and missing pieces, and there were holes in different places on the shirt. She bought me a brand spanking new identical one; the right size and everything. She said "give me the old one so I can throw it away." She immediately saw my reluctance to comply. Even though I had a new and better shirt, I still wanted to remain where **I am comfortable** — in that old ragged shirt.

Ever been there?

There are times at work when I want things unchanged. I want to remain where **I am comfortable**. Like when leadership wants to re-organize, or integrate some new technology or program. I know that change will benefit me, but I still want to remain where **I am comfortable**.

Sound familiar?

That is *not* where the *LORD* wants His servants to remain, even in our workplace. He is in the business of getting rid of the old (the comfortable and ragged) and creating new amazing possibilities. He is comfortable changing us, changing our relationships, our work habits, our perspectives and goals. Then He gives us the power of His Holy Spirit to make us comfortable in the midst of it all.

So as a *Christian* public servant, I am leaning to trust when He tells me to get rid of the old and the ragged, because I know something new and amazing is headed my way. At work and elsewhere, **I am comfortable** with *that*!

How about you?

PRAYER

Father, may I rest comfortably in Your sovereign hand, and may I glorify You in my life, my family and at my job. In Your Son's name, I pray. Amen.

—Bill Dudley

Week 45, Day 3

APPETITES OF THIS WORLD

READING

John 4:31-34 Meanwhile, the disciples were urging Jesus, "Rabbi, eat something." But Jesus replied, "I have a kind of food you know nothing about." "Did someone bring him food while we were gone?" the disciples asked each other. Then Jesus explained: "My nourishment comes from doing the will of God, who sent me, and from finishing his work.

REFLECTION

As incredible as it may sound, I want you to consider not worrying so much about today's work schedule and project deadlines. There are weightier matters to deal with, like the work God has placed before you.

I'm not suggesting that you should forget what needs to be done today at the office, but the **appetites of this world** are meant to distract us from our mission to serve the Lord. Never satisfied, the **appetites of this world** return vigorously and ferociously. They never quit.

Today at work, take a moment to eat the *Bread from Heaven* and drink from the *Everlasting Fountain* — become sustained for the real work the Lord gives you and your coworkers.

PRAYER

Lord, help me to trust You for my daily bread and my other needs. Then, strengthen me and my coworkers to do the good work that You have laid out before us. In Your name, I pray. Amen.

—Stan Best

Week 45, Day 4

REMAIN CONTENT

READING

Philippians 4:11-12 Not that I was ever in need, for I have learned how to be content with whatever I have. I know how to live on almost nothing or with everything. I have learned the secret of living in every situation, whether it is with a full stomach or empty, with plenty or little.

REFLECTION

It is extremely easy to become envious when coworkers and peers are getting raises and promotions around you — when you are not. This can certainly lead to distance and resentment towards those who are only striving to achieve the best for themselves and their families.

You have to remember that, while this may not be your time, your Father in Heaven has not forgotten you. Though your journey may seem long, and even tiresome, it will be exactly what it needs to be in order to get you where He wants you to be.

Today, **remain content** in your current role, perform to the best of your abilities, and know that there are no limits to what you and your God can do!

PRAYER

Lord, help me to **remain content** with what I have, and also thankful for each and every blessing that You have given me. Please continue to bless me with the gift of patience to endure whatever trials and tribulations I face along this journey. I know that You have more blessings for me than I can ever imagine, and there is no limit to what I can achieve. In Your name, I pray. Amen.
—Cassandra D. McLendon

Week 45, Day 5

THE TIME I HARVEST

READING

Leviticus 19:9-10 When you harvest the crops of your land, do not harvest the grain along the edges of your fields, and do not pick up what the harvesters drop. It is the same with your grape crop—do not strip every last bunch of grapes from the vines, and do not pick up the grapes that fall to the ground. Leave them for the poor and the foreigners living among you. I am the LORD your God.

REFLECTION

You know, scripture directs us to leave some of our hard work for those in need. That's easy in some professions. Auto dealers might raffle away company cars for charity. A computer company might donate some product to an inner-city or rural school. Farmers might dedicate a portion of their harvest to homeless missions. Companies might take a portion of profit and create a private foundation.

But what happens when the harvest is more conceptual than material?

As a public servant, my job fits that description. Doesn't yours? My workday is generally dictated by the Outlook calendar, a software package, and a smart phone. Like most of you, I don't actually make or create anything in my job. And even when I do, it doesn't belong to me because it already belongs to the citizens. Like you, my harvest tends to involve only *the reaping of time* that gives concrete direction and application to others.

But as a *Christian* public servant, I can leave for the needy some of **the time I harvest**. I'll still work just as hard, and be just as productive, but I will leave open a little bit of my daily calendar so that I may better give to the needy: the phone call that comes out of the blue, the urgent cry for help from a coworker, the inquiry from a confused citizen. Who knows, a weekly portion of **the time I harvest** from my own lunch break might easily be donated to a soup kitchen.

I know I can't leave all **the time I harvest**, but if I *do not strip every last bunch of grapes from the vines,* my work vineyard will better serve Him and His people.

PRAYER

Lord, by Your plan, I am where I am. My job is ultimately established by You. Please help me to remember always that I am here to serve You and Your people. I am expected to use my gifts and talents to help others see Christ in this world — in their own personal world. Help me to carve out a small portion of **the time I harvest** for those in need, whether they are in my office or in my community. I am expected to complete my work harvest in ways that glorify You. I need Your help! In Jesus' name, I pray. Amen.

—Larry Ketcham

Week 46, Day 1

TO SAY NO

READING

Psalm 33:5(a) He loves whatever is just and good;

REFLECTION

If you're like most public servants, you will spend part of today delivering bad news.

Maybe you will need **to say no** this morning to someone requesting specific vacation dates because the selected dates don't fit into the needed schedule. Perhaps this afternoon you will have **to say no** to a subordinate you can't keep, or to an applicant you can't hire, because of funding cut-backs. This evening you may be forced **to say no** to a woman with children fleeing an abusive man — someone who just wants an already-filled space at a secure safe house rather than risk another evening of being caught at a less-secure homeless shelter.

To your face or behind your back, in all likelihood, your decision will result in you being cursed as hardhearted, unfeeling, or — worse yet — bureaucratic. You may even be called un-Christian.

Fact is, having **to say no** is more common in the public service than the luxury of saying yes. And, as a *Christian* public servant, this may be one of those days when no luxuries are afforded.

Hang on and trust Him and His promises. Weather the storm of criticism and second-guessing that comes part-in-parcel with the job. God is pleased with tough decisions when they are based on justice and made with righteousness. Doing what is just — and doing so in a righteous way — may not feel very just and right to you or the recipient of the bad news. It might be hard for anyone to understand the decision in the short-term.

But remember, He loves us when we are led by Him to behave in a just and good manner. He will be faithful — even when tough situations give us no choice but **to say no**.

PRAYER

Father, be with me today as I carry out my tasks. Help me to seek justice and to act righteously; to say yes when I can and no when I cannot. Help me to know that all things work together for Your good for those who love You and trust You — even when understanding is missing. Help me to accept criticism humbly and to show Your face through me, even when I am saying no. Above all, thank You for the gift of justice. In His name, I pray. Amen.
—Mary Manjikian

Week 46, Day 2

FIRST RULE OF MANAGEMENT

READING:

Proverbs 3:5-6 Trust in the LORD with all your heart; do not depend on your own understanding. Seek his will in all you do, and he will show you which path to take.

REFLECTION

I work in a juvenile probation office. There, it's important that the environment remains as pleasant and peaceful as possible because probation officers deal with kids that come with a lot of tragic circumstances. While directly affecting the juvenile, this baggage can also have devastating consequences on the minds and hearts of probation officers.

I have seen special supervisors who, understanding this situation, find ways to keep the stress manageable for each probation officer. They know every decision is important; every action may have long-term consequences for both worker and client-citizen. They seem to understand that decisions should never be made in a vacuum. Many quietly pray throughout the day.

From watching those around me, I have learned the **first rule of management**: *seek Christ first* and trust Him to guide your actions.

Whether or not you work in an environment like mine, it is important for all supervisors to know that decisions should never be made in a vacuum. The most effective supervisors understand this, and the best follow that **first rule of management**: they *seek Christ first*.

Your workplace situation may seem impossible. Circumstances may well be unchangeable and devastating for both those who serve and those you serve. Supervisors quietly demonstrating that **first rule of management** will set the tone for others and, in doing so, adjust the workplace atmosphere for the betterment of all.

Today at work, practice that **first rule of management**: *seek Christ first*.

PRAYER

Eternal Father, the Author of everything I imagine and the Finisher of everything I touch, I ask You to guide all supervisors today. Let each seek and acknowledge You. Give each the courage to practice Your **first rule of management**, as the workplace culture is rebuilt and repaired in such a way to glorify and please You. In Your Son's name, I pray. Amen.

 —Deyonta T. Johnson

Week 46, Day 3

LIVING WATER WON'T LET YOU DOWN

READING

John 6:27b Spend your energy seeking the eternal life that the Son of Man can give you.

John 4:10 Jesus replied, "If you only knew the gift God has for you and who you are speaking to, you would ask me, and I would give you living water."

REFLECTION

Each day you see advertisements about energy drinks. They come in a variety of names, but they all report to revive you when your tank is on empty. I've always been afraid to drink them, but I'm told that some give you a short burst of energy and wear off in an hour or so. Other brands will help for a couple of hours, but may wear off when you need them most. The fact is, none of them last a very long time. They can let you down.

Energy drinks may help your body when it's on empty, but what about your spirit? Certainly, your spirit also needs replenishing. Jesus reminds us that we should spend our energy seeking eternal life. And, when our spiritual tank is on empty, He offers *that energy drink called Living Water*. But, unlike those earthly energy drinks, **Living Water won't let you down**!

At work, you need both kinds of energy to think, speak, and act. But spiritual energy is most important when it comes to building the public service as He wants it; to serve citizens and clients as He wants you to serve them; to help coworkers in ways that truly please Him.

At work today, don't be afraid to take a big gulp of *that energy drink called Living Water*. Drink it down! There's no limit to its supply, and its Supplier guarantees that **Living Water won't let you down**!

PRAYER

Father in Heaven, give me bodily and spiritual energy to make my words and actions pleasing to You and to Your flock. Use the energy You give me to touch lives that need Your presence. When I tire, quench my thirst with living water. For it is in the awesome name of Jesus that I pray! Amen.
— Ellen C. Stamm

Week 46, Day 4

LAND OF TROUBLED HEARTS

READING

John 14:1 Don't let your hearts be troubled. Trust in God, and trust also in me.

REFLECTION

Perhaps the greatest temptation any of us face is the temptation to believe in ourselves; to believe that it is all up to us. In calmer, more reflective moments, we know this is not true. But when the funding is slow in coming, or we are faced with difficult personnel matters or any other of the myriad difficult situations that a public servant faces, it is easy to fall into *the trap of believing in ourselves*; of believing that it is all up to us.

Succumbing to this temptation leads straight to the **land of troubled hearts**. In this land, a troubled heart is an agitated heart, and an agitated heart is a confused heart. There is no way to quantify the staggering amount of *anguish* sown in this land by people with troubled hearts.

As *Christian* public servants, our God-given task is to *sow peace and justice in the world*. We can only do so when we remember in Whom we trust — when we remember that it is not up to us. As you ready for work today, know that God is involved in our work, and He is already involved in those whom we serve. If we trust in Him, we can evacuate the **land of troubled hearts**.

PRAYER

God of grace, this day help me to remember that it is not all up to me. Remind me anew that You are at work in my job, in my life and in our world. In Jesus' name, I pray. Amen.
— Tom Duley

Week 46, Day 5

WHAT MATTERS MOST

READING

Titus 2:7 In everything set them an example by doing what is good. In your teaching show integrity, seriousness.

REFLECTION

There's an old adage: *you never know who is watching, so do your best*. Certainly God is always watching, but who else is watching us at work, school, or in any other setting? We might be surprised at who is taking notes and trying to learn from us.

As a mother, it's easy for me to take for granted that I always have an audience of three impressionable small children. That is, until they repeat something I've said that doesn't sound acceptable coming from their mouths...then again, it didn't sound acceptable coming from mine, either.

I cringe at the realization that I sometimes lack integrity. Do you ever feel this way?

In those instances, I wish I had gotten over my own self and had instead been a good example through the power of Christ. It would be great if I could just remind myself, or have a friend and coworker lovingly remind me, that there are people watching and I need to remember that integrity is **what matters most**.

On the day I retire, I want to be remembered as a *Christian* public servant who exhibited integrity in every situation, no matter how small or large. And no matter who was watching.

Today at work, integrity is **what matters most**.

PRAYER

Lord, please help me remember that in every situation, whether at work or home or school, I need to be an example to those around me. Help me to remember that integrity is a direct attribute of You, and I should always try to reflect You in me. In Your name, I pray. Amen.
  —Sarah Majeske

Week 47, Day 1

BATTLE OF THE BREAK ROOM

READING

Ephesians 4:15 Instead, we will **speak the truth in love**, growing in every way more and more like Christ, who is the head of his body, the church.

REFLECTION

A couple of days ago, several coworkers were chatting in the break room. A health policy issue in my country came up and discussion gravitated to debate between two coworkers, an atheist and a Christian. It started friendly enough, but escalated to an abrasive level. The Christian was truthful about her Bible-based position, and she appeared to be winning the argument with quicker responses and better articulated ideas. But she also appeared to be somewhat of a bully, cutting off the atheist's words and almost smirking each time she felt she scored a "point".

She may have won the **battle of the break room**, but I'm not sure about the war for that atheist's soul. Her aggressive manner and condescending attitude certainly diminished being Christ-like. She drowned out any Good News about our Lord.

What if my Christian friend addressed the situation with greater humility and grace? What if I and the other Christians had intervened with love?

I guess we all fell into the stereotype of the modern-day Christian: neither silence nor outspokenness makes us appear *Christ-like*. Neither draws attention to the Truth of His love, mercy, humility, and grace.

When we *speak the truth in love*, the stereotype is broken and the Christian narrative becomes the better story. When we *speak the truth in love*, we become better witnesses of our faith.

The next time the **battle of the break room** commences, do not remain silent; do not be a bully. Whatever the truth is, speak it in love.

You never know what war will be won.

PRAYER

Lord God, let Your servant speak the truth with a humble and gracious attitude, seeking first to emulate our Savior, Jesus Christ. In the flurry of the day, strengthen Your servant to overcome the propensity to cast judgments, mock the opposition, or remain silent. Bless the conversations of Your servant this workday so that the truth may be spoken only in love. In Your holy name, I pray. Amen.

—Katherine Zasadny

Week 47, Day 2

THAT KIND OF PUBLIC SERVANT

READING

Matthew 6:1-4 Watch out! Don't do your good deeds publicly, to be admired by others, for you will lose the reward from your Father in heaven. When you give to someone in need, don't do as the hypocrites do—blowing trumpets in the synagogues and streets to call attention to their acts of charity! I tell you the truth, they have received all the reward they will ever get. But when you give to someone in need, don't let your left hand know what your right hand is doing. Give your gifts in private, and your Father, who sees everything, will reward you.

REFLECTION

It becomes synonymous in public life to always ensure that your constituents know you are doing good to help them. After all, isn't that how we're elected? We all have worked with, or have been, **that kind of public servant** who sends out a press release every time he does the smallest good deed. If not a press release, you can count on an e-mail-of-boast.

It's not about press releases or e-mails. It's not about getting seen doing the right thing. After all, a person of character should do the right thing, even when no one is looking.

Is there an opportunity for you to be *a true public servant* today?

I know I have plenty opportunities and don't always live up to what God tells me to do, as a *Christian* public servant. I think I'm too busy or the person might not appreciate what I'm doing for them. Some days I'm just tired, but that is no excuse for God's work.

Take the time today to perform *one random act of being Christ-like*, and when you perform that random act, don't tell anyone. Don't send out that press release. Don't write that e-mail. Don't tell a coworker.

God doesn't want you to be **that kind of public servant**.

He wants you to be His *Christian* public servant.

PRAYER

Mighty God, thank You for giving me the opportunity to serve You and my fellow man. I know I take this opportunity for granted. Humble me to know that it is Your work I am doing and not my own. Help me to live up to the example set by Your Son. In the Awesome and Holy name of Jesus Christ, I pray. Amen.

 —Scott Conger

Week 47, Day 3

TAP-HAMMER

READING

Mathew 5:39(b) If someone slaps you on the right cheek, offer the other cheek also.

John 2:15(a) Jesus made a whip from some ropes and chased them all out of the Temple.

REFLECTION

The workplace is perhaps the most difficult turf from which to follow and glorify God. Because of that, there are many models designed to help us be *Christian* public servants. Nowadays we hear a lot about one particular model: *servant leadership.* We are told to lead from a position of sacrifice, with an eye toward healing and love, being empathic about the desires of others. We are told to do this because this is what Christ did.

Don't get me wrong. The model of servant leadership can be useful, but one tool never remedies all problems. If we keep using a **tap-hammer** each and every time, when perhaps a *jack hammer* or a *wrench* or maybe a *crowbar* is needed — well, things can only get worse.

Far too many *Christian* public servants enter workplace engagements with only a **tap-hammer** called "servant leadership." They eagerly seek ways of compromise and turn the other cheek in all situations. Constant use of that **tap-hammer** makes so-called servant leaders ripe pickings for other practicing Christians who perhaps have a clearer understanding of the *servant role* in defending and advancing that which the Master has given them in their own work unit.

Sadly, servant leadership is often confused with *self-flagellation.* The more I passively suffer, the more my work unit humbly accepts an unchallenged outcome, the more I glorify God.

Jesus taught with a variety of tools — from the **tap-hammer** of turning the other cheek to the *jack hammer* of cleaning house at the temple. At times, His *wrench* twisted tightly and was not empathic toward others. His *crowbar* did not always seek consensus or love with those trying to usurp the turf of the church.

Yes, the workplace is perhaps the most difficult turf from which to follow Him. After all, your workplace flock is always at risk — budget reductions, potential RIFs, mission drift, the threat of external agency encroachment.

In that scheduled encounter today, what tool will you use? Compromise and empathy? Or, will you overturn tables and use whips?

Jesus used all of the above, and God was glorified with each.

Today at work, do not be afraid to use the appropriate tool that glorifies God.

PRAYER

Father God, Your Son has given guidance through a variety of teachings and examples. Let me choose wisely and appropriately what tools to use in defending and advancing my agency, my coworkers, and those I am called to serve. In Jesus' name, I pray. Amen.

—James D. Slack

Week 47, Day 4

CANNOT DO THIS ALONE

READING

Exodus 18:17-18 "This is not good!" Moses' father-in-law exclaimed. "You're going to wear yourself out—and the people, too. This job is too heavy a burden for you to handle all by yourself.

REFLECTION

We **cannot do this alone**. It is only arrogance and pride that tells us we can. Others have been called to serve as well, and we must rely on their gifts to complete the mission. Does that mean that they will do it exactly as you want? Probably not. They will do it as they deem best, and that is exactly what your agency needs.

The Body of Christ is made of different parts for a reason: diversity in gifts ensures all needs are met. If we try to do everything ourselves, we will not "only wear ourselves out," but we will prevent the Body working well together.

As you go to work today, remember you **cannot do this alone**.

PRAYER

Lord, thank You for those at work with whom You have surrounded me. They help me in so many ways, including seeing that this is not all about me. It is a wonderful thing to see others openly serve with a servant's heart. In Your name, I pray. Amen.

—Stan Best

Week 47, Day 5

FAR GREATER PURPOSE

READING

Luke 10:20 But don't rejoice because evil spirits obey you; rejoice because your names are registered in heaven.

REFLECTION

I once got a very high award during my military career. The temptation was to believe that it was all about me. While it would have been easy to "wallow in my greatness," I knew the medal was about the accomplishments of the men and women who worked with me. They really deserved that award.

But that medal had a **far greater purpose** in that it was the result of the *change that Jesus brought in my life* — giving me the work ethic, the leadership abilities, and the wisdom to apply His principles of success. And yet, I know that there is *a greater award in my future*, and that is where I need to keep my focus.

Jesus reminded his followers of that very principle. They were rejoicing in the success of their work of healing and casting out devils — by the power that was given them through Jesus. He reminded them it was not about what they were able to do, it was about *what they were given*; the award of eternal life. He reminded them that His was a **far greater purpose** for sending them out and giving them power: it was to bring the kingdom of heaven to others so they might also receive *the award of eternal life*.

In our jobs and ministry as *Christian* public servants, it is easy to fix our sights on awards and commendations — and don't get me wrong, awards and commendations are not evil. They are an honorable encouragement, one that the Lord himself promises to those who honor Him.

Yet remember, our work has a **far greater purpose** than getting recognition. It is about showing Jesus to the world, through our daily words and actions as *Christian* public servants, so that others may receive that *award of eternal life*.

PRAYER

Lord Jesus, thank You for the work You did that resulted in allowing me to receive the gracious award of heaven as my eternal home. Lord Jesus, empower me to be an agent of hope to others in my workplace so they may also receive that same award. It is in Your name that I pray. Amen.
    —Bill Dudley

Week 48, Day 1

SALT THAT SEASONS OUR WORKPLACE

READING

Matthew 5:13a You are the salt of the earth.

REFLECTION

I watched in disbelief as Nurse Cathy was berated by a physician for simply starting an IV in the only place that she could, in the inner elbow. (I am told by many medical clinicians that this is not the most preferable site for an IV.) After investigating the arm for what seemed like forever, Nurse Cathy decided that this was the most effective site.

I could not help but wonder why Cathy did not respond to that physician. Why didn't she explain her actions? Why didn't anyone else come to her defense? What kind of team was this? After all, everyone knew that this particular physician was a handful. Moreover, all who were present were aware of the fact that Nurse Cathy made the right decision and that the physician was out of order. How could it be that someone who did not deserve to be treated so shamefully could simply smile and say "I have to do what is best for the patient." There was never an unkind word about the physician who acted so ungracefully.

My curiosity about her peaceful response to an angry physician prompted me to question what it was about her that was different. *What I did not realize at the time was that God was using Nurse Cathy to draw me closer to Him.*

As weeks passed by, I found myself clinging to Nurse Cathy. I quietly observed her as she interacted with patients, coworkers, physicians and hospital administrators. I noticed that Cathy consistently exhibited a *calming joy* that made everyone want to be around her. I finally asked Cathy the reason for the joy that she had. She responded with words that would change my life. "Connie, *Jesus Christ is the reason for the joy that I have.*"

Over the next few months, Nurse Cathy and I spent time together talking about Jesus Christ and His transforming power. Approximately 6 months later, I gave my life to Christ. *My life has not been the same since.*

When I look back over the initial incident that transpired between Nurse Cathy and that physician, I realize that *ministry is not just for the pulpit.* As workplace ministers we have a unique opportunity to show the love of Christ in our actions and words. In fact, it is through *our Christ-like actions* that we can become that **salt that seasons our workplace**.

PRAYER

Heavenly Father, please help me to be the salt that adds the season of righteousness to my workplace. Let my light so shine that others will see my good work and glorify You. Allow me to draw those who don't know You through my actions. Father, I thank You for allowing me to minister daily to my coworkers, clients and citizens. Help me to continually be strengthened for every good work. In Jesus' name, I pray. Amen.

—Consuella S. Tynes

Week 48, Day 2

SPEAK AND ACT ACCORDINGLY

READING

Matthew 7:12 Do to others whatever you would like them to do to you. This is the essence of all that is taught in the law and the prophets.

REFLECTION

The Golden Rule is a familiar verse to Christians. It is the "Gold Standard" for fairness and, as such, it is a mandate on how to treat others. Yet we know it is often difficult to apply this simple verse in the rush of daily life: the guy who wants to cut in front of you in the long line of cars waiting patiently in the narrowed lane on the freeway; that woman who lets her Basset Hound soil your front lawn every morning; the nightly Acid-Rock concert sponsored by "those kids" in the apartment next to yours. Man, it's enough to make you "wanna Shout!" along with the Isley Brothers!

The same is true at work.

Serving the public presents challenges that are as diverse as people are varied. And, as if you didn't know, not all citizens are happy campers when it comes to the government! Some do not realize that equity and fairness require regulations to be applied in the same way for each case. They think, it's fine to have rules that keep other people in order and to maintain order for everyone else — but those rules should not apply to "me" in "my situation".

They may become angry.

Jesus gave us a simple rule for interacting with people who cross our paths today. His rule applies to us more than "seventy times seven" because we serve the public. We are to use this Gold Standard with all persons, not just with the "nice" ones.

At work today, think about how you would feel — and then **speak and act accordingly**.

PRAYER

Dear Lord, keep me mindful of the way I treat others. Give me strength where needed to do what I would want done to me. In Your name, I pray. Amen.

    —R. Keith Jordan

Week 48, Day 3

RIGHT KIND OF FRUITS

READING

Galatians 5:22-23 But the Holy Spirit produces this kind of fruit in our lives: love, joy, peace, patience, kindness, goodness, faithfulness, gentleness, and self-control. There is no law against these things!

REFLECTION

It's wonderful how the Holy Spirit knows the **right kind of fruits** needed in our lives to do His work! If you're like me, you arrive at work with *love, joy, peace, kindness,* and *goodness* just begging to be released. Yet you know how it goes. You want really want to splash others with the juices of these fruits, but people start looking at you as if you're crazy. Sometimes they even ask, "What are you so happy about?" Most haven't a clue as to what they're missing, and many simply aren't in the mood to find out what He is offering!

Thank God for the fruits of *patience* and *self-control* because too often you really have to guard your enthusiasm. After all, to show coworkers the *love, joy, peace, kindness,* and *goodness* of Christ takes time and strategy. So your conversations become a little careful and gauged. They're so near the fruit; it would be a shame to scare them away! And your workplace prayers become focused on the fruits of *faithfulness* and *gentleness* so that your actions do no harm to what the Holy Spirit is trying to do.

Oh, it's difficult to maintain *patience, self-control, faithfulness,* and *gentleness* when *love, joy, peace, kindness,* and *goodness* want to burst out, make you go crazy, and splash everyone! There is no law against sharing these fruits, but you don't want to lose anyone in the process.

Is the Holy Spirit sharing His fruits with you at work today? Be glad that He produces many fruits — the **right kind of fruits** — that you need to share Christ with others. So go ahead and unleash your enthusiasm, but be careful. Splash others with *love, joy, peace, kindness,* and *goodness* — guided with *faithfulness, gentleness* and, above all, *patience* and *self-control.*

Prayerfully, your coworkers will want all that He produces — the **right kind of fruits** to be *Christian* public servants!

PRAYER

Holy Spirit, thank You for all the fruits you give to me so freely. Grant me wisdom to share them with others so that they come to know the Father. Let them seek the **right kind of fruits** needed to glorify You. In Jesus' name, I pray. Amen.

    —Ellen C. Stamm

Week 48, Day 4

CHRIST-LIKE GLASSES

READING

Acts 8:1; 3(a);10:34-35 Saul was one of the witnesses, and he agreed completely with the killing of Stephen... . But Saul was going everywhere to destroy the church... . Then Peter replied, "I see very clearly that God shows no favoritism. In every nation he accepts those who fear him and do what is right.

REFLECTION

It was *one of those moments*. You know — when God, in His own fatherly way, reminds you of an essential truth that is pivotal in moving you to the next level in your walk. It was a Friday, and He certainly gave me *one of those moments*!

I try to set aside time each morning for God before I begin my workday. My routine always includes reading the e-mail devotional, *The Christian Public Servant*.

On that Friday, the devotional did more than just set the tone of my day. It changed me. The author talked of the need to forgive people. Yet I got confused because there were terms like "cell" and "prison." I just couldn't figure it out until I got to the bottom of the devotional. The author was not only someone in prison, but also someone on *death row*. I mean *someone on death row*! I thought, "How could someone like him be allowed to write a devotional for someone like me?"

But God immediately reminded me that He could use *anyone*. My thoughts ran to Saul, a self-proclaimed enemy of Christ who watched approvingly as Stephen was stoned to death for his faith. Christ still pursued Paul with a passion. God also reminded me of Peter as he learned that our Father loves everyone. Peter learned that spiritual pride is something we cannot allow the enemy to use to prevent us from seeing the work God is doing!

For that brief moment, I let my own spiritual pride get in the way of seeing this death row author for what he is today. I didn't know him when he arrived at death row back in 1993. I only know this man today. I confess, I have corresponded with him several times, and what I see is a human. A man who struggles like all followers of Christ — *walking Christ-like in a world broken* and filled with sin. But I also know, through his words, that someone saw past his brokenness. Someone saw a human being whom God wanted to bring out of darkness and into the light.

Today and every day, I say a prayer for those who work to bring Christ's love to the broken. I also say a prayer for this death row author and the work God has called him to do in his place of work for as long as God allows him to do it. God uses the words and the life of a man on death row to teach someone like me the importance of seeing people through **Christ-like glasses**.

As this workday begins, may God give all of *us one of those moments*. May He remind us to see people through **Christ-like glasses**.

PRAYER

God, thank You for those who accept Your call to radically change their own lives so You may use them to bring the Light and Life to others in a broken world. Help us to see people through **Christ-like glasses**. Provide us with Your wisdom and grace to share Your love with those the world calls unlovable. In Your Son's name, I pray. Amen.
— Jenny Sue Flannagan

Week 48, Day 5

NOW REPRESENT JESUS

READING

Colossians 3:17 And whatever you do or say, do it as a representative of the Lord Jesus, giving thanks through him to God the Father.

REFLECTION

Every day I wake up, I ask the Lord to give me *His wisdom and strength* to walk in love and mercy with others — even when it hurts.

Why do I pray that prayer? Because I no longer represent me - Mr. Jimmy Davis, Jr.

No. I no longer represent me. I have not for some time. I **now represent Jesus**.

And if I **now represent Jesus**, I must have *His wisdom and strength*. I need these especially when I represent Him to the ones around me who can be so difficult to forgive and love. I need *His wisdom and strength* especially when I represent Him to the old me: the one I find hardest to forgive and love. The one who tries to show up again every now and then.

No! I no longer represent Mr. Jimmy Davis, Jr. I **now represent Jesus**.

Who do you represent?

Today at your work, forget your name tag; forget that uniform that you may wear. Forget the brand of that car you drove to work. Forget your status or job title — whether it be worker, or officer or boss. Forget you are a Mr. or Mrs. or even a Dr.

Forget all that. Today, do not represent you.

In or out of your office, regardless of who you talk to or the problems you face, use *His wisdom and strength* to represent Him the same way He represents you — with His love and mercy.

Even before work starts today, say to yourself — commit to God — I **now represent Jesus**.

PRAYER

Father, in the name of Jesus, I pray. Give me Your grace so I can go anywhere, or go nowhere, and represent You so someone can see Jesus through my words and actions. Amen.

—Jimmy Davis, Jr.

Week 49, Day 1

NOT TO LOSE SIGHT OF HIS YOKE

READING

Matthew 11:28-30 Then Jesus said, "Come to me, all of you who are weary and carry heavy burdens, and I will give you rest. Take my yoke upon you. Let me teach you, because I am humble and gentle at heart, and you will find rest for your souls. For my yoke is easy to bear, and the burden I give you is light."

REFLECTION

Well, it's another Monday morning. Shortly everyone will be filing into the workplace. In my office, some coworkers will look in shock at the piles on their desks, as if the paperwork had given multiple births over the weekend, and instantly they will become weary. The week is only beginning, and yet some will act as if all hope is lost. Me? The last thing I do each night is to put away all my paperwork so I am not easily shocked when I first walk in the next morning.

It's true; the stress levels can get a bit much around here. While it's easy for me to join the hopeless and weary each morning, I try my best to remember where my strength comes from and Who can give me rest. I try **not to lose sight of His yoke** in the anxiety of the workday.

Eliminate that which you can, rest in your faith in the Lord, and Monday mornings tend to go a lot smoother. Today at work, try **not to lose sight of His yoke**.

PRAYER

God, help me to find restoration and rest in You. Help me not to allow workday anxieties to drain me and find me lost from Your yoke. In Your Son's name, I pray. Amen.

　　　—Malcolm Jones

Week 49, Day 2

PLAY MOSES

READING

Exodus 39:43 Then Moses inspected all their work. When he found it had been done just as the LORD had commanded him, he blessed them.

REFLECTION

It was a large project, with many small and intricate tasks along with a lot of heavy lifting. The entire "staff" was involved in one way or another. No task was more important than another task. No worker more important than other workers.

And when completed to the glory of God, Moses blessed all of them! Now, how amazing was that?

I wonder how Moses blessed them. Certainly with prayer. But did he take them out for lunch? Did he bring in donuts the next day? Did he give them a pat on the back? What about a simple but heartfelt *thank you*?

How amazing would it be *now*, for any type of leader, to **play Moses**? To pray about a project, to conduct the project for the glory of God, and then bless everyone who helped complete the project — planners, engineers, project managers, associates, laborers, secretaries, custodians, parking attendants, security — all had something to do with the project and its success.

Hey, you can **play Moses**!

You don't have to be an executive in the organization. You can pray about the jobs others are doing around you; pray that everyone in your agency performs for the glory of God, and just be thankful for work finished. You don't even have to wait for some spectacular project, like a civic Tabernacle, to be designed and completed. All daily activities, small and large, are important if lifted in prayer and conceived and accomplished in ways pleasing to God.

You don't even need to invest in lunch or donuts to **play Moses**. A private prayer, a heartfelt "thank you," and a pat on the back — all go a long way! Today at work, **play Moses**!

PRAYER

Lord, please help me to be thankful for the jobs others around me are doing. Let me encourage someone today for no reason other than because I want to be a blessing to others as You are to me. Give me a grateful heart at all times. In Jesus' name, Amen.

—Sarah Majeske

Week 49, Day 3

KNOWS AND PLANS

READING

Jeremiah 1:5a I knew you before I formed you in your mother's womb.

Jeremiah 29:11 "For I know the plans I have for you," says the LORD. "They are plans for good and not for disaster, to give you a future and a hope."

REFLECTION

I have been struggling with fear lately, especially having completed my MPA degree. Where will I be in a month from now? In a year from now? Will I find the right job? Will I have a job? Will I be able to acquire the things we all dream about? Will I acquire that which I need?

It's so easy to get caught up in trying to be materially satisfied. It's even easier to foster fear when you're not sure you'll have the basics you need. I have to remember that it's not about what I want *for* me, but it's about what God wants *from* me. After all, *He knows me best*!

You may be struggling with an issue in your workplace. Will you get that promotion? Will you get that raise? Is your job meaningful enough? Will you even have a job a year from now?

You and I need to take assurance that God has both of us exactly where He wants us today so we can do exactly what He has called us to do today. And with diligence and prayer, He will guide both of us to where He needs us tomorrow.

As you work today, and as I search for a place to work today, we both need to take comfort in the fact that our Lord **knows and plans** for you and He **knows and plans** for me.

Sure, we're both struggling with fear. But He **knows and plans**. And that gives us a hope and ensures us a future.

And guess what? Today I got a phone call. I got the job He wanted me to have!!!! All that worrying... all that fear...truly, He **knows and plans**!!

PRAYER

Heavenly Father, the weight of the world is so easy to take on but hard to carry. Thank You for being my burden bearer. Thank You for setting me apart. Thank You for Your ways not being my ways, but much higher ways, O Lord. Thank You for not allowing my current circumstance to hinder my divine destiny. Thank You for turning today into tomorrow!!!! I will be who You have called me to be — today and tomorrow! In You, I have a future and a hope. In Jesus' name, I pray. Amen.

—Crystal Featherston

Week 49, Day 4

WALK THE WALK

READING

Matthew 28:18-19a Jesus came and told his disciples, "I have been given all authority in heaven and on earth. Therefore, go and make disciples of all the nations..."

REFLECTION

Christ has given us the *Great Commission* to make disciples of all nations. Yet, as *Christian* public servants, we are constrained by laws and constitutions of the countries in which we live and work. In some nations, Christianity is outlawed and Christians are viewed as enemies-of-the-state. Even in democratic nations, the secularist culture typically tries to place informal restrictions on proselytizing.

So, how do we **walk the walk**? How do we follow the Great Commission when there is a gap between His word with man's law? Are we to withhold our evangelizing, a command from God, because of earthly documents and customs?

No one can stop us from loving God with all our hearts, souls, minds and strength. Yet remember: the power of the words, of the Word, and of the Holy Spirit is enough. If we use the trappings of power and prestige from our public offices, or take abusive advantage of a captive audience in a break room, we are either doing so because we doubt that power, or for our own egos. Besides, regardless of national setting and law — *our example* remains a powerful evangelizing force. Those we meet will come to know that we are Christians, and the way we conduct ourselves will bring either glory or shame to the name of our Lord.

So we really don't need words to **walk the walk**. St. Francis once said that we should *pray constantly* and use words *only when necessary.* Despite laws and customs — despite where we are called to live and serve — we can preach the *reality of Christ* by loving our neighbors, caring for those in need, being good stewards of human, material and financial resources — and by maintaining high moral standards.

As *Christian* public servants, we can **walk the walk** every day at work yet *talk the talk* only when necessary.

And today is a great day to **walk the walk**!

PRAYER

Lord, thank You for showing me how to live a godly life, and how to preach the Gospel. I pray for the strength to be a good disciple at work today, and for the humility to know that all authority in heaven and on earth has been given to You, and that it is Your power on which I depend. In Your name, I pray. Amen.

    —Allen Stout

Week 49, Day 5

HEROES OF FAITH

READING

1 Corinthians 13:7 Love never gives up, never loses faith, is always hopeful, and endures through every circumstance.

Romans 8:18 Yet what we suffer now is nothing compared to the glory he will reveal to us later.

REFLECTION

It remains easy to serve God when we have plenty — a job, a career, more than enough to eat, family who loves us, a warm bed to greet us at the end of the work day, and a healthy body that allows us to enjoy so many of the blessings of life.

But what if one of those blessings is stripped away? What is our reaction to God when pain of a disease, or perhaps anxiety over a pregnant teenage daughter, torments us night and day? Or, when the healing or remedy just does not come as we pray?

I have walked along side some **heroes of faith** that bear pain, often in silence, with such amazing strength of purpose. They walk never giving up, keeping faith in the midst of personal terror, hopeful for the answers, and enduring the suffering knowing that only when He has finished His perfect purpose will His glory be revealed.

What amazes me is the love these **heroes of faith** so willingly give in the midst of the silent pain they bear. Truly they are an encouragement to others.

At work today, look around. There are **heroes of faith** near you — coworkers and the people you serve — giving lovingly and faithfully in the midst of the silent pain they bear.

How can you show them *your* love today?

PRAYER

Abba Father, provide strength to me through Your Spirit, encourage me through Your promises, empower me through Your word, and let me make an eternal impact on each immortal soul that You give me the divine opportunity to engage. At work today, may You be glorified in the way I love others. In Your Son's name, I pray. Amen.

—Bill Dudley

Week 50, Day 1

ADVISERS BRING SUCCESS

READING

Proverbs 11:14 Without wise leadership, a nation falls; there is safety in having many advisers.

Proverbs 15:22 Plans go wrong for lack of advice; many **advisers bring success**.

REFLECTION

I've been working on a grant application for funding for a river corridor. The project has life safety issues with flooding concerns, but it would also provide incredible trails and recreation opportunities. Economic factors are also pertinent.

Sadly, this will be the third attempt. Previous applications scored well, but not quite what was necessary to bring home an award letter. The phrase, "third time's a charm" comes to mind, but that sort of optimism is out of place.

We need to compile a winning application, and past efforts relied on one project feature while apparently underplaying other concerns. So we are gathering a team of various parties interested in the project, and we are letting the strongest components lead. We want to present a broader overview that can only come from the help of diverse and wide-ranging community support. We hope this application will be successful.

Do you resist working in teams? I used to think a team with differing interests would add difficulty to the process. I now fully recognize that a team with a broad base of interests is solid and strong, bringing incredible insights.

As a *Christian* public servant, I should have recognized the importance of teamwork. After all, as scripture states, many **advisers bring success** to workplace plans.

PRAYER

Lord, You created me to live and work in community. It is most often my pride and arrogance that leads me to strike out on my own. I convince myself that I can do things alone. God, You have so many ways to get my attention and, unfortunately, repeated failure is one of Your more effective ways at forcing me to stop what I am doing and rethink! Help me, Lord, to repent, turn away from pride, and work in community. In Your Son's name, I pray. Amen.
—Larry Ketcham

Week 50, Day 2

PRIORITIZE RATHER THAN BALANCE

READING

Ecclesiastes 3:1, 11b For everything there is a season, a time for every activity under heaven.... . Yet God has made everything beautiful for its own time.

REFLECTION

Even before I read scripture, my dad taught me about seasons. He had many. He served two years, under-aged, in the U.S. Navy during World War II. He then married and started a family while laboring 16 hours a day for 20 years, 400 feet down in a sandstone quarry. He then became a foreman in a sandstone mill, while driving a bus for Oberlin College. Meanwhile, he earned his high school diploma and was elected to the village council. Dad had *many* seasons.

And, as scripture promises, everything was beautiful *in its own time*. With Sunday's off, we went to church. We played catch on Saturdays and went camping for his annual one-week vacation. He always had time to share lunch with me at the mill where he worked, and he never missed my school activities. But he *never felt guilty* about working so hard to provide for his family.

In today's world, my dad wouldn't fit in. Now, we are made to feel guilty about focusing on work. Talk-show pop psychologists say that, like our diets, work & play must be "balanced."

But life isn't like that, is it? Granted, there're always important things to do and relationships to nurture, but balancing everything requires the art of juggling. Problem is, people go crazy trying to juggle everything and end up mediocre on all fronts. And when we juggle, we worry so much about dropping things that we don't enjoy the many seasons of work, family, and church.

The world says "juggle — go on, you can balance and it's good for you!" But scripture calls us to engage in *seasons — many seasons*. There are seasons when we *have* to build. Hard work is necessary — civilization doesn't exist without it — and public service is the most honorable kind of hard work. There are also seasons to embrace loved-ones, and seasons when we are born, healed from sickness, and die. Thinking in terms of *seasons,* rather than balance and juggling, helps *prioritize* what is needed each day. All endeavors are valuable but, once prioritized, they may not be of equal value in any given season.

So you have my dad's permission — and the calling of scripture — to **prioritize rather than balance**. Burn the midnight oil, without guilt or apology, to complete the particular work project "season". Remember: it's dangerous to juggle other things while burning that oil!

Remember also: as my dad and I discovered, as scripture promises, He will make everything beautiful *in its own time*. **Prioritize rather than balance**, and you will enjoy, without mediocrity, the many seasons of work, family and church. You won't miss your daughter's soccer game, and you won't have to juggle work while watching the game from your lawn chair!

PRAYER

Father God, let me truly be blessed in each of Your seasons throughout my life. With each day, Your seasons can change so quickly. Let me not balance, but give me strength to focus on each season that I am in. For Your glory, I do not want to be mediocre in any season for they all belong to You. Today at work, let me not juggle, but have faith that You will make everything beautiful *in its time*. Amen.
 —James D. Slack

Week 50, Day 3

FOR HIS SAKE, NOT YOURS

READING

Matthew 5:16 In the same way, let your good deeds shine out for all to see, so that everyone will praise your heavenly Father.

REFLECTION

As a public servant, you have a platform that many can see. What better way to spread the gospel of Jesus Christ!

Oh, I realize that laws, customs and constitutions may restrict proselytizing. But regardless of where you live and work in this world, today is a great workday to glorify His name!

But wait a minute! My supervisor won't let me place a bible on my desk, let alone have a cross or fish symbol on it. I can't even talk about scripture in our break room. How can I shine my light and glorify His name in my workplace?

The answer is both simple and difficult. You must be kind, helpful, just, and considerate **for His sake, not yours**. Use His word to direct your path when you have to make an important decision. When there is turmoil at work, call on Him to give you peace and understanding so that you can better communicate with your coworkers to solve those problems. Do all this each workday **for His sake, not yours**, and others will "catch on" and see a light shining through you that truly glorifies our Lord.

Actions **for His sake, not yours**, do indeed speak louder than words. Therefore, live your life in a way that is worthy of Him. Live your professional life on the principles and commandments of His word.

Whether you are a manager or custodian, a fire-fighter or teacher, a secretary or a mayor - you have been placed in public service **for His sake, not yours**. Without even saying a word, God will let others see His good through you!

Today at work, let your light so shine — **for His sake, not yours**.

PRAYER

Lord, today at work, use me as Your vessel to show others the good work that can be done only if they follow You. Let my light shine so brightly that others will see You in me and glorify Your name. It is in Your name, that I pray. Amen.
—Cassandra D. McLendon

Week 50, Day 4

PERSONALIZE AND ENGAGE

READING

Philippians 3:17 Dear brothers and sisters, pattern your lives after mine, and learn from those who follow our example.

REFLECTION

A Christian life is more than righteous thoughts about the way life and living should be; there is biblical life/morality that we must **personalize and engage**. Biblical exemplars become models for how a Christian life can be lived.

As I seek to influence my workplace to the glory of God, I need to ask: what does Christian discipline look like in my setting? What does it look like in your setting? How do the preparative disciplines take form and *daily expressions* become a part of our own individual character?

Paul and other influential Christians are exemplars on whom we can depend for answers. Our task is to **personalize and engage** them in our profession and in our daily work-life.

God has uniquely equipped each of us. With God's faithful partnering in the process, the burden is ours to discover and deliver — to **personalize and engage**.

PRAYER

Father, through me, may others see Your faithful love lived-out in my devotion to You and expressed in genuine concern for them. Infuse Your character *in* me as I exercise Your spiritual life *for* me. May the examples of godly people in biblical stories and historic Christian exemplars touch my soul as life-living models, with whom I may join in authenticity to glorify You. In Your Son's name, I pray. Amen.
—Chris Summers

NOTHING COMPARED

READING

Isaiah 43:18 But forget all that — it is **nothing compared** to what I am going to do.

REFLECTION

I have had professional success in a secular world. I made money. I had the house, the car, the technology, and all else "successful" people care to have. But it was not enough.

I had a hole. I was empty. Life was not pleasurable. I was missing something. God knew all that before I did.

And then I met Him.

He gave me hope. He gave me strength. He taught me that all of those "things" meant nothing without Him. I guess you could say, He gave me *a new work-calling*.

So I did as the verse commands.....I forgot *all of that* and began to live a life more honoring of Him: in my new work, in my new ministry, in my new me.

His word does not lie. What happened before (in my old line of work) is **nothing compared** to what has happened since I began to follow Him.

As this workweek grinds down, remember: whatever you think you have — that may be wonderful and fine. But it is **nothing compared** to what He will do if you simply follow Him.

PRAYER

Lord, help me to continue Your work. Help me to remember that the past is **nothing compared** to what You are going to do in me. Help me to see You and have faith in where You call me to go. In Jesus' name, I pray. Amen.

    —Tajuan McCarty

Week 51, Day 1

BLIZZARD IN OUR WORKPLACE

READING

Isaiah 1:18 "Come now, let's settle this," says the LORD. "Though your sins are like scarlet, I will make them as white as snow. Though they are red like crimson, I will make them as white as wool."

Psalms 51:7 Purify me from my sins, and I will be clean; wash me, and I will be whiter than snow.

REFLECTION

Where I live, we recently experienced our first snow fall of the season. Getting to work was a little treacherous, but the weather also served notice of a potentially depressing time of the year. You see, around the Great Lakes, winter is a season of continual *gray and cloudiness.*

But with the first snow fall, I am reminded of how my God sees me. White, *white as snow*! Not the red crimson sin that put my Savior on the cross; not the evil wickedness that deserves a black desolate hell. No, my God sees me as *clean*, pure and white — just like each unique snowflake. And have you ever had the opportunity to see the snow fall at night? There is nothing gray about it! It *glistens* as a perfect diamond.

That's what God wants to do through you and through me, *glisten in this dark world.* Not just shine a little light, like the Sunday school song; no, not just a little flicker but a bold, brilliant, diamond that *glistens in this dark world.*

Don't know about you, but I think it's time for a **blizzard in our workplace.** Regardless of the season where you live, it's the perfect time for Christians to join together & show this world what it means to be children of the King — ones who have been washed *whiter than snow*. Children of the King — ones who actually *glisten in this dark world*!

At work, let us rid this day of the gray and cloudiness. Let today be the day when you stop judging & start loving like Jesus loves, stop holding grudges & start forgiving like our Father forgives, and stop denying passageway & start encouraging others like the Holy Spirit encourages you. Today at work, let our God move us in mighty ways with eternal dividends. Today at work, let us truly *glisten in this dark world*! Let you and me be the first snowflake diamonds that start a **blizzard in our workplace**.

PRAYER

Dear God, thank You for forgiving me of my sin that is as filthy rags, and for using Jesus' blood to wash me as white as snow. Please use me in my workplace and in this world to draw people closer to You. Let me love like You love, forgive like You do, and encourage those who You bring into my path today. In Jesus' name, I pray.

—Debra Neal

Week 51, Day 2

KNOCK FIRST

READING

Matthew 7:8b And to everyone who knocks, the door will be opened.

REFLECTION

Funny how we hesitate to bring prayer into the workplace. It's as though we think God has a limit on how small or how large a request needs to be for Him to take it seriously.

Wishing for a raise? In the middle of a rough meeting? Can't unscrew the lid from a canister or unjam the copy machine? Can't remember the name of your supervisor's third husband? We often stifle blessings and remedies when we do not **knock first** on His door for help.

God does not have a list of things you can and can't ask for. He is pleased when His children depend on Him for *everything*. It's a sign of ultimate dependence on the Only One.

So at work today, **knock first** on His door. In His time and for His plan, that door will be opened.

PRAYER

Dear God, give me courage to knock on Your door when I am in need. No matter how little or how large, let me not be ashamed or afraid to make my request known before You. In Your Son's name, I pray. Amen.
    —Joycelyn N. Biggs

Week 51, Day 3

UNEXPECTED STILLNESS

READING

Job 3:26 I have no peace, no quietness. I have no rest; only trouble comes.

REFLECTION

Leadership includes crisis management but, dear Lord, there must be a reprieve! I mean, it can't be this reactive all the time.

Budget cuts have reduced staffing until everyone is working at least a job-and-a-half. Overtime - a requirement rather than a choice. Morale is low. Everyone is — just — so — tired. The only comfort I have is the hope that my staff really sees me working as hard as they.

Does this sound familiar?

It feels absurd to suggest that anyone should take time during the workday for reflection. After all, you and I know that such precious time simply doesn't exist.

Yet, insisting that "peace" be an integral part of the workday will help you be a more focus-centered manager. Making "stillness" an integral part of the staff's day will certainly help them tackle the impossible tasks you must lay before them. Having a short mental break will make everyone better *Christian* public servants.

So today at work, find a minute of **unexpected stillness**. Take that minute for yourself, and empower each staff member to do the same. Trouble will still be there when you return, but the madness will be just a little more sane. The Lord will use that time of **unexpected stillness** to transform you into who He needs you to be for the remainder of the workday.

PRAYER

Father, show me how to be still today — just for a minute or two — to allow You to transform me into who and what You call me to be. Help me learn not to borrow trouble and to be faithful to Your word. In Your Son's name, I pray. Amen.

—Stephanie L. Bellar

Week 51, Day 4

BEFORE YOU GO TO WORK

READING

Proverbs 8:17 I love all who love me. Those who search will surely find me.

REFLECTION

I love my job. It's very rare that I wake up and think, "Man, I just don't want to face what's waiting for me at work today." So I guess I am pretty blessed.

Yet there are days when the world has beaten me down — so much so that I wake up and think, "I just want to lay here in my warm bed and sleep." On those days, my physical drowsiness wants to drag me over into spiritual drowsiness. I even feel like skipping my morning devotion.

If I give into that temptation, of skipping my morning devotion, the day is destined for disaster. So, in those early hours, even if I don't really feel like it, I know I still must seek Him. And when I do, He shows up and changes my entire attitude. He changes my entire day!

If you seek Him **before you go to work**, it sets in motion a pattern of seeking Him throughout the rest of the day. You'll seek Him to clarify your thoughts as you go into a meeting. You'll start to seek Him for wisdom when you have to apply accountability to a subordinate. You will seek Him to reveal the divine opportunities you will have during the day to share His truth with others. If you seek Him **before you go to work**, you will seek Him throughout the workday because you realize that, without Him, there is nothing but failure waiting to happen.

So regardless of how hard it is to get up in the morning, I pray you will rise and seek Him **before you go to work**. Believe me, miracles lie just around the corner!

PRAYER

Father, thank You for loving me. Thank You for always being there when I seek you. Use me this workday to proclaim Your love to others and to live Your love to others, so they will be encouraged to seek You also. In Jesus' name, I pray. Amen.

—Bill Dudley

Week 51, Day 5

KNOW IT ALL

READING

Romans 12: 3b-6a Don't think you are better than you really are. In his grace, God has given us different gifts for doing certain things well.

REFLECTION

It's Friday and, if you're like me, you're feeling a bit overwhelmed with your assignments and responsibilities. In my area of work, local government, complex accounting and finance regulations mean that no one can **know it all**. I know I can't, and I bet it's the same where you work.

When I'm feeling clearly out of my comfort zone of expertise, I ground myself in humility and recognize that God really does not expect me to **know it all.** Otherwise, I would think more highly of myself than my fellow workers who have the gifts and abilities that I may not have.

Especially on Fridays, lean on Him and your coworkers who are part of the body of Christ. If your workplace is like mine, you are blessed to serve with talented individuals whose gifts are varied, and together, you can serve effectively to accomplish the work for the good of the community.

So the next time you're feeling "out of your league," humbly rely on teammates' strengths and talents to teach you and help you. And, on a day like today, you will get in better position to tackle the challenges that are bound to arrive come Monday!

PRAYER

Dear God, on this Friday, reassure me that I do not need to **know it all**. I only need to know some of it, and trust that others know some of it, too. Only You, after all, **know it all.** Today may I lean on You and humbly seek the help of my coworkers. That way, together we can best serve the citizens in ways that bring honor and glory to You. In Jesus' name, I pray. Amen.

—Lou Lassiter

Week 52, Day 1

WHICH PATH TO TAKE

READING

Proverbs 3:5-6 Trust in the LORD with all your heart; do not depend on your own understanding. Seek his will in all you do, and he will show you which path to take.

REFLECTION

As this work-week begins, do you feel like you're walking on a tightrope or near a precipice? Not sure which way to turn? All the work that wasn't completed last week... That unfinished grant proposal... The scheduled meetings this week... That deadline just around the corner.

Good Lord, there's a *lot* to be anxious about, isn't there!

You know, trust is a rare commodity in today's society — given the breakdown of values and principles, we shouldn't be surprised. It's the same in the public service, regardless of where you work in this world. Trust is particularly taxing when so much may be at stake.

Trusting is the most difficult act, especially when we serve an *unseen* God. The awesome news, however, is He wants us to *focus on Him,* in the difficult times as well as in the good times, and trust Him unconditionally in all our paths.

As a *Christian* public servant, all you need to do is submit to Him and trust in Him.

This workweek, He *will* show you **which path to take**.

PRAYER

Thank You, Lord, for showing me **which path to take** in every facet of my life, including my work this week. Give me strength and courage to submit to You. I trust and love You with all my heart and soul. In Your name, I pray. Amen.
        —Lyse-Ann Lacourse

Week 52, Day 2

DON'T RUN WITHOUT GOD

READING

Luke 24:31 Suddenly, their eyes were opened, and they recognized him. And at that moment he disappeared!

REFLECTION

I woke up early this morning to study, but there was no electricity. Can you believe it? Not only could I not hit the books, I also had no coffee, no cell phone, and no computer. And I couldn't see anything in the dark! As they say, *you don't know what you have until it's gone.*

It's not just the loss of electricity this morning. It seems I spend my whole life rushing from one urgency to the next. I have to ask, do I lose sight of God in the darkness of my urgencies? I mean, when the electricity goes out in my life, is that the time when I really want to be blind to Him?

Just like our brothers on the road to Emmaus, we often get so caught up in the here and now that we *fail to see what God intends for us to see.* Jesus walked the road with those brothers and, just like us, they did not recognize Him. I guess they were too busy talking about the Urgency that just happened. So He stayed until they realized Who stood before them. This is the amazing thing about our God: *He is so incredibly patient!*

Today you will have urgencies that will cause you to run to work or run to your next class. You may run to the coffee machine, you may run to get that project completed, or you may run to pick up the phone. Whatever urgency that makes you run, **don't run without God**. He is the God who is standing by your side even when you ignore Him. He is the God who is with you even when you try to fix the urgencies all by yourself. He is the God who is working for you even when your electricity is not. He is the God who is the Most Patient One.

As this workday begins, **don't run without God**.

PRAYER

Lord, You remind me to remain faithful to You. But sometimes I stray, don't I. Today draw me close to You, Lord. Don't let me or my work get in Your way. Open my eyes to Your blessings, and help me to include You in every situation. In Your name, I pray. Amen.

—Stephanie van Straten

Week 52, Day 3

SPECIAL RESPONSIBILITY

READING

Titus 3:1 Remind the believers to submit to the government and its officers. They should be obedient, always ready to do what is good.

Matthew 5:9 God blesses those who work for peace, for they will be called the children of God.

REFLECTION

Recently I had to calm down a citizen who felt that one of my coworkers had been rude. It seems she drove her car through barricades and into a construction site. Simply put, she placed herself in danger, as well as others in the area. This citizen was upset at my coworker's alleged unnecessary abruptness in explaining the situation. She had phoned two other city staff members, multiplying her frustration, before she reached my voice.

I fully understood her frustrations — but likewise, I understood my coworker's good intentions about ending quickly a potentially dangerous situation. So it became one of those long phone calls, but well worth it in the end. This charged encounter turned into a pleasant conversation about what should be done the next time barricades are set.

As public authorities, we know it can be difficult dealing with some citizens — especially those who insist on driving through barricades! But as *Christian* public servants, we have this **special responsibility** to remember that they (collectively) are the rulers — even the barricade runners! We need to be obedient of them, when our authority permits, and we must always be *the doers of their good*. Scripture requires this of us and, when a fracas rises, we are called to be *the peacemakers*.

Today you, too, may have one of those long encounters with at least one of our rulers. You may have to play the peacemaker in the process. Know that, as a *Christian* public servant, you truly are a child of God and can therefore handle this **special responsibility**.

PRAYER

Dear Jesus, please help me to remain focused on doing good for my rulers and, when necessary, keeping the peace! Today may I take the time to truly listen to those I serve, using only Your wisdom in seeking remedy. In Your name, I pray. Amen.

—Larry Ketcham

Week 52, Day 4

UNFINISHED STORY

READING

Philippians 1:6 And I am certain that God, who began the good work within you, will continue his work until it is finally finished on the day when Christ Jesus returns.

REFLECTION

As a public servant, I know that the phrase "unfinished project" tends to communicate a negative message to many citizens. It's at best something potentially good, but without yet having a sure outcome. Simply put, it is an **unfinished story**.

In the public service, it's common to juggle a multitude of unfinished projects. You probably left a couple on your list at the close of business yesterday, and rest assured they are still on that list this morning! Getting each off your list requires working with colleagues, department heads, partnering agencies and, in many cases, volunteers, boards, community groups, and individual citizens. Just receiving responses to e-mails and phone calls, let alone finding that one date where everyone can meet in the same room, causes delays. Coordination is key in today's public and nonprofit sectors, but it sure does complicate the completion of projects!

And here you sit wondering if your work will prove worthwhile. Will each unfinished project finally get completed and off your list? That, of course, remains to be seen!

But as a *Christian* public servant, know that one unfinished project can remain on the list indefinitely — *YOU*. God is working on you daily — right this very moment — shaping you bit-by-bit into something He can use for His glory at your workplace.

So while unfinished projects remain on my list, I take comfort knowing I am on His list. He is working things out in me for His good. He is in charge of my **unfinished story**!

PRAYER

Dear Lord, thank You for working on me today. I surrender to You all my cares surrounding my own work. I am so grateful for Your mercy and Your favor. Bless me with Your wisdom to guide me at every step in my job and in my career. Mold me into something useful for Your kingdom. In Jesus' name, I pray. Amen.

—Courtney Christian

Week 52, Day 5

LONG FOR THE LORD —
FOR HIS SAKE, NOT MINE

READING

Proverbs 18:10 The name of the LORD is a strong fortress; the godly run to him and are safe.

Psalm 42:1 As the deer longs for streams of water, so I long for you, O God.

REFLECTION

Perhaps the toughest part of being public servants is dealing with those citizens and clients who stubbornly refused professional advice and mentorship when it could have done some good. Hence, we too often see the consequences of students who long ago rejected the help of a teacher, or the youngster who ignored a counselor's path away from destructive behavior. We witness the ramifications of a homeless man who chose drug-addiction over the mentorship once given by a social worker, police officer, or pastor. We see the results of the incarcerated who chose in earlier times to run from the guidance of many.

Yes, it's difficult being a public servant. We grow sickened watching the potential of life shatter in the face of unwillingness to seek timely remedy offered by so many at so many turns. Remedy — or a way out — is only sought when the person hits bottom.

But are you or I any different than, well, "them"? After all, do we not act the same way towards God? We know God is the source of the greatest remedies to life's problems, but it often takes our own poor choices to drive us to Him. Oh sure, we sometimes rejoice in celebration; we may occasionally even fall to our knees in gratitude. But how many more times do we ignore His mentorship and advice because we think we can get away with it? Then, and only then, we run to Him in the hope of finding a way out of *the mess of our own mistakes*.

I need to **long for the Lord — for His sake, not mine**. I need to seek His streams of remedy each day without waiting to run desperately to Him for a fix or a favor that may no longer be part of His plan. If I cannot do that, why should I be surprised when others refuse to take earthly, professional advice and mentorship when they mistakenly think they don't need it?

As I drive to work today, how I pray my soul will **long for the Lord — for His sake, not mine**. Only then might I truly be a *Christian* public servant.

PRAYER

Father God, please forgive that I come to You so often not in worship and gratitude but only because I chronically and persistently need something after I ignored Your mentorship. I know, Father, that You want to bless me beyond my imagination but please help me come to You in awe as well as in need. In Christ's name, I pray. Amen.
   —Karl Thoennes III

About the Contributors

Alexander, Deanna — Week 34, Day 2
>County Supervisor, Milwaukee, Wisconsin USA
>M.A. Candidate
>Robertson School of Government
>Regent University
>Virginia Beach, Virginia, USA

Amiel, Anne-Marie — Week 32, Day 2; Week 36, Day 3
>Risk Manager
>Columbus Consolidated Government
>Columbus, Georgia USA

Anderson, M. Evangeline — Week 41, Day 1
>Senior Access to Information & Privacy (ATIP) Advisor
>ATIP Secretariat
>Natural Resources Canada
>Ottawa, Ontario, Canada

Arbitter, Angela — Week 4, Day 2; Week 24, Day 4; Week 31, Day 1; Week 39, Day 4
>Master of Public Administration (MPA) Candidate
>Robertson School of Government
>Regent University
>Virginia Beach, Virginia USA

Bellar, Stephanie, Ph.D. — Week 3, Day 1; Week 15, Day 4; Week 22, Day 2; Week 41, Day 4; Week 51, Day 3
>Dean of the Graduate School
>University of Central Arkansas
>Conway, Arkansas USA

Best, Stan — Week 17, Day 3; Week 41, Day 3; Week 45, Day 3; Week 47, Day 4
>Past Community Lay Director
>Tidewater Emmaus Community
>Virginia Beach, Virginia USA

Biggs, Joycelyn N. — Week 30, Day 4; Week 35, Day 5; Week 51, Day 2
 Public Affairs Specialist
 Marine Corps Logistics Base Albany
 Albany, Georgia USA

Boisselle, David — Week 8, Day 2; Week 15, Day 2; Week 35, Day 4; Week 37, Day 1
 Director of Military & Veterans Affairs
 Regent University
 Virginia Beach, Virginia USA

Brandon, TaQuesha — Week 10, Day 5; Week 42, Day 2
 MPA Candidate
 Robertson School of Government
 Regent University
 Virginia Beach, Virginia USA

Brown, Christie, MPA — Week 11, Day 5; Week 26, Day 4; Week 42, Day 5; Week 44, Day 3
 University of Alabama at Birmingham Health System
 Birmingham, Alabama USA

Bryer, Thomas A., PhD. — Week 6, Day 3
 Director, Center for Public and Nonprofit Management
 School of Public Administration
 University of Central Florida
 Orlando, Florida USA

Butler, Steve — Week 23, Day 2; Week 26, Day 5; Week 38, Day 3
 U.S. Department of Justice
 Washington, DC USA
 Doctoral Candidate
 School of Communication
 Regent University
 Virginia Beach, Virginia, USA

Carlos, Louis A., LT — Week 3, Day 4
 Patrol Services Commander
 Santa Fe Police Department
 City of Santa Fe
 Santa Fe, New Mexico USA

Carr, Krystiana — Week 13, Day 1
 Human Resources Assistant
 U.S. Army ROTC Program
 Hampton University
 Hampton, Virginia USA
 MPA Candidate
 Robertson School of Government
 Regent University, Virginia Beach, Virginia USA

Christian, Courtney — Week 2, Day 3; Week 27, Day 3; Week 29, Day 1;
Week 33, Day 2; Week 35, Day 3; Week 52, Day 4
    City Administrator
    City of Leesville
    Leesville, Louisiana USA
    Master of Public Administration (MPA) Candidate
    Robertson School of Government
    Regent University
    Virginia Beach, Virginia USA

Cooney, Kevin, Ph.D. — Week 5, Day 4; Week 36, Day 2; Week 38, Day 4
    Visiting Professor
    Ritsumeikan Asia Pacific University
    Beppu, Japan

Conger, Scott — Week 47, Day 2
    City Council Member
    District 5
    City of Jackson
    Jackson, Tennessee USA

Coetzer, Thea G.D. — Week 6, Day 2; Week 12, Day 1
    Head: Disaster Management Centre
    Emergency Services Department
    City of Tshwane Metropolitan Municipality
    South Africa

Cornibe, Savanna Faith, M.A. — Week 39, Day 2
    Research Fellow
    Commonwealth Foundation
    Harrisburg, Pennsylvania USA

Crone, Loren LT — Week 18, Day 5; Week 26, Day 1; Week 29, Day 3
    Chaplain, USN
    Marine Corps Embassy Security Group
    Marine Corps Base Quantico
    Quantico, Virginia USA

Davis, Jimmy Jr. — Week 7, Day 5; Week 12, Day 5; Week 17, Day 5; Week 19,
Day 5; Week 24, Day 5; Week 25, Day 5; Week 27, Day 5; Week 31, Day 5;
Week 33, Day 5; Week 37, Day 5; Week 39, Day 5; Week 41, Day 5; Week 48,
Day 5
    Z-557 Unit N-10
    Death Row
    Holman Correctional Facility
    Atmore, Alabama USA

Denis, Suzanne — Week 5, Day 3; Week 22, Day 4
　　　Directrice de la qualité et du développement de l'expertise
　　　Centre régional de réadaptation La RessourSe
　　　Gouvernement du Québec
　　　Gatineau, Québec, Canada

Dickens, Logan — Week 9, Day 2; Week 33, Day 1
　　　MPA Candidate
　　　Robertson School of Government
　　　Regent University
　　　Virginia Beach, Virginia USA

Doster, Erika D., PA-C — Week 1, Day 2; Week 13, Day 3; Week 26, Day 2;
Week 34, Day 3
　　　Plastic Surgery
　　　Charlie Norwood Veterans Administration Medical Center
　　　Augusta, Georgia USA

Dudley, William (Bill), MPA — Week 4, Day 4 ; Week 17, Day 1; Week 21,
Day 4; Week 31, Day 3; Week 36, Day 4; Week 42, Day 3; Week 45, Day 2;
Week 47, Day 5; Week 49, Day 5; Week 51, Day 4
　　　Logistician
　　　U.S. Department of Defense
　　　Naval Base Norfolk
　　　Norfolk, Virginia USA

Duley, Tom — Week 2, Day 5; Week 6, Day 4; Week 13, Day 2; Week 46, Day 4
　　　Minister of Missions
　　　Bluff Park United Methodist Church
　　　Hoover, Alabama USA

Esteves, Tammy, Ph.D., — Week 16, Day 1; Week 41, Day 2
　　　MPA Program
　　　Troy University
　　　Troy, Alabama, USA
　　　Consultant and Speaker, The Aaron Principle

Featherston, Crystal — Week 6, Day 1; Week 9, Day 5; Week 15, Day 3; Week
34, Day 1; Week 49, Day 3
　　　Budget and Management Analyst
　　　City of Virginia Beach
　　　Virginia Beach, Virginia USA

Flannagan, Jenny Sue, Ed. D. — Week 16, Day 2; Week 48, Day 4
　　　School of Education
　　　Regent University
　　　Virginia Beach, Virginia USA

Garnes, LaShonda — Week 4, Day 1; Week 8, Day 5; Week 20, Day 1; Week 25, Day 1; Week 27, Day 4; Week 29, Day 5; Week 36, Day 5
> Senior Fiscal Analyst
> Public Works & Utilities
> City of Wichita
> Wichita, Kansas USA

Gaston, Sam — Week 2, Day 1; Week 19, Day 3
> City Manager
> City of Mountain Brook
> Mountain Brook, Alabama USA
> Practitioner-in-Residence/Online
> The Master of Public Administration (MPA) Program
> Robertson School of Government
> Regent University
> Virginia Beach, Virginia USA

Gordon, Michael J., Ph.D., LL.M. — Week 19, Day 2
> Policy & Bylaws Fellow
> University of Nevada, Las Vegas
> Las Vegas, Nevada USA

Graber, Jason David — Week 31, Day 4
> MA Candidate
> Robertson School of Government
> Regent University
> Virginia Beach, Virginia USA

Grogan, James — Week 2, Day 2
> Mayor
> City of Dawsonville
> Dawsonville, Georgia USA

Hankle, Dominick D., Ph.D. — Week 18, Day 3; Week 22, Day 5; Week 38, Day 2; Week 44, Day 4
> College of Arts and Sciences Psychology Program
> Regent University
> Virginia Beach, Virginia USA

Holley, H. Frank — Week 7, Day 2
> Pastor, Oak Grove United Methodist Church
> Chesapeake, Virginia USA

Hollingsworth, Brooke — Week 25, Day 4
> MPA Candidate
> Robertson School of Government
> Regent University
> Virginia Beach, Virginia USA

Johnson, Deyonta T. — Week 19, Day 1; Week 34, Day 4; Week 46, Day 2
Street Law Program Assistant
Virginia Dept. of Juvenile Justice- Norfolk Court Service Unit
Norfolk, Virginia USA
MPA Candidate
Robertson School of Government
Regent University
Virginia Beach, Virginia USA

Jones, Jennifer — Week 38, Day 1
Green Youngstown Coordinator
City of Youngstown
Youngstown, Ohio USA

Jones, Malcolm — Week 5, Day 5; Week 10, Day 4; Week 49, Day 1
Local Probation Officer
Norfolk Criminal Justice Services
Norfolk, Virginia USA
MPA Candidate
Robertson School of Government
Regent University
Virginia Beach, Virginia USA

Jones, Zachary — Week 11, Day 4
Recruiter, Regent University
MPA Candidate
Robertson School of Government
Regent University
Virginia Beach, Virginia USA

Jordan, R. Keith — Week 12, Day 3; Week 32, Day 5; Week 48, Day 2
Food Safety Specialist Sr.
Office of Dairy and Foods
Virginia Department of Agriculture and Consumer Services
Virginia Beach, Virginia USA

Ketcham, Larry — Week 1, Day 5; Week 13, Day 5; Week 15, Day 1; Week 19, Day 4; Week 30, Day 1; Week 43, Day 4; Week 45, Day 5; Week 50, Day 1; Week 52, Day 3
City Engineer
City of Laramie
Laramie, Wyoming USA
Master of Public Administration (MPA) Candidate
Robertson School of Government
Regent University
Virginia Beach, Virginia USA

King, Mary Anne — Week 27, Day 2; Week 45, Day 1
Executive Director
Laura Crandall Brown Ovarian Cancer Foundation
Birmingham, Alabama, USA

King, Stephen M., Ph.D. — Week 21, Day 1; Week 23,
Day 5; Week 39, Day 1
>Professor and R. Philip Loy Endowed Chair of Political Science
>Taylor University
>Upland, Indiana USA

Kohm, Lynne Marie, J. D. — Week 27, Day 1
>John Brown McCarty Professor of Law
>School of Law
>Regent University
>Virginia Beach, Virginia USA

Krider, David Week 28, Days 1-5
>former mayor/ex-convict
>Brother-in-Christ

Lacourse, Lyse-Ann — Week 1, Day 3; Week 17, Day 4; Week 21, Day 5; Week
42, Day 1; Week 52, Day 1
>Administrative Coordinator/Coordonnatrice administrative
>Office of the Chief Actuary/Bureau de l'actuaire en chef
>Office of the Superintendent of Financial Institutions/Bureau du surintendant
>des institutions financières Government of Canada/Gouvernement du Canada,
>Ottawa, Canada

Lantz, Jonathan, Week 8, Day 1
>MPA Candidate
>Robertson School of Government
>Regent University
>Virginia Beach, Virginia USA

Lassiter, Lou, CPA — Week 51, Day 5
>Assistant County Administrator
>County of Chesterfield
>Chesterfield, Virginia USA

Lewis, Dyteya, MPA — Week 20, Day 3
>Director of Advancement and Stragetic Relations, Park Place School
>Norfolk, Virginia USA

Lindsley, Art — Week 21, Day 3
>Vice President of Theological Initiatives
>Institute for Faith, Work & Economics
>McLean, Virginia USA

Lowther, Adam B., Ph.D. — Week 24, Day 3; Week 33, Day 4
>Research Professor
>Air Force Research Institute
>Maxwell Air Force Base
>Montgomery, Alabama USA

Luchun, Melinda — Week 17, Day 2
>Program Supervisor
>Communications and Technology
>City of Norfolk
>Norfolk, Virginia USA

Lyvers, Glenn, BPH — Week 35, Day 1
>CEO - Instant Access Corp.
>Mishawaka, Indiana USA
>MPA Candidate
>Robertson School of Government
>Regent University
>Virginia Beach, Virginia USA

Majeske, Sarah — Week 36, Day 1; Week 44, Day 1; Week 46, Day 5; Week 49, Day 2
>MPA Candidate
>Robertson School of Government
>Regent University
>Virginia Beach, Virginia USA

Manjikian, Mary, Ph.D. — Week 46, Day 1
>Associate Dean
>Robertson School of Government
>Regent University
>Virginia Beach, Virginia USA

McCarty, Tajuan — Week 4, Day 5; Week 12, Day 4; Week 23, Day 3; Week 24, Day 2; Week 37, Day 3; Week 50, Day 5
>Founder
>The WellHouse
>Birmingham, Alabama USA

McLendon, Cassandra D., MPA — Week 3, Day 3, Week 13, Day 4; Week 18, Day 1; Week 42, Day 4; Week 45, Day 4; Week 50, Day 3
>Performance Improvement/Accreditation
>Children's (Hospital) of Alabama
>Birmingham, Alabama USA

Meconnahey, Christopher Sean, MPA — Week 29, Day 2; Week 38, Day 5
>Robertson School of Government
>Regent University
>Virginia Beach, Virginia USA

Mitchell, C.A. — Week 5, Day 1
>Chief of Police
>Christian Broadcasting Network/Regent University Campus Police
>Virginia Beach, Virginia USA

Monnin, Rachael — Week 43, Day1
 MPA Candidate
 Robertson School of Government
 Regent University,
 Virginia Beach, Virginia USA

Moyo, Angelina — Week 22, Day 3; Week 30, Day 3
 M.A./J.D. Candidate
 Robertson School of Government/School of Law
 Regent University
 Virginia Beach, Virginia USA

Neal, Debra — Week 8, Day 3; Week 31, Day 2; Week 34, Day 5;
Week 51, Day 1
 6th Grade Teacher
 South Amherst Middle School
 Firelands School District
 South Amherst, Ohio USA

Nohe, Martin — Week 29, Day 4
 Board of County Supervisors
 Coles District
 Prince William County, Virginia USA

Nystrom, Trevor — Week 11, Day 1
 MPA Candidate
 Robertson School of Government
 Regent University
 Virginia Beach, Virginia USA

Patterson, Kathleen — Week 11, Day 3; Week 32, Day 1; Week 43, Day 3;
 School of Business & Leadership
 Regent University
 Virginia Beach, Virginia USA

Pincus, Stephen, M. A. — Week 5, Day 2; Week 8, Day 4; Week 10, Day 3;
Week 20, Day 4; Week 24, Day 1; Week 32, Day 3; Week 44, Day 5
 Battalion Chief
 City of Newport News Fire Department
 Newport News, Virginia USA

Plummer, Dwayne — Week 16, Day 4
 Teaching Assistant
 Special Education
 SECEP Center (School)
 Virginia Beach, Virginia USA
 MPA Candidate
 Robertson School of Government
 Regent University
 Viriginia Beach, Virginia USA

Pulsford, Meredith — Week 9, Day 4; Week 18, Day 4
    People Department Manager
    McDonalds Corporation
    Virginia Beach, Virginia USA
    MPA Candidate
    Robertson School of Government
    Regent University
    Virginia Beach, Virginia USA

Roberts, Gary, Ph.D. — Week 7, Day 1
    Robertson School of Government
    Regent University
    Virginia Beach, Virginia USA

Saunders, Kathryn — Week 7, Day 3
    Head Soccer Coach
    Texas Southern University
    Houston, Texas USA

Scaife, Wilisha G. — Week 11, Day 2
    Department of Elementary Education
    Ball State University
    Muncie, Indiana USA

Schenkel, Adam — Week 14, Day 2; Week 26, Day 3
    MPA Candidate
    Robertson School of Government
    Regent University
    Virginia Beach, Virginia USA

Shields, Patricia M., Ph.D. — Week 18, Day 2
    Department of Political Science
    Texas State University - San Marcos
    San Marcos, Texas USA

Shultz, David LT — Week 9, Day 3; Week 30, Day 5
    US Navy EOD
    MBA Candidate
    Kenan-Flagler School of Business
    University of North Carolina USA
    Virginia Beach, Virginia USA

Slack, James D., Ph.D., Ph.D. — Week 3, Day 2; Week 10, Day 1; Week 16,
Day 3; Week 33, Day 3; Week 47, Day 3; Week 50, Day 2
    Robertson School of Government
    Regent University
    Virginia Beach, Virginia, USA

Slack, Janis Dunn, M.Ed. — Week 39, Day 3
    Program/Operations Coordinator
    Intercampus Interactive Telepresence System
    University of Alabama System
    Birmingham, Alabama USA

Slack, Samuel Douglas Drake — Week 9, Day 1
    Intern
    Police Department
    Mountain Brook, Alabama USA
    Criminal Justice Major
    Auburn University
    Auburn, Alabama USA

Slack, Sarah Ashley — Week 14, Day 1
    MSW Candidate
    University of Alabama
    Tuscaloosa, Alabama USA

Smith, Martha, M.A., J.D., SPHR — Week 23, Day 4; Week 43, Day 2
    Vice President for Human Resources and Administration
    Regent University
    Virginia Beach, Virginia USA

Smidt, Corwin, Ph.D. — Week 40, Days 1–5
    Research Fellow
    The Henry Institute
    Calvin College
    Grand Rapids, Michigan, USA

Stamm, Ellen C. — Week 7, Day 4; Week 46, Day 3; Week 48, Day 3
    Secretary 3
    Department of Affirmative Action/Contract Compliance
    City of Toledo, Ohio USA

Stephens, Jim — Week 12, Day 2; Week 37, Day 4
    Associate Professor Emeritus
    College of Education
    Georgia Southern University
    Statesboro, Georgia USA

Stout, Alan — Week 4, Day 3; Week 44, Day 2; Week 49, Day 4
    Director, Inland Empire Campus
    University of La Verne
    La Verne, California USA

Summers, Chris — Week 6, Day 5; Week 16, Day 5; Week 21, Day 2; Week 23, Day 1; Week 43, Day 5; Week 50, Day 4
> W.C. Holman Correctional Facility
> Alabama Department of Corrections
> Atmore, Alabama USA

Theroux, Paul — Week 20, Day 5
> Maintenance Program Manager
> U. S. Department of Defense
> Naval Base Norfolk
> Norfolk, Virginia USA
> MPA Candidate
> Robertson School of Government
> Regent University
> Virginia Beach, Virginia USA

Thoennes, Karl III — Week 1, Day; Week 52, Day 5
> Court Administrator
> Sioux Falls, South Dakota USA

Tynes, Consuella S., M.Div. and MPA — Week 48, Day 1
> Coordinator, Workforce Management
> Christian Broadcasting Network
> Virginia Beach, Virginia USA

Van Straten, Stephanie — Week 1, Day 4; Week 22, Day 1; Week 52, Day 2
> Third Year Bachelor of Medicine and Surgery
> University of Witwatersrand
> Johannesburg, Gauteng, South Africa

Villamarin, Carlos — Week 15, Day 5
> Police Chaplain/Capellán de la Policía
> Colombia National Police/ Policía Nacional de Colombia
> Bogotá, Colombia

Whelchel, Hugh — Week 20, Day 2; Week 25, Day 2; Week 30, Day 2; Week 32, Day 4; Week 35, Day 2
> Executive Director
> Institute for Faith, Work & Economics
> McLean, Virginia USA

Whitman, Matt — Week 3, Day 5; Week 37, Day 2
> City Councillor
> District 13 Hammonds Plains St.
> Margarets Bay
> City of Halifax
> Halifax, Nova Scotia Canada

Wooten, Sabrina, M.P.A. — Week 25, Day 3
    Executive Assistant to the Office of Bishop McBath
    Calvary Revival Church
    Norfolk, Virginia USA

Zasadny, Katherine — Week 2, Day 4; Week 10, Day 2
    MPA Candidate
    Robertson School of Government
    Regent University
    Virginia Beach, Virginia, US

Subject Index

a tongue with a flame of fire — Week 30, Day 5
accomplish infinitely more — Week 1, Day 4
advisers bring success — Week 50, Day 1
all—stars — Week 37, Day 4
all the motivation — Week 44, Day 3
allow God's best — Week 26, Day 2
always bring hope — Week 29, Day 1
always preparing you — Week 14, Day 4
always His season — Week 23, Day 4
always right — Week 6, Day 3
answer lies in hope — Week 8, Day 5
appetites of this world — Week 45, Day 3
as Christ serves us — Week 41, Day 3
at the heart — Week 7, Day 5
authority I walk in — Week 5, Day 1
battle of the break room — Week 47, Day 1
be there with your heart — Week 8, Day 3
bearer of second chances — Week 24, Day 2
beautiful feet — Week 1, Day 2
become proud — Week 37, Day 1
before you go to work — Week 51, Day 4
begin the day again — Week 7, Day 2
beyond your job description — Week 9, Day 2
Big Dance — Week 26, Day 1
bit more sacred — Week 3, Day 1
bless the listener and please our Lord — Week 7, Day 4
blizzard in our workplace — Week 51, Day 1
both rational and crazy — Week 1, Day 1
both stranger and friend equally — Week 11, Day 3
brave enough — Week 35, Day 1
bring Christ alive — Week 13, Day 2
building for our success — Week 19, Day 3

but what about Me — Week 10, Day 2
but you can choose faith — Week 21, Day 5
call on the Lord — Week 18, Day 2
cannot do this alone — Week 47, Day 4
can't afford to dawdle — Week 26, Day 3
cause others to wonder — Week 25, Day 4
chaplains do not carry rifles — Week 29, Day 3
Christ-like glasses — Week 48, Day 4
Christ's servant — Week 39, Day 4
Christian cord to braid — Week 42, Day 5
chronically unlovable — Week 22, Day 4
clean and lean house — Week 31, Day 4
cost of doing something — Week 39, Day 5
deeper quiet — Week 4, Day 3
desperately dependent and prepared — Week 7, Day 3
despised work neighbor — Week 43, Day 3
direct your path — Week 30, Day 4
do what He would do — Week 3, Day 4
do what it says — Week 13, Day 4
do what we say — Week 15, Day 1
do well — Week45, Day 1
do your job — Week 24, Day 1
donkey on which He rides — Week 6, Day 2
don't slip and fall — Week 3, Day 3
don't run without God — Week 52, Day 2
don't worry about it — Week 18, Day 4
dreadful morning — Week 34, Day 1
entertaining an angel — Week 35, Day 5
establish our hearts — Week 21, Day 1
faith trumps anything — Week 36, Day 2
fallen fire fighters and police officers — Week 39, Day 2
far greater purpose — Week 47, Day 5
first rule of management — Week 46, Day 2
first set ablaze the fire inside — Week 32, Day 3
fixers find repose — Week 13, Day 3
fly that flag unceasingly — Week 6, Day 5
for God's glory and praise — Week 31, Day 1
for His sake, not yours — Week 50, Day 3
for the tough times — Week 29, Day 4
forget that box — Week 13, Day 5
give thanks to Him — Week 13, Day 1
give that Light to everyone — Week 37, Day 5
go — Week 40, Day 3
go beyond the technicalities — Week 39, Day 3
go with them two miles — Week 33, Day 2
God of Monday miracles — Week 39, Day 1

God's intended results — Week 27, Day 4
good gossip — Week 2, Day 4
good novel — Week 28, Day 5
good to be His dog — Week 38, Day 3
grow, advance, and serve — Week 29, Day 2
guard our hearts and tongues — Week 44, Day 1
hang on to that string — Week 30, Day 1
harmony, relationship and community — Week 44, Day 2
heaviness of the impersonal — Week 43, Day 5
heroes of faith — Week 49, Day 5
highest calling — Week 40, Day 2
His public servant — Week 38, Day 1
hit the ball as hard as we can — Week 12, Day 1
holding pattern — Week 25, Day 3
hope in the Lord — Week 16, Day 4
hopelessly homeless, friendless, and family-less — Week 10, Day 3
how are you known — Week 14, Day 3
how long to wait — Week 26, Day 5
hump day is doable — Week 20, Day 3
I am comfortable — Week 45, Day 2
important stuff — Week 10, Day 1
in the frying pan — Week 33, Day 4
in the shadow — Week 22, Day 3
just another Monday — Week 36, Day 1
just doesn't make sense — Week 11, Day 4
just wait patiently — Week 2, Day 2
just who is this Jesus — Week 15, Day 3
knock first — Week 51, Day 2
know God is God — Week 5, Day 3
know it all — Week 51, Day 5
knows and plans — Week 49, Day 3
land of troubled hearts — Week 46, Day 4
lesson to be learned — Week 16, Day 2
lessons unlearned at city hall — Week 28, Day 3
let God be in control — Week 20, Day 5
like that man in the synagogue — Week 27, Day 3
little spark of light — Week 21, Day 4
Living Water won't let you down — Week 46, Day 3
loneliness, strangeness, and disconnectedness — Week 18, Day 5
long for the Lord - for His sake, not mine — Week 52, Day 5
make our efforts successful — Week 42, Day 2
make things work — Week 9, Day 4
more measured response — Week 32, Day 5
most important tool — Week 38, Day 5
mighty workplace warrior — Week 17, Day 3
misfortune into fortune — Week 23, Day 1

more discipline than churning — Week 22, Day 2
need to hear His voice — Week 41, Day 4
neither your heaven nor your hell — Week 10, Day 4
no limits on acts of love — Week 12, Day 3
no matter what happens today — Week 29, Day 5
no option but to stand — Week 37, Day 3
no pain on God's watch — Week 41, Day 1
no reason not to trust God — Week 27, Day 1
no surer safety net — Week 43, Day 2
no vacations — Week 25, Day 5
not gonna forsake you — Week 19, Day 1
not our choice — Week 40, Day 1
not people, but the Lord — Week 10, Day 5
not to lose sight of His yoke — Week 49, Day 1
nothing compared — Week 50, Day 5
nothing more than His scum — Week 24, Day 5
now represent Jesus — Week 48, Day 5
old-self way — Week 11, Day 2
on the court hot — Week 12, Day 4
on troubled seas — Week 44, Day 4
one particular person — Week 2, Day 1
only after it's too late — Week 4, Day 2
only to bless, not to curse — Week 33, Day 5
only way to stop the pain — Week 28, Day 4
original job description — Week 30, Day 2
pass by on the other side — Week 17, Day 4
pass that cup of hope — Week 4, Day 5
passage through your desert — Week 26, Day 4
perfect number of watts — Week 25, Day 1
person God intended — Week 5, Day 5
personalize and engage — Week 50, Day 4
plainly on tablets — Week 43, Day 1
play Moses — Week 49, Day 2
playing by His rules — Week 42, Day 3
practice that answer — Week 7, Day 1
pray and think quickly — Week 19, Day 4
preachers, plumbers and prostitutes — Week 8, Day 4
pretty important — Week 17, Day 1
prioritize rather than balance — Week 50, Day 2
profess a Protector's heart — Week 15, Day 5
pulling weeds — Week 1, Day 5
pursuit of good work — Week 21, Day 3
put up guideposts — Week 23, Day 3
quiet corner in the cave Week 22, Day 1
reading the bible can put you to sleep — Week 43, Day 4
really good knock-knock joke — Week 23, Day 2

rejoice in the midst of the chaos — Week 36, Day 5
remain content — Week 45, Day 4
responsibility to be — Week 12, Day 2
reverse networking — Week 3, Day 5
riding right next to you — Week 36, Day 4
right field at the right time — Week 31, Day 5
right kind of fruits — Week 48, Day 3
rooted and built up in Him — Week 9, Day 5
rule over others righteously — Week 38, Day 4
run the race publicly — Week 8, Day 1
run to win — Week 15, Day 2
run up the debt — Week 14, Day 2
salt that seasons our workplace — Week 48, Day 1
secret of living in every situation — Week 32, Day 4
see us as Jesus — Week 6, Day 4
seek first and last His advice — Week 20, Day 4
seek to see the Lord at work — Week 32, Day 1
self-made — Week 37, Day 2
set aside shame — Week 12, Day 5
someone needs to see me — Week 17, Day 5
someplace else — Week 35, Day 3
speak and act accordingly — Week 48, Day 2
speak the truth — Week 44, Day 5
special responsibility — Week 52, Day 3
spread that message — Week 40, Day 4
standing in the freezing rain — Week 3, Day 2
see the picture differently — Week 42, Day 4
simplifying question — Week 5, Day 4
steel door slamming shut — Week 34, Day 5
substitution of listening — Week 5, Day 2
take the stress — Week 9, Day 1
tap-hammer — Week 47, Day 3
temptation is simply an invitation — Week 28, Day 1
that kind of public servant — Week 47, Day 2
that other kind of sweet perfume — Week 27, Day 5
the time I harvest — Week 45, Day 5
the way you do your work — Week 25, Day 2
think of our Example — Week 34, Day 3
those two simple words — Week 8, Day 2
thoughts of wishing — Week 24, Day 4
to say no — Week 46, Day 1
top of your task list — Week 2, Day 3
true feast, not just lunch — Week 1, Day 3
truly great for God — Week 19, Day 2
trust in that power — Week 15, Day 4
unexpected stillness — Week 51, Day3

unfinished story — Week 52, Day 4
wake up and look around — Week 41, Day 5
walk away from that tomb — Week 38, Day 2
walk the walk — Week 49, Day 4
walking in the midst — Week 6, Day 1
wear your heart first — Week 14, Day 1
we are not our own — Week 21, Day 2
weights and measures — Week 34, Day 2
what are you afraid of — Week 31, Day 2
what are you wired for — Week 31, Day 3
what matters most — Week 46, Day 5
what nature — Week 33, Day 3
what true religion is all about — Week 32, Day 2
what you don't do — Week 27, Day 2
whatever you do — Week 20, Day 2
when the sun doesn't even shine — Week 19, Day 5
when to say "no" — Week 4, Day 4
where help comes from — Week 20, Day 1
where is your brother — Week 11, Day 1
which path to take — Week 52, Day 1
who am I — Week 28, Day 2
who sees your light — Week 11, Day 5
Why did I doubt — Week 35, Day 4
willing vessel — Week 41, Day 2
without memory — Week 34, Day 4
work at hard work — Week 18, Day 3
work at living in peace — Week 14, Day 5
work deeply matters — Week 35, Day 2
work with enthusiasm — Week 16, Day 1
work within the attitude of Christ — Week 4, Day 1
working for the Lord — Week 30, Day 3
workplace hope of Jesus Christ — Week 17, Day 2
workplace prayer group — Week 42, Day 1
workplace seeds — Week 18, Day 1
workplace show & tell — Week 9, Day 3
worry get in the way — Week 33, Day 1
Y should I care — Week 16, Day 3
your words and actions — Week 40, Day 5
you work for Christ — Week 36, Day 3

About the Editors

William (Bill) Dudley earned the Master of Public Administration (MPA) degree from the Robertson School of Government at Regent University. Bill is a retired 32-year Naval Officer and ordained minister. By day, he works for the Department of Defense, and his evenings and Sundays are spent as a singer/songwriter and Worship Pastor for the Virginia Beach Beacon Baptist Church. He resides in Virginia Beach, Virginia with his lovely wife, Annette.

Christopher Sean Meconnahey earned the Master of Public Administration (MPA) degree from the Robertson School of Government at Regent University. He earned the Bachelor of Science degree from Old Dominion University. Chris is considering either a career in city management or a career in academia. Chris lives near family in Virginia Beach, Virginia.

James D. Slack Ph.D., Ph.D., is a professor in the Robertson School of Government at Regent University where he directs the Master of Public Administration (MPA) Program. He teaches in the areas of public policy, public administration, and Christian foundations of government. Dr. Slack writes on death policy and life policy. His most recent book is *Abortion, Execution and the Consequence of Taking Life*, Transaction Publishers, Second edition. He splits living between Chesapeake, Virginia and Hoover, Alabama – where his lovely wife and children reside.

CPSIA information can be obtained at www.ICGtesting.com
Printed in the USA
LVOW08s0028250715

447619LV00002B/431/P